The Little Book of the Holy Trinity

A New Approach to Christianity, Indian Philosophy, and Quantum Physics

Shelli Renée Joye, Oblate, OSB, Cam.
B.S. Electrical Engineering
M.A. Indian Philosophy
Ph.D. Philosophy and Religion

D1611530

Published by the Viola Institute
Viola, California

Dedicated to my teachers and mentors
in East/West philosophy and religion:
Dr. Haridas Chaudhuri (1913-75) and
Chögyam Trungpa Rinpoche (1939-1987); and
to my mentor in psychonautics, Dr. John C. Lilly (1950-2001),
and to my priest friends and mentors:
Fr. Bede Griffiths, Order of Saint Benedict, Camaldoli,
Fr. Robert Hale, OSB, Camaldoli,
Fr. Bruno Barnhart, OSB, Camaldoli,
Fr. Thomas Matus, OSB, Camaldoli,
Fr. John Takahashi, Orthodox Church of America;
also, to my friend and spiritual brother,
Dr. Stephen Keith Watson (Dhruva),
Librarian of the Sri Aurobindo Ashram, Pondicherry;
and to my dear family: Alyssa, Jason, and Teresa,
my father, Lt. Col. Kenneth Edward Joye, USAF,
my mother, Jeanette Margaret Faltinow Joye,
and the love of my life and editor Susanne Cathryn Rohner,
and to Stella, our black cat, and Nuggles, our green Macaw.

The Little Book of the Holy Trinity:
A New Approach to Christianity,
Indian Philosophy, and Quantum Physics. -- 1st ed.

ISBN-13:   978-09988785-0-8
ISBN-10:   09988785-0-2

Cover painting: image by Shelli Renee Joye, acrylic & oil.

The different traits here taken into account are brought together to form a tress which represents one of the deepest intuitions man has had and is still having, from different points of view and with different names: the intuition of the threefold structure of reality, of the triadic oneness existing on all levels of consciousness and of reality, of the Trinity.

We are not saying that the idea of the Trinity can be reduced to the discovery of a triple dimension of Being, nor that this aspect is a mere rational discovery. We are only affirming that the Trinity is the acme of a truth that permeates all realms of being and consciousness and that this vision links us together.

> Raimundo Panikkar,
> *The Trinity*
> *and the Religious Experience of Man,* 1973, xi.

By the same author:

The Little Book of Consciousness: Holonomic Brain Theory and the Implicate Order

Dr. Joye has not only created a map of consciousness; she has created a map of reality. Everything we call reality is experienced in consciousness, known in consciousness, and is in fact a modified form of consciousness. Reading this book will move you beyond physical materialism into better understanding the realities of consciousness.

— — **DEEPAK CHOPRA**, **M.D.**,
Endocrinologist, founder of The Chopra Center, and author of
You Are the Universe with the physicist Menas Kafatos

Tuning the Mind: The Geometry of Consciousness

Shelli Joye's integrative masterpiece, *Tuning the Mind*, reads like insane science fiction—quantum black holes, a universal center that's everywhere and nowhere, the dark energy holoflux, and of course, the mysterious Teilhardian isospheres. But the strange thing is, it's not insane, nor is it fiction. It's a novel and refreshing scientific take on the role of consciousness in the physical world. Well worth the read.

— — **DEAN RADIN**, **Ph.D.**,
Chief Scientist, Institute of Noetic Sciences (IONS), and author of
*Supernormal: Science, Yoga, and the
Evidence for Extraordinary Psychic Abilities*

iv

Introduction

There are many mysteries associated with religious symbols in every culture down through the ages, but prominent among these are the numinous mysteries of the Holy Trinity. Widely recognized and revered by both Orthodox Christians and Roman Catholics, the Holy Trinity is invoked in the private and communal prayer of 2.2 billion Christians. At this very moment there must be tens of thousands of Christians around the globe in the act of "signing themselves" (touching the three central fingers of the right hand to forehead, heart and each shoulder in making "the sign of the cross") while reciting silently or audibly the three manifestations of the Holy Trinity, "In the name of the Father, and of the Son, and of the Holy Spirit."

Yet those same Christians would likely be surprised to learn that an additional billion people also pray to the Holy Trinity, with great devotion, *even though they are not Christians.* Deep reverence for the Trinity can be found in India as *Sacchidānanda* (an elision of the three Sanskrit metaphysical terms, *Sat-Chit-Ānanda,* words individually translated as "Existence" (God), "Consciousness" (the Son), and "Love" (the Holy Spirit).

This term, *Sacchidānanda,* encapsulates the Vedantic metaphysics of the Trinity in texts composed as early as the 4th century CE, and perhaps it is not an accident that it was in this very same century that early Christians in Constantinople (381 CE) codified the doctrine of the Holy Trinity in the Nicene Creed, which has ever since been recited daily by Christians.

What may be more surprising to many is the existence of yet another 400 million humans, neither Christian nor Hindu, who frame their belief within a Buddhist Trinitarian context, viewing the Holy Trinity in metaphysical terms of what is referred to as the "three Bodies of Buddha," the *Nirmaṇakāya*, the *Dharmakāya*, and the luminous *Sambhogakāya* (three Sanskrit terms which translate as the Immanent, the Transcendent, and the Clear Light "body of bliss" which bridges space-time and transcendence).

Yet all of these mutual Trinity-acknowledging Christians, Hindus, and Buddhists would be even more surprised to learn that millions of Muslims also revere the Holy Trinity as a central doctrine in their faith. Among the five million Sufi Alawites living in Syria, Turkey, and Lebanon, the Holy Trinity is honored as the three intersecting, hypostatic emanations of the One God. A common Alawite prayer is the recitation: "I turn to the Gate, I bow down before the Name, and I adore the Meaning."[†]

This book presents a multidimensional, cross-cultural, picture of the Holy Trinity, related in the context of my own life story. It does this through a trans-disciplinary method called "the integral approach" discussed in the first chapter. By comparing and contrasting approaches to the Trinity as seen from the following three widely different perspectives, new and interconnecting patterns begin to emerge:

- Teilhard de Chardin's Christian vision of the Omega Point and the Noosphere,
- Sri Aurobindo's Vedantic Trinitarian metaphysics of the threefold *Sacchidānanda*, and
- David Bohm's nondual physics of "the Whole."

Several of the concepts, particularly those that are central to modern quantum physics and Indian metaphysics, might at first glance seem challenging for the average reader. However, the material as presented does *not* require any deep or extensive

---

[†] Abi-Talib, *Al-Saheefah Al-Alawiyah or The Alawite Book*, 17.

educational background in philosophy or modern physics. The numerous diagrams and figures that have been included provide sufficient visual detail for acquiring a wider and deeper understanding of ideas that are to be discovered in the Trinity.

The Little Book of the Holy Trinity has been written with the hope that the confluence of ideas from multiple subject areas will provide sufficient detail so that the reader might be rewarded with a deeper appreciation, broader understanding, and closer connection to the transcendent mystery that is referred to as the Holy Trinity. It is also hoped that a consideration of the parallel ideas presented here, converging upon this central metaphysical mystery that has arisen in multiple cultures, might lead to a more ecumenical understanding, acceptance, and reverence for all expressions of the Holy Trinity. In this I feel in full accord with the words of the Spanish Roman Catholic priest, Raimundo Panikkar, in speaking of his own book on the Trinity:

> My aim at present is simply so to enlarge and deepen the mystery of the Trinity that it may embrace this same mystery existent in other religious traditions but differently expressed. The Trinity, then, may be considered as a junction where the authentic spiritual dimensions of all religions meet.[‡]

Each of the five chapters in this book is approximately fifty pages long and biographical in nature; the chapters do not have to be read in sequence. A summary chart is presented in Chapter V, the concluding chapter, which offers a direct comparison of fourteen Trinitarian structures associated with four major religions and the writings of ten philosopher-mystics. For those with an interest in mathematical derivations,

---

[‡] Panikkar, *Trinity and the Religious Experience of Man*, 42.

Appendix A, "The Fourier Transform," discusses the subject of imaginary numbers, the derivation of Euler's Law, and the Mandelbrot set of Real and Imaginary numbers. Appendix B, "Icons and the Holy Trinity," is a brief discussion of traditional icons depicting aspects of the Holy Trinity, both Christian and Vedantic.

A Note on Ecumenism

> Some years ago, Fr. Bede Griffiths, a Camaldolese Benedictine monk from Great Britain and an Oxford graduate, had gone to India where he developed an ecumenical ashram open to Christians, Hindus, Moslems, Buddhists, and God-seekers of any sort. His experience soon convinced him that the supposed polytheism of the bulk of India's population was only an illusion caused by the various depictions of God inherited from India's ethnic and regional diversity, each of which mirrored one or another aspect of nature—all of it stemming from the one God.[§]

[§] Kropf, *A Response to Contemporary Atheism*, 149.

CONTENTS

"Trinity" is a common name in many cultures, philosophies, and religions. We find trinities everywhere. The dogma of the Christian Trinity is not a dead dogma incapable of growth. The Christian dogma of the Trinity has been respectfully kept closed under seven keys for almost the last millennium and a half of Christian history. It may be all the best for Christians to receive some inputs, stimuli and provocations from an intercultural approach, which is the cultural imperative of our times. I am convinced that, if more fully deepened and unfolded, the traditional Christian idea of the Trinity opens immensely fruitful perspectives for our times.

Raimundo Panikkar, The Gifford Lectures,
Trinity and Atheism:
The Dwelling of the Divine in the Contemporary
World, 1989, 56.

I. Quest for the Holy Trinity

My own fascination with the Holy Trinity began with the place of my birth, an emerald green tropical island seven miles off the northeastern coast of Venezuela, the island of Trinidad. Originally the island was called the "Land of the Hummingbird" by its indigenous inhabitants, the Arawaks (Fig. 1), who have dwindled as an ethnic group since the time of Columbus, and are now extinct among the islands of the Caribbean where they once ruled.

Figure 1. *Arawaks in 1880, waiting to meet the Governor.* [1]

An Island Named Trinity

Trinidad was discovered by the Europeans with the sighting of three enormous volcanic peaks on the southeastern peninsula of the jade green island, first spied by a lookout on Trinity Sunday (so the legend goes) in 1498, during the third crossing of the Atlantic by Columbus, a full six years after his initial discovery of the Americas.[2]

First Sighting of Trinidad, 1498

While this confluence of Trinity Sunday (a Catholic holy day dedicated to the Holy Trinity) and the sighting of the three volcanic peaks[3] makes it understandable that Columbus should name the island "Trinidad" (the Spanish word for "Trinity"), the even stranger truth is that Columbus had already, prior to the departure of his third voyage from Spain to the New World, vowed to name the first new island he hoped to discover "Trinidad" in honor of the Holy Trinity.[4]

It was as a child in St. Philomena's convent school near London that I first heard the Catholic concept of the Holy Trinity from my teachers, Irish and German nuns. However, any explanation of the underlying reality of the Trinity was never attempted other than to tell us that the Trinity was a great and wonderful mystery, consisting of some deeply mystical relationships among three aspects of the one God: God the Father, God the Son, and God the Holy Ghost. My only concept of a ghost at that time was of Casper, the Friendly Ghost, from an animated cartoon of the same name! Though confusing to a six-year-old (like many things introduced at that age), I was somehow able to accept this explanation at face value. In subsequent years, I tried to supplement my understanding by thinking that perhaps the Trinity might have something to do with the "Three Wise Men" who visited the baby Jesus while he lay in his manger in Bethlehem, or perhaps that it had something to do with the three crosses on Calvary that day when Christ died.

The overtly physical act of making the "sign of the cross" at the beginning and end of prayer, and performed numerous times during church liturgical services, reinforced the idea that this Holy Trinity must certainly be an important and central mystery of Christianity (at least in Roman Catholic and Eastern Orthodox churches). Strangely, however, there was little explanation of the Holy Trinity nor any mention of its meaning or history in Catholic school, nor even in Sunday school.

Yet I found myself, even at this early age, beginning to notice things that came in threesomes, such as the "Three Blind Mice" song we sang in first grade, or the "Three Musketeers" watched on our tiny black-and-white television, "Goldilocks and the Three Bears," and the three children of Donald Duck: Huey, Dewey, and Louie. Early in my life I began to detect this pattern in what seemed to me to be mysterious configurations, and I wondered if there might be some deeply hidden connection between the fact that I had been born on the island of Trinidad and this recurring pattern of threes.

Christian Metaphysics and the Trinity

While the mystery of the Trinity has never been entirely absent from Christian thought, neither has it been explicitly discussed. As Fr. Bruno Barnhart, a Benedictine monk and scholar has observed:

> It has seldom been expressed in its purity and autonomy within the Christian tradition. This

strange suppression is parallel to the ambivalence of mainstream Christianity toward mysticism.[5]

Aside from a few rare groups of monastics such as the Benedictines, mysticism has remained a marginal pursuit in the Catholic Church. According to Fr. Bruno (himself a member of the Camaldolese Benedictine hermits, founded by St. Romuald in the 10th century CE):

> Solitude, silence, and contemplative prayer have seldom remained the central concerns in a Roman Catholic monasticism which has become engaged very largely in pastoral, cultural, and educational activities.[6]

Vatican II

Like many young adults, leaving their familiar family life routines to become college students, my participation in the Catholic church diminished soon after leaving home to study in a distant city. My American ancestors, originally immigrants from Poland, Germany and Ireland, had all been practicing Roman Catholics; my grandfather and his father before him had both been altar boys, assisting the priest at Sunday Mass. But I must confess that I only infrequently attended church services on Sundays, overwhelmed with my heavy academic workload. With regular homework in engineering, physics, chemistry, and math, and long reading assignments in English and world history, I spent most of my free hours on Sunday mornings and afternoons studying in the Rice library, trying to keep up with my course work.

But it was Vatican II that added impetus to weaken my Catholic roots. I can still recall one morning at the age of six when my first teacher, an Irish nun named Sr. Mary Bernadette, told us that somewhere on the planet the Holy Mass was even now being recited in Latin. She went on to assure us that if ever

4

we should find ourselves traveling in a foreign country, wherever we were, we would be able find a Catholic church nearby in which we could hear the Mass being said by the priest using the same Latin words that our grandparents and great-grandparents had heard and recited every Sunday. Sr. Mary Bernadette also assured us that the Mass would always be recited in Latin this way until Judgment Day (which seemed like a long way off to me). Having been sufficiently motivated, we then began to practice memorizing the Pater Noster ("Our Father") in Latin. It was a great accomplishment when we were eventually able to recite the words of the prayer, along with the priest and congregation during Mass, in the "original Latin" (or so we thought, though I have since heard that Jesus likely spoke to his disciples in a dialect of Aramaic and Hebrew, not Latin).

What I learned of Vatican II,[7] concluding in 1965 during my first year of college, seemed to turn upside-down everything about my religion that I had been taught by the nuns. The extensive changes in the Mass seemed to have negated the foundational ideas which I had learned at such an early age from Sr. Mary Bernadette, and which I had practiced for eighteen years. Suddenly every church throughout the world was required to change the position of the altar itself by moving it away from its former place against the wall. From now on the priest would be able to look out over the people from the other side of the altar while performing the Mass. This radically contradicted what I had been taught by the nuns, that the priest and the people all face the altar together, in the same direction, because behind the altar was a little special compartment, called the Tabernacle or sanctuary, a special place where the blessed hosts of bread were kept, a place where we were told that God lived.

An even more shocking change to me was the decree that the Latin Mass would no longer be recited in the Latin language!

Henceforth, Latin would be discouraged everywhere throughout the Catholic world, and replaced through recitation of the Mass using translations from the Latin into local languages and dialects. Suddenly I recalled images of the Tower of Babel story in a picture book I had seen, where everyone was shown to be confused, speaking in totally different languages; "babbling" was the term that came to be used. I could only imagine how my grandfather would have reacted had he been alive to comment upon these modern innovations, which abruptly ended traditions that I assumed went back many centuries in our family of Catholics.

But the ultimate shock, for me, was the introduction of folk music and guitars into the liturgy of the Mass. One Sunday morning I managed to find a Catholic church within walking distance of campus, only to discover, in the middle of the Mass (being recited in English of course), that suddenly an acoustic guitar began to play, accompanied by an accordionist and a folk singer. Perhaps the intention of all these changes was to make worship more relevant to the 1960s, but it all seemed to me jarringly discordant, certainly not conducive to the solemnity of mind I had been taught was required for serious prayer and contemplation of the holy mysteries. The effect of these changes in the church I had known and within which I had prayed with my family for the first eighteen years of my life, was both shocking and profound. My familiar childhood religious experiences and practices were suddenly slipping rapidly into the past, as was my familiar family environment.

Poetry and Metaphysics

Fortunately, blessed with good teachers in London and later in northern Virginia, I had also acquired a love for English literature, and particularly for the lyrical poetry of Wordsworth, Byron, and Keats. Although most of my courses were from the physics, mathematics, and engineering departments, I made it an almost religious practice to enroll in at least one English literature or poetry class each semester. These elective classes became like a breath of fresh air for my beleaguered psyche, filled as it was with equations, graphs, logic and technical jargon, and I remember convincing my academic advisor to approve these elective courses by saying that they "improved my intellectual health by keeping me balanced." Doing this came with a penalty in time, however. The typical engineering program was scheduled to require a minimum of four years to complete, but with all of my elective literature and poetry courses, it took me five and a half years as a full time student to complete my engineering program requirements.

One spring semester I enrolled in a senior English course, focused exclusively upon the poetry of Byron, Shelley, and Keats. I recall taking many breaks when studying physics or math, and going out into the backyard, lying on a blanket in the grass under an oak tree and reading *Endymion*, a richly symbolic 4,000-line poem by John Keats (1795-1821) written in Italy when he was only twenty-three.[8] Endymion was a handsome shepherd, the great-grandson of Deukalion, a survivor of the Great Deluge, and the moon goddess, Selene, who falls in love with Endymion and eventually grants him a wish: that he will remain immortal, young and beautiful forever but only if he agrees to live within the dream world of deep sleep. The rich imagery of *Endymion* led me into deep and forgotten areas of thought and feeling that I immediately associated with my childhood religious experiences at Mass, listening to mysterious Latin prayers and visualizing Biblical stories. I had moved into a period during which it seems that reading and thinking about poetry had become my new religious practice.

My Journey from Physics to Metaphysics

It was during the following summer of 1967 in California, having just completed my third year of studies, that I first experienced with vivid clarity those realms of awareness described by mystics and poets, perceptions far beyond my normal range of feeling and perception, far beyond anything I could ever have previously imagined.

This unexpected deeper experience of consciousness began around a small campfire on a lovely Pacific Ocean beach just south of Big Sur, California, at around midnight on a clear July night, shortly after ingesting three small yellow tablets of LSD-25 ("Owsley acid"). Having just completed a spring term of mathematics and electrical engineering (as well as an English Romantic poetry course), my vision of the universe was deeply influenced by such things as frequency charts, Fourier and Laplace transforms, electromagnetic theories describing invisible energy waves, and Greek nature gods. Suddenly all of these dry paradigms became vividly alive for me, overlaid and energized with the direct visual, auditory, and tactile experience of other entities in an enormous sea of energy. Astonished, I found myself floating on the vast depths of oceans of consciousness that I had never noticed, lying beyond the shores of my own familiar mind, and I suddenly realized that we (meaning every-*one* and every-*thing*) are all immersed in planetary and galactic fields of energy swirling in and out of our own limited islands of awareness.

Several years later, in a book written by the medical psychonaut[9] John Cunningham Lilly (1915–2001), a physician, neuroscientist, psychoanalyst, psychonaut, philosopher, writer and inventor. In one of his books, I came across a description that resonated intensely with my recollections of "what it was like" under LSD. Here Lilly briefly describes his own initial experience with LSD in one of his carefully designed light-

8

proof, sound-proof isolation tank floating in body-temperature water:

> I am a small point of consciousness in a vast domain beyond my understanding. Vast forces of the evolution of the stars are whipping me through colored streamers of light becoming matter, matter becoming light. The atoms are forming from light, light is forming from the atoms. A vast consciousness directs these huge transitions.
>
> With difficulty I maintain my identity, my self. The surrounding processes interpenetrate my being and threaten to disrupt my own integrity, my continuity in time. There is no time; this is an eternal place, with eternal processes generated by beings far greater than I. I become merely a small thought in that vast mind that is practically unaware of my existence. I am a small program in the huge cosmic computer. There is no existence, no being but *this* forever. There is no place to go back to. There is no future, no past, but *this*.[10]

My own experiences under the influence of LSD-25 had opened my eyes to a completely new paradigm of what it might mean to exist on this planet, among the stars, as a "conscious being." Something had suddenly thrown wide open the shutters of the universe; no longer could I regard the real world in the relatively constricted ranges I had inherited from previous generations, and which I had unquestioningly adopted as the boundaries of reality.

While I was able to continue in my role as an engineering student, completing my engineering program the following year, the intense psychonautic experiences on the beach at night in the ocean of consciousness had kindled a flame of enthusiasm for exploring and understanding consciousness as a phenomenon in its own right. No longer was my fascination focused so exclusively upon radio and laser communication theory; I found that I could not stop thinking about the word "consciousness." I pondered what a deeper understanding of the concept might imply for my own religious practices, for prayer and for mystical experiences beyond the state of simply "being awake." Indeed, I had acquired my first taste of "psychonautics," of sailing beyond the edge of the familiar into a heretofore concealed "ocean of consciousness" within which we all exist, yet as invisible to us as water is to fish swimming in the ocean.

However it was only a few months later, one October night in the Texas hill country, thirty miles southwest of Austin, that I was confronted with even stranger phenomena than those I had experienced during my LSD-catalyzed night on the beach; a startling and unexpected apparition in the Texas forest reinforced my new fascination with trying to explore and understand the intersections of science and mysticism.

The Light in the Forest

It was around midnight in the hill country of Texas, at a place known as Hamilton Pool, twenty miles west of Austin, above an ancient crack in the earth known as the Balcones Fault. Fed by a 50-foot waterfall, the large pool of water had been created when the limestone dome over an underground river had collapsed during a quake many millennia past.

Four of us had come to swim after a week of final exams at the University of Texas. The night was quiet except for the chirping of small frogs, and pale clouds obscured the stars. After swimming in the deeper parts of the pool, not far from the small waterfall, we soon gathered by the edge of the pool talking quietly.

The first noticeable sign of something unusual was the abrupt cessation of the frogs' peeping, that incessant forest murmuring mixture of crickets and frogs on a summer night. Abruptly they stopped, leaving only the sound of the small waterfall across the pool from us.

Soon, a barely perceptible glow appeared far down the creek back to our right, where a creek flowed from the pool into the Pedernales River almost about half a mile to the west. The light, growing and fading in rhythmic pulsations, bobbed slowly up and down along the creek, obscured by intervening pine trees and brush. We sat in silence, backs against a large boulder on the shore of Hamilton Pool, both mesmerized and nervous. We were familiar with ominous urban legends that circulated in Austin, warning of nighttime horror in the forested hill country to the west of Austin, stories of people alone in the woods at night who had mysteriously vanished, echoed some years later in the movie, *The Texas Chainsaw Massacre* (1974).

Figure 2. *Hamilton Pool, southwest of Austin, Texas.*

At long last, emerging from the obscuring brush, what appeared to be a spherical object of pale opal phosphorescence came into view, floating high above the creek. Gently glowing and slowly pulsing, the orb majestically moved along the rim of the cliff overhanging the pool of water. After what seemed to be an eternity, the softly glowing spherical shape reached the waterfall, and after rising slightly and moving closer to the falling water, the apparition slowly dipped three times, bobbing and weaving in a stately rhythmical pattern above the water before the falls, like some gigantic moth in the night. Eventually it resumed motion along the sheltering rim, moving ever closer to us where we sat on the pebble-strewn beach, speechless, paralyzed, more in awe than in fear.

Finally, after what seemed an eternity, it reached us where we sat on the shore, our backs pressed against the cool boulder. There it paused, hovering, about ten feet above us, a small, silent, spherical galaxy of tiny bright stars and glowing filaments, flashing and flickering. Within the mysterious, luminous orb could be seen patterns, like thin contrails, all bound within a spherical shape approximately a meter in diameter, about the size of a large beach ball. Time stood still. I held my breath, speechless, in awe verging on disbelief for what seemed an eternity. At last it began again its slow, bobbing movement away from us, continuing its journey above the beach edge until it reached the creek draining the pool. Then it continued west, above the creek, in a slow stately fashion, moving into the swampy forest where it had first appeared.

What I felt and perceived beneath the apparition is difficult to recall, yet alone relate. I remember clearly hearing peculiar whistling sounds and the distinct sensation of electrical snappings of some sort in my head. At the same time I felt an intensity of a kind I had never previously experienced. It was apparent that here, in the unbroken silence of this remote Texas countryside, far from any town or city, we had encountered a mystery beyond anything I had previously considered or discovered in any of my books.

In the following days the three of us could not stop talking about what we had seen. Had we seen a UFO? Or was this the same experience of something historically referred to as a wood spirit, leprechaun, fairy, demon, or angel? In its movement around the pool we all agreed it had moved with direction and intent, and seemed to have displayed an awareness. It was alive, clearly, though not made of any identifiable material or substance; it had appeared as a transparent sphere, manifesting glowing electric sparks and lines in visibly changing swirls, as might be seen in holographic moiré patterns (Fig. 3).

Figure 3. *Moiré Patterns in Spherical Volume.*

We agreed that as the sphere hovered above us the impression was one of benevolent curiosity. Could this have been some kind of machine? Its movements did not seem machine-like, but gave the impression of intelligence, particularly in the lovely "dance" it made in front of the waterfall, and later as it hovered directly above us, twinkling and glowing in pastel aurora-like colors. The sphere seemed to be considering us, observing us intently. The next morning we all agreed that we had been both terrified and amazed, like deer caught in car headlights, we had frozen, and could neither move nor think nor react.

Many years later, during what had become my lifetime study of consciousness, in a search for corroborating material, I was fortunately able to find descriptions of similar encounters in the writings of both John Blofeld (1913–1987) and Aleister Crowley (1875–1947).[11,12]

Born in London in 1913, Blofeld was fascinated by Buddhism and contemplation from an early age. He traveled to China in 1937, spending the next decade visiting remote monasteries and sacred mountains in China, Mongolia, and Tibet. In *The Wheel of Life: The Autobiography of a Western Buddhist,* Blofeld relates that he once visited the Temple of Wutai Shan on a mountain of the same name in northern China, sacred to the Bodhisattva of Wisdom, Wénshū (文殊 in Chinese). The temple was renowned for the fact that (according to the Buddhist monks there) *bodhisattvas* could often be seen floating down from the mountain top in the form of spheres of light, and special meditation platforms had been constructed so that the balls could be observed by contemplatives. Here Blofeld relates his experience on the mountain of Wutai Shan:

> At last we were ready. Fully dressed, we wound quilts about us like cumbrous shawls and walked out into the monastery compound. The ascent to the door of the tower occupied less than a minute. As each one entered the little room and came face to face with the window beyond, he gave a shout of surprise, as though all our hours of talk had not sufficiently prepared us for what we now saw. There in the great open spaces beyond the window, apparently not more than one or two hundred yards away,

innumerable balls of fire floated majestically past. We could not judge their size, for nobody knew how far away they were, but they appeared like the fluffy woolen balls that babies play with seen close up. They seemed to be moving at the stately pace of a large, well fed fish aimlessly cleaving its way through the water; but, of course, their actual pace could not be determined without a knowledge of the intervening distance. Where they came from, what they were, and where they went after fading from sight in the West, nobody could tell. Fluffy balls of orange colored fire, moving through space, unhurried and majestic—truly a fitting manifestation of divinity![13]

Blofeld continues in an attempt to categorize what he and his companions had seen that night:

I do not know if this extraordinary sight has ever been accounted for "scientifically" and I am not much interested in such explanations. It is far lovelier to think of them as divine manifestations, however prosaic their real nature may be. But is it prosaic? Marsh gas, you say? Marsh gas right out in space, a thousand or more feet above the nearest horizontal surface and some hundreds of feet from the vertical surface of a cold, rocky mountain innocent of water? Surely not. Human manipulation? Yes, if you first suppose two or three hundred men all clothed in black and able to swim slowly through space. Fire flies? Even supposing they were really much closer than they seemed, fireflies almost the size of small footballs? I doubt it very much. And why should these gases or flies appear only between midnight and two in the morning? The belief that the Bodhisattva thus manifests himself to the faithful is no easier to accept than the theories just disposed of, but is it more difficult? I do not know. Assuming that a Wisdom Force does exist in the universe as a separate entity—separate, that is, on the plane of differentiated phenomena—it is still difficult to understand why it should manifest itself materially in the form of slowly moving balls of fire. I really do not know. What remains? Silence, perhaps, is best.[14]

Aleister Crowley, the English painter, theosophist, and mountaineer recorded in his biography the details of a similar experience of a seemingly-living sphere of light. He describes a sphere of light which entered his hut by a lake in Scotland during a violent thunder storm. He writes that at first he thought it must be St. Elmo's fire, balls of light often seen hovering about the top masts of sailing ships during thunder storms at sea, but the one that appeared to have entered his cottage during a storm seemed clearly to be alive as it moved in a stately procession around the room, as if studying the environment, then dashing straight toward Crowley's face, only to stop suddenly, and after what seemed to be an interminable period, finally moving slowly back out of the hut and vanishing into the storm.

The impact of the strikingly otherworldly apparition at Hamilton Pool upon my 21-year-old recently-acquired physics and electrical engineering mindset, following that summer's LSD experience on a California beach, opened my eyes to an entirely new dimension for exploration and research. How could I have seen and experienced these things so vividly, phenomena of nature (or super-nature) that were never referred to by any of the current sciences? The occurrence at Hamilton's Pool had rocked my scientifically indoctrinated sensibilities, abruptly opening my eyes to a wide new range of dimensions for both scientific and experiential exploration, regions far beyond the current maps so carefully explored by physicists, biologists, and radio engineers.

In Search of the Miraculous

Nine months later I graduated with my degree in electrical engineering and left Texas for New York, where I soon found my first job as an electrical engineer in the World Trade Center, on the 64th floor of the north tower. While I worked during the day as a design engineer, my evenings and weekends were primarily filled with efforts to expand my understanding of the phenomenon of consciousness.

Being an avid reader since an early age, I spent many Saturdays searching through the stacks of the New York Public Library in the center of Manhattan, one of the largest libraries in the United States, second only to the Library of Congress in Washington, D.C. At the time I was searching through subject areas that dealt primarily with psychology and science, hoping to find material relevant to consciousness and in particular to "out of the ordinary" experiences. One Saturday morning I noticed a book someone had left on a reading table, and I opened it and began reading. The title of the book was *In Search of the Miraculous: Fragments of an Unknown Teaching,* and I was surprised to learn that the author was a mathematician, a Russian named Pyotr Demianovich Ouspensky (1878–1947).[15] Having always been impressed by technically credentialed writers, I checked the book out of the library and, with a mixture of awe and reverence, spent the rest of the weekend reading Ouspensky's book in my loft on Canal Street in lower Manhattan. Here I found a deep, articulate discussion of experiences and concepts that dealt directly with the subject of consciousness that now so fascinated me. Up until then I had assumed that all books fell into one of two categories, technical nonfiction and fiction. Yet here was a book written by a technically trained professional mathematician, describing his experiences during a three-year exploration of consciousness and search for "the miraculous" under the guidance of his teacher, a Greek-Armenian Orthodox Christian named George Ivanovich Gurdjieff. Reading the first page, I was immediately captivated, finding in Ouspensky's opening passages, word for word, a description perfectly mirroring my own search. Ouspensky writes here of his search for the miraculous:

> I had said that I was going to "seek the miraculous." The "miraculous" is very difficult to define. But for me this word had a quite definite meaning. I had come to the conclusion a long time ago that there was no escape from the labyrinth of contradictions in which we live except by an entirely new road, unlike anything hitherto known or used by us. But where this new or forgotten road began I was unable to say. I already knew then as an undoubted fact that beyond the thin film of false reality there existed another reality from which, for some reason, something separated us. The "miraculous" was a penetration into this unknown reality. And it seemed to me that the way to the unknown could be found in the East.[16]

This book by Ouspensky opened my eyes to an entirely new category of writing that I had not previously imagined existed, and I realized that what I was seeking might be found in the "esoteric" subject areas of mysticism, occultism, theosophy, and Asian religions and philosophies; all of these were subject areas I had never before been introduced to in high school or university courses, as they were generally ignored by the scientifically trained communities. Nor had the nuns ever mentioned such subjects, as their focus had been, it seems, to teach us to defend Catholicism in arguments with Protestants.

In addition to suddenly "discovering" an entirely new range of reading material to be explored, I soon acquired the habit of attending various lectures and workshops dealing with meditation and the esoteric; New York in the early '70s had become a confluence for new age teachers, authorities on esoteric contemplative practices, and over the next several years I was able to study with a number of seemingly authentic teachers, including Swami Satchidananda Saraswati, Chögyam Rinpoche, John Lilly, and Alan Watts. But during my five years in New York I had no idea that there might also be rich mystical traditions and teachings within my own Christian roots, and so my focus was upon absorbing theory and techniques regarding mysticism and psychonautics primarily from Buddhist, Taoism, Hindu and Native American traditions.

Perhaps it was synchronicity, but I was fortunate to be living on East Sixth Street, only three blocks from an amazingly esoteric bookstore run by the publisher, Samuel Weiser.[17] Weiser's bookstore offered many hundreds of books on such topics as Christian mysticism, Vedanta, Theosophy, Yoga, Buddhism, Sufism, medieval metaphysics, magic, shamanistic traditions, and a wide variety of esoteric religious teachings from many cultures; there, I spent many hours after work and on Saturday mornings browsing the shelves in my search for coherent theories of consciousness that might be compatible with what I knew of radio theory, physics, and quantum mechanics.

Tuning the Mind

During this time I was living in the Lower East Side, in a two room flat on the fifth floor of a five story walk-up in the Lower East Side of New York (Avenue 'A' and E. 6th Street). The neighborhood was full of Indian vegetarian restaurants and an influx of a young and noisy immigrants. At work in the World Trade Center, I had befriended the only other person I have ever known to have come from Trinidad, a young engineer named Rudy Israel. For many years he rented a fifth floor apartment on East 6th Street in the city, where he could party with friends in privacy (he lived with his parents in Queens), but as he was getting married, he bequeathed me the apartment. It was a strange place, and a rough neighborhood at the time (gentrified now). The rent was exceedingly cheap, at $ 21/month, so I decided to accept Rudy's offer.

Each floor at 530 E. 6th Street had it's own social ecology. As I entered the building up the stairs from the sidewalk to the first floor, I passed an apartment which always seemed to have the door partly open and restrained with a chain, revealing a blue light coming from within and a few African-Americans living there (rumored to sell drugs). The second floor housed an apartment with a Puerto Rican couple, often sounding as if fighting, and rumored to be a pimp and his girl. The third floor housed a strangely quiet man from Poland, who had covered his door with sheet metal. For the first year he would only whisper to me when greeted in the hall, but acting paranoid, as if someone were listening to us. Eventually he trusted me enough to invite me one day into his apartment for Oolong tea. I learned that he had helped design cooling systems for MIG fighter planes under the Soviet occupation as a young engineer, but had escaped with his brother over the mountains via a cross-country skiing adventure. On the fourth floor was a very old lady who lived alone, and apparently passed away alone during my second year there, only to be discovered a week later when a smell was detected in the hallway near her apartment. Though it was a challenge when carrying heavy groceries, my apartment on the 5th floor had the advantage of lowering most of the noise of the city neighborhood, and my inner room was wonderfully quiet, especially at night.

One late evening I was in my inner room doing my usual stretching exercises, trying to maintain a shoulder stand posture (*sarvāṅgāsana*) for 10 minutes as part of my *hatha yoga* practice. Part of the exercise was to move into the pose, then to become as quiet as possible, practicing internal silence.

This required making an effort to attenuate every thoughts that might arise, to detach from and not follow memories as they began to form, nor to allow any inner dialogue to resume streaming. The goal was to open up the bandwidth of awareness and to remain receptive, just listening. Suddenly, out of the silence, I heard a singular loud, high pitched tone which seemed to be located somewhere within my cranium. I noticed that as I focused my awareness on the sound it seemed to coalesce into a point while substantially increasing in volume! I quickly feared I might be experiencing a brain aneurism in progress. But as I soon discovered that by maintaining my focus, I was able to coax the sound into growing louder and more distinct, my fears were transformed into awe at this audible tone coming from within. Even more strange was that accompanying the sound sensation was a sensation of "touch" detectible within this tiny region located somewhere within the upper right-hand quadrant of my brain.

Then things became even more strange. After noticing the initial "bright" sound, additional "points" of sound of distinctly different pitch began to rise into awareness *in other locations in my cranium.* I gently lowered myself from my shoulder-stand position and, ending my hatha yoga for the night, lay down under a blanket in the dark. For many hours that night I could not sleep, totally fascinated in focusing upon and listening to the sounds that would variously increase in volume according to the degree that I would be able to direct my attention toward them. I noticed, however, that as soon as I would begin consciously thinking "about them" or "thinking in words," letting my attention begin to stray, they would subside and contact would be lost. I quickly learned that by gently dropping my train of thought which seemed so insistent on thinking, classifying, etc., I was able once more enter the silence and the tiny sounds would suddenly peek out of the silence once more, and increase in volume in what was clearly a feedback loop, a sort of reverberation responding to my search. The tones were quite pure, high pitched, and I suppose most people would classify them as a "ringing in the ears." Several months later I discovered the term "tinnitus," which was defined by medical science as any perceived sound not brought in by the ear canal. Since perception of these sounds seemed to bother people, doctors decided that it must be an disease of the hearing system with an unknown (yet to be determined) source.

Nevertheless, by now being quite serious in my efforts to explore the phenomenon of "consciousness" by any means possible, catalyzed by the unknown dimensions I had experienced on LSD and the Austin forest encounter with the glowing sphere of living light, I was completely fascinated by what was happening that night in my top floor apartment. I found that by trying to ignore a particularly dominant bright sound and trying to focus on a fainter, more obscure sound ("further away from" or "behind" the first) the second sound would immediately grow louder in volume and become easier to focus upon using this inner focal-sense mechanism. Here was direct cause and effect, albeit in an internal domain of consciousness among some kind of living experiential fields of energy dynamics. All that night I lay awake in the dark, moving from sound to sound within my head, as each would rise and fall, almost as if each had an independent volition of its own. I experienced strong emotional oscillations between exaltation verging on disbelief, and terror that I might be damaging my neuronal centers, perhaps even encouraging (or experiencing) a brain damaging hemorrhage.

As an electrical engineer, I had often listened to various single sinusoidal tones generated by equipment in laboratory sessions, yet this was not a single tone but a confluence of tones faintly making up a background of the perceived, sensed audio range, like those aforementioned "peepers" in the forest at night at Hamilton's pool. It was at specific points in space within my cranium, that from time to time a tone would arise with exponential sharpness high above the background level, to become a bright point, like a beacon, upon which, if I were able to sustain focus for a few moments, would become markedly louder with an accompanying intense tactile sensation.

During the course of what seemed a very long night my body grew hot and sweated profusely, soaking the sheets in what I assumed might be a fever caused by whatever was happening in my brain. I went through what seemed to be a long period of deep fear, suspecting that I had somehow damaged my nervous system. Yet, since that first night listening to the inner sounds, I have never experienced a headache or discomfort of any kind within my cranium.

Some time in the early morning hours I fell asleep. When I awoke it was with great relief to find that my mind seemed to be back to normal, having returned to its familiar mode of verbalized thoughts, chatting away merrily once more. However I now lived with these new memories and realization that something singularly strange had occurred, something I had never been prepared for and which I had never previously encountered in books nor in life's experiences.

I continued to practice *hatha yoga* but spent increasingly long periods in silent meditation, finding that, now, I was able to fairly easily contact these resonant inner sounds. I began the practice of focusing upon them while falling asleep, and found that when I would begin to awaken from a dream in the middle of the night, I was able to quickly re-enter the dream world by following these mysterious bright inner sounds.

My training in physics and electrical engineering led me to believe that these internal sounds were sine waves, not some sort of random noise. The tones also appeared to manifest in narrow spectrums centered about fundamental frequencies. For a time, I conjectured that they might be mechanical resonances within the physical structures of my inner ear. At the time I worked as an engineer for the Port Authority on the 64th floor of the World Trade Center, and began to experience, with great surprise, one of the high pitched sounds flare up in my cranium whenever I approached certain electronic equipment, computer screens, or even certain vending machines. At such moments I found myself internally verbalizing, with some humor "incoming," a phrase widely heard in the media at that time, from the front lines in Vietnam.

Over the next few weeks I noticed that, during my meditation sessions, if I concentrated awareness within different physical/spatial locations within my body, such as the heart or the throat, perceptually different sounds would arise in different locations and patterns, though the sounds were most clear and pronounced in the central region of my brain.

I soon concluded that the source of these perceived inner sounds must be of an electromagnetic nature, possibly the vibrations of a neuronal plexus within my nervous system resonating with electromagnetic modulations of our Earth's electromagnetic energy fields, or in the case of vending machines, the harmonic frequencies of some internal electrical radiation emanating from their circuitry, transformers, etc.

In bookstores I began to browse through books on anatomical structures of the brain and the central nervous system. This was the age before the internet, but luckily I was living in New York City, and had access not only to the New York Public Library, but to many bookstores with medical sections. I was soon able to obtain excellent material with technical illustrations and x-ray photographs of internal physiological structures. I used these to visualize, with as much detail as possible, those internal areas, usually corresponding with the Indian chakra system, while meditating in the dark.

Over several years this process, concentrating and visualizing within areas of my body and focusing on the sound tones as they would arise, became a main source of meditative practice for me, and the inner sounds tones grew ever more richly complex and often markedly louder in volume, and began to produce distinct tactile sensations of flowing nature, unlike the sensations felt in the external senses of touch, vision, taste, and hearing.

On weekends I would also search for books for guidance in silent meditation, and in the process discovered the *Patañjali's Yoga Sutras*. My first copy was a translation with commentaries by Professor Ernest E. Wood (1883–1965), having the rather impressive (and long) title of *Practical Yoga, Ancient and Modern, Being a New, Independent Translation of Patañjali's Yoga Aphorisms, Interpreted in the Light of Ancient and Modern Psychological Knowledge and Practical Experience*.[18] I was thoroughly impressed that Wood had first been educated in the "hard" sciences of chemistry, physics and geology, and only later had he become so thoroughly fascinated by yoga and meditation that he undertook to become a Sanskrit scholar. Wood's translations of the Sutras seemed to me to be the perfect manual for the type of meditative exploration that had become my passion. After carefully studying Wood's translation for several months, I found a different translation of the *Yoga Sutras* by a professor holding a PhD in chemistry, Dr. I.K. Taimni (1898–1978).[19] To my surprise, many of the translations and commentaries differed markedly between the two books. This led me to attempt an understanding of each word in the context of my own experiences and practices.

As a direct consequence of the three major experiences that steered my interest from physics to metaphysics (i.e., the experience of LSD at night on the beach, the light in the forest at Hamilton's Pool, and detection of the "inner sounds" in my New York apartment), I had discovered in the *Yoga Sutras*, what seemed to me to be an exceedingly useful, highly detailed, and integrated set of instruction and theory for psychonautic exploration through the means of prayer, meditation, and specific psychophysical exercises. More than simply a detailed handbook of "how to meditate," Patañjali's *Yoga Sutras* presents a theory-practice continuum that includes, in the words of the scholar Ian Whicher, "effective definitions, explanations and descriptions of key concepts and terms relating to *theoria* and *praxis* in Yoga."[20]

Patañjali's sutras can be likened to a set of charts for navigation within the ocean of consciousness, much in the same way as the "rutters," written compilations of collected sailing experiences shared among Portuguese mariners, were used to cross oceans to new worlds prior to the development of scientifically calibrated nautical charts in the 14th and 15th centuries. The Portuguese rutters contained not only sketches, charts, and maps from first-hand accounts and direct observation; they also a wealth of practical tips for exploring the new world oceans, pointing out such things as dangers to avoid, steering directions, and other practical instruction for those setting out upon ocean voyages. In a similar fashion, Patañjali's sutras can be viewed as a collection of practical information, a rutter for those choosing to leave their egos anchored behind and setting out for exploration upon the vast oceans of consciousness. Patañjali's *Yoga Sutras*, is thus a compendium of integrated sailing instructions for the psychonaut. We are all immersed in various oceans of consciousness but, like fish swimming in water, to us the waters of consciousness are invisible. And like fish in water, we often experience confusion, both as individuals and collectively, when powerful, seemingly

26

invisible currents of consciousness take hold and sweep us away to unfamiliar depths and strange regions of thought and sensation.

Within the next few months I found more than the first two published translations I had acquired, and with Samuel Weiser's help, I had soon acquired English translations of Patañjali by more than a dozen individuals, each one expressing widely different interpretations of many areas of the *Yoga Sutras*. I soon realized that to develop my own understanding of this classic of contemplative yoga in the context of what I had been taught in physics, electronics, and communication theory, I would need to study Sanskrit in order to understand the *sutras* more precisely.

Influenced by my recent direct experiences of the numinous during prayer, meditation, and LSD, far outside of the domains of laboratory science, I found myself becoming somewhat of a "black-sheep engineer," moving beyond a technical, materialist view of the world. My motivation was growing exponentially to explore consciousness in depth, *both* academically and experientially, and to understand the numinous in terms of modern science. This passion to explore the unknown regions of consciousness soon altered any previous career goals I might have had, replacing them with this new effort to understand not only my numinous direct experiences, but to pursue the deeper mysteries related to the core of my early religious teachings, and in particular the mysteries which had been presented as the Holy Trinity.

For some time I wondered where I might find the means to study the Sanskrit language in New York. However, in 1973 the answer arrived during a three-day workshop on Asian traditions and contemplation, led by Alan Watts, a brilliant teacher of Asian studies who was visiting from California. During the introduction to the workshop, Alan mentioned that during the fall he would be teaching graduate academic classes in Asian philosophy at the California Institute of Asian Studies (CIAS) in San Francisco. He described the school as unique in that the teachers at CIAS were both academically as well as experientially qualified to teach in their respective subjects. I soon contacted the Institute and received a catalog, and to my amazement, not only were Sanskrit language courses part of the curriculum, but one of the teachers of Indian philosophy at the school was Dr. Rammurti Mishra, the author of a 538-page treatise in what I considered to be one of the most detailed translations of the *Yoga Sutras*.[21]

I soon applied for admission to the California Institute of Asian Studies, though with some trepidation, concerned that my academic background in physics and engineering might not meet with approval for acceptance into an academic philosophy department. However to my delight I received a formal letter of admission, and the following spring, having worked for five years as an electrical design engineer in New York, I found myself travelling to San Francisco to enroll in a program of comparative Asian philosophy and religion. At last I would be able to study Sanskrit and Indian philosophy in a formal setting!

To the surprise of everyone I knew, I left my lucrative engineering job in New York to become a fulltime student in San Francisco. That autumn of 1974, in evening classes at the California Institute of Asian Studies, I was soon happily absorbing rich new paradigms supporting my efforts to discover new connections between physics, religion, and philosophy. One major new concept was introduced to me during my first class with Dr. Haridas Chaudhuri, a concept I had never heard of before, which he called *integral nondualism*.[22] Later I was to learn that this was his translation of Sri Aurobindo's Sanskrit term, *purna advaita*. This novel idea of integral nondualism was nothing like the separative, materialist, analytical approach I had steeped in as an undergraduate science student. This new way of viewing things grew ever more rich during my following semesters of study at the Institute, and this "integral perspective," or "aperspectival awareness," is also key to the development of the material presented in the following chapters.

An Alternate Way of Seeing

Quite often in life, in trying to understand abstract things, it is useful to find alternate perspectives. Analogies and stories often provide new insight into what previously seemed obscure or impossible to grasp. Many stories, particularly folk tales, convey meaning through simple analogy, which often leads to that wonderful "Aha!" moment as deeper levels of a puzzle suddenly click into place.

In the world of the sciences, the most common alternate way of seeing can be found in the tools of mathematics. The scribbled equations on parchment do not seem at first glance in any way to model the falling apple seen by Newton, but this mathematical lens suddenly gave Newton a way to see the pattern, to directly grasp the dynamism of an apple as it falls to the ground. Such may also be the case of our effort to obtain a deeper, clearer understanding of that which Christians revere as the Holy Trinity and Hindus see as Sat-Chit-Ananda.

The following chapters in this book offer major alternate perspectives from which we may enhance our approach to this mysterious "Holy Trinity." We first explore contemporary questions of nonduality and East/West thought from a Christian perspective in Chapter II, "Trinitarian Christianity," through the ideas of the Benedictine Camaldolese monks—Fr. Bruno Barnhart at a monastery in California, and Fr. Bede Griffiths at his ashram-monastery in South India. The section ends with an integrative look at the concepts in Christianity and evolutionary science set forth by the paleontologist/priest Pierre Teilhard de Chardin.

A alternate yet parallel perspective to the Christian approach to the Holy Trinity is presented in Chapter III, "Trinitarian Vedanta." Here the discussion compares the metaphysical concepts found in the Christian Holy Trinity to the nondual Vedantic experience of the Trinity which emerged in the ancient culture of India, as it has been translated into English and explained in 20th-century terms by the Oxford-educated Bengali, Sri Aurobindo Ghose.

In Chapter IV, "Trinitarian Quantum Physics," a third approach to the Holy Trinity can be found in concepts developed by 20th-century quantum physicists, and in particular from among the cosmological theories of the American quantum physicist David Bohm, who himself spent years in public dialog with the Indian sage Jiddu Krishnamurti.

Please note that *none of the chapters in this book need to be read sequentially*; each chapter presents ideas developed by one individual in the context of their life's biographical material.

The Integral Approach: Three Perspectives

Most would agree that it is rare to find serious discussion of Indian philosophy, cosmological quantum physics, and Christianity within the same context. It is rare to find authorities in any one of these subjects with the time or interest into delving more than superficially into the other two. However this book takes an "integral approach" to these three disciplines in order to derive a deeper understanding of each through the discovery of transdisciplinary relationships.

Academics are discovering now, in the early 21st century, that excessive focus and specialization results in a human knowledge that is becoming increasingly fragmented. The Biblical story of the Tower of Babel comes to mind: each domain of knowledge speaks its own language, using concepts supported within its own highly technical and acronym-laden field of academic specialization. Cross-discipline dialog and basic communication thus has become greatly impaired, if not impossible. According to the systems thinker, Edgar Morin, the problem seems to be both fragmentation and lack of integration:

> An influx of knowledge at the end of the 20th century sheds new light on the situation of human beings in the universe. Parallel progress in cosmology, earth sciences, ecology, biology and prehistory in the 1960s and 1970s have modified our ideas about the universe, the earth, life and humanity itself. But these contributions remain disjointed. That which is human is cut up into pieces of a puzzle that cannot form an image. . . . The new knowledge, for lack of being connected, is neither assimilated nor integrated. There is progress in knowledge of the parts and paradoxical ignorance of the whole.[23]

The integral approach in this book assumes that valid data may be found beyond the traditional methodologies which compartmentalize knowledge and lose the connection with other areas of understanding. An integral method examines information from multiple and often disparate domains, seeking to perceive correlations between them, resonances among disparate domains of knowledge that might lead to conceptual bridges between these otherwise relatively isolated, compartmentalized knowledges.

Sri Aurobindo's Integral Perspective

Historically, this integral methodology stems from a combination of integral philosophy and integral theory.[24] The Cambridge-educated Indian philosopher, Aravinda Ghose (1872–1950), later known as "Sri Aurobindo," was possibly the first writer to use the word "integral" extensively in his own writings on consciousness and evolution:

> Aurobindo is often credited as the first to use the term "integral" in connection with evolutionary philosophy. However, Harvard sociologist Pitirim Sorokin also began using the phrases "integral philosophy" and "integralist" in this connection at around the same time as Aurobindo. In fact, it appears that Sorokin, Aurobindo, and Gebser each originally adopted the term "integral" independently without knowledge of its use by others.[25]

Early in 1950, Dr. Frederic Spiegelberg (1897–1994), the academically renowned professor of Indian philosophy at Stanford University, began working with the British philosopher and writer Alan Watts (1915–1973) to establish a new center of East-West studies in San Francisco. Spiegelberg had travelled to South India the year before to study with the Indian mystic Ramana Maharshi at his ashram, and, during a two-week retreat in nearby Pondicherry, had also met with the scholar/mystic Sri Aurobindo. The meeting had a profound effect on Spiegelberg, as can be seen in the following dedication to Aurobindo in Spiegelberg's next book:

> To Sri Aurobindo for having X-rayed the author for five seconds lasting an eternity and for thereby calling forth the atman within as the only reality which he notices in any visitor.[26]

In his search for a scholar from India to head his new East-West studies center, Spiegelberg wrote to Sri Aurobindo, asking if he might suggest a suitable candidate to head his East-West research center, someone well versed in both Western and Indian philosophy. Aurobindo wrote back with the strongly worded recommendation of Dr. Haridas Chaudhuri, who was at the time a full professor and the Chair of Philosophy at the University of Calcutta, and who had written his dissertation on Aurobindo's integral philosophy. Spiegelberg managed to persuade the young professor to leave Bengal and relocate with his family to San Francisco, where Chaudhuri soon began teaching with Watts and Spiegelberg at what eventually became the graduate school known as the California Institute of Asian Studies (CIAS). The school changed its name in 1980 to the California Institute of Integral Studies.[27] At CIAS, Chaudhuri and Spiegelberg developed a new approach to the philosophy which Aurobindo often termed *purna advaita,* a Sanskrit concept that Chaudhuri translated as "integral panentheism" or "integral nondualism."

According to Sri Aurobindo's view, expressed clearly in his 1100-page work *The Life Divine,* evolutionary energy is to be found simultaneously manifesting in the cosmos of space–time *as well as* in a transcendent region, beyond time and space. But more even more significant was his teaching that it was possible, through direct contemplative practice, for individuals to *experience* these regions integrally connected in one unified and nondual whole.[28] In his student years at Cambridge, Sri Aurobindo, fluent in the French language, became acquainted with the writings of Henri Bergson, who in 1911 published *Creative Evolution.*[29] In *Creative Evolution,* Bergson argues for "intuition" as being of primary significance in any approach to exploring directly the phenomenon of consciousness. He writes that he regards intuition as being a mode of conscious awareness *beyond* the domain of an intellectual consciousness, and goes on to criticize modern epistemologies for discounting the use of intuition, while instead choosing to enforce the primacy of intellect:

> In the humanity of which we are a part, *intuition* is, in fact, almost completely sacrificed to intellect. . . . *Intuition* is there, however, but vague and above all discontinuous. It is a lamp almost extinguished, which only glimmers now and then, for a few moments at most . . . feeble and vacillating, but which none the less pierces the darkness of the night in which the intellect leaves us.[30]

Sri Aurobindo's integral perspective can be seen as one that requires going beyond the intellect to employ additional modes of apprehension such as, perhaps, that which Bergson terms *intuition,* and the entire range of supersensible perception implied in the Sanskrit term *samādhi,* described at length in *Patañjali's Yoga Sutras.* To understand the whole (including the physicist David Bohm's "Whole") requires a wider perspective than that offered by the analytical and separative intellectual cognition of the brain-evolved mind.

Gebser's Integral Perspective

A contemporary of Aurobindo, the German cultural historian and evolutionary philosopher Jean Gebser (1905–1973), writing in Switzerland in the 1940s, developed another approach to integral philosophy. Laying out his theory of an integral consciousness in his book *The Ever-Present Origin,* Gebser develops a theory of the evolutionary emergence of a new mode of consciousness which he calls "the 'aperspectival (arational–integral)' consciousness."[31] Gebser's motivating objective was to foster what he called an incipient "integral aperspectival consciousness."[32]

Gebser's spoke primarily through the lens of cultural anthropology, but his integral methodology is far ranging. In Gebser's approach can be seen a search for meaning through the discovery of *transdisciplinary* connections, and here, in an essay entitled "Cultural Philosophy as Method and Venture," Gebser explains the importance of *an integral effort* for uncovering "meaning-giving connections:"

> It is a scientific attempt, particularly distinctive of our epoch, to appraise the multiplicity of cultural endeavors, that is to say, to uncover meaning-giving connections . . . it could contribute toward the abolition of the feeling of isolation which today not only reigns in the various scientific disciplines but which is generally prevalent.[33]

Another prolific thinker taking an integral approach to philosophical inquiry is the German Indologist Georg Feuerstein, who in discussing Gebser's methodology, describes how Gebser's aim can be seen encapsulated in the term *synairesis*, "an intelligent realization of reality proceeding from the accomplished transparency of all modes of cognition."[34] In fact, Feuerstein tells us, it is Gebser's *synairesis* that can free us from the limited bounds of scientific realism. Feuerstein here comments:

> Gebser also makes it clear that his panoramic orientation is not a mere synthesis, which would only be part of the kind of systematization peculiar to the mental-rational consciousness. He speaks of his methodology as aiming at *synairesis*, which is an integral understanding, or perception, of reality. . . . *Synairesis*, then, describes an intelligent realization of reality which proceeds from the accomplished transparency of all the various modes of cognition.[35]

Gebser coins yet another term to describe his methodology, *systasis*, a term implying a process whereby partials merge or are merged into a whole:

> *Systasis* is the means whereby we are able to open up our consolidated spatial consciousness to the integrating consciousness of the whole. This integrating consciousness enables us to perceive and present the integrity or integrality of the whole.[36]

By contrast, scientific materialism, the driving force behind contemporary technological miracles, has relied thus far upon a limited intellectual focus, almost exclusively applied to statistical subsets, measurements and observations abstracted from the whole. Physics and the hard sciences have seldom explored nor investigated reports of the many phenomena that cannot be measured nor observed in time and space. Materialists have no way to consider such things as love, faith, compassion, or consciousness itself, and thus it is left to the nonscientifically trained academic specialties, who are without the tools that might bridge the gap between space-time dimensions and loving dimensions. Yet there is hope; previously it was a rare theoretical physicist who would investigate the multidimensional "whole" as a starting point, as did Einstein and Bohm, yet this limitation is gradually being recognized by small segments of the scientific community, as Feurstein remarks here:

> Avant-garde scientists admit the need and indeed are looking for a new "paradigm" that, hopefully, will do justice to the multidimensionality of humanness.[37]

Gebser's opus, *The Ever-Present Origin*, leads the way into this new multidimensional research methodology, which he refers to as the integral, multiperspectival approach. From a wider mix of academic and historical perspectives than that traditionally taken by material science, the focus becomes one of discovering and verifying new patterns through a *synairesis* emerging from multiple disciplines.[38]

According to Gebser, what he calls the integral approach leads to the acquisition of a panoramic, multiperspectival view which can present the observer with a newer, more detailed map—and a richer understanding of—the subject being explored.

Gebser subsequently called this newly emergent mode of consciousness "integral consciousness." Once activated, the integral perspective leads directly to transformatively new insights. Here, Gebser clarifies his aperspectival approach by referencing it here as a "new spiritual attitude:"

> The aperspective consciousness structure is a consciousness of the whole, an integral consciousness encompassing all time and embracing both man's distant past and his approaching future as a living present. The *new spiritual attitude* can take root only through an insightful process of *intensive awareness*. This *attitude* must emerge from its present concealment and latency to become effective.[39]

Wilber's Integral Perspective

Another significant contribution to and example of this evolving integral approach can be found in the writing of the American philosopher Ken Wilber, who expresses his own theories of an integral philosophy here in his 1996 book, *A Brief History of Everything*:

> If we look at the various fields of human knowledge— from physics to biology to psychology, sociology, theology and religion—certain broad, general themes emerge about which there is very little disagreement. If we take these types of largely agreed upon orienting

generalizations from the various branches of knowledge . . . and if we string these orienting generalizations together, we will arrive at some astonishing and often profound conclusions, conclusions that, as extraordinary as they might be, nonetheless embody nothing more than our already agreed upon knowledge.[40]

Wilber integrates material from far-ranging disciplines, including psychology, Asian philosophy, and to a lesser extent, the sciences. In so doing, he presents an approach that he terms Integral Methodological Pluralism (IMP), in which multiple perspectives are brought together in an effort to elicit a deeper understanding of consciousness.[41] The methodology of IMP stresses the idea that all articulated understandings are like fingerprints in their uniqueness. They are context-based: formed within specific cultural epochs, and molded by particular academic, experiential, and cultural-historic background environments. It is from this milieu that each individual attempts to forge new, clarified self-referential maps of understanding.[42]

Wilber's methodology can be seen to work by juxtaposing historically older paradigmatical frameworks alongside newer paradigms. In *A Brief History of Everything*, for example, Wilber outlines contemplative maps of consciousness accumulated by Indian Vedantic contemplatives over many millennia, and then supports these with fundamental considerations of nonduality as described by quantum physicists. He then brings into focus the resulting overlay by expressing them in terms of various transpersonal theories articulated by modern psychologists.[43]

In addition to the inclusion of such wide-ranging source material, Wilber applies the use of an epistemological capacity which he calls "vision-logic," consisting of an integration of intellectual capacity with intuition in order to bring about the recognition of new relationships among radically distinct perspectives.[44] While Wilber's *vision-logic* echoes the central methodological ideas of intuition as developed by Henri Bergson, it also clear that Wilber embraces the discipline-bridging interdisciplinary method of *synairesis* associated with Gebser's integral approach.[45]

Integral Approaches to the Holy Trinity

The short history of the integral method according to Aurobindo, Gebser, and Wilber has been discussed in the previous 10 pages to help the reader appreciate the trans-disciplinary ecumenical approach to the Holy Trinity developed in the following sections of this book.

In Fig. 4 can be seen a visual outline of the integral method applied in the following chapters to more fully understand the Holy Trinity. The diagram presents the three approaches taken here: Christianity, Vedanta, and Physics.

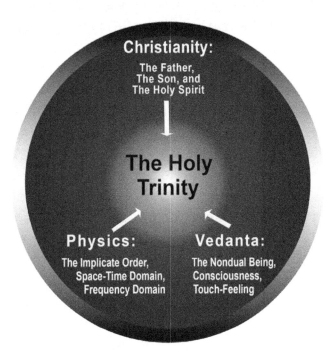

Figure 4. *An Integral Approach to the Holy Trinity.*

These approaches are clarified in the following chapters:

Chapter II –> Trinitarian Christianity

Chapter III –> Trinitarian Vedanta

Chapter IV –> Trinitarian Quantum Physics

But first we conclude this chapter with a review of the historical roots of the Holy Trinity and a discussion of several key metaphysical concepts that were not available to previous generations in their explorations of this mystery.

Historical Approaches to the Trinity

The archetypal image of the Holy Trinity, one that has been a globally familiar concept for millennia, is even now a living article of faith for over three billion contemporary human beings. The majority of two billion Christians and one billion Hindus on the planet in the early 21st century share the belief that God manifests Himself/Herself/Itself in *three distinctly different modes* or hypostases.[46]

This is not a new belief among human beings, for we find among the earliest writing in Egypt, some 5,000 years ago, explicit references to the Trinity: "All gods are three: Amun, Re and Ptah, whom none equals. He who hides his name as Amun, he appears to the face as Re, his body is Ptah."[47] Why do we find this recurring Trinitarian structure at the root of so many metaphysical world views? According to the renowned scholar of comparative religion Raimundo Panikkar, "My surmise is that it is *reality itself* that discloses itself as Trinity."[48]

Yet the Trinity, this fascinating and sublime mystery, so widely revered and intuited by generations of humans throughout history, is currently regarded merely as a minor object of inquiry among the limited number of academic specialties of anthropology, literature, history and theological studies. In a 1940 lecture, Carl Jung deplored the fact that this Trinity has been so exclusively relegated to theology and history that it is no longer, in general, even thought about:

> From a series of reactions, it has become clear to me that educated readers take exception to the psychological discussion of Christian symbols, even when these discussions carefully avoid questioning the symbols' religious value. . . . A notion like the Trinity belongs so much to the realm of theology that today, of the secular disciplines, history alone deals with it. People have even largely stopped thinking about a concept like the Trinity, which is so difficult to picture.[49]

This book addresses Jung's concerns by presenting in details a comprehensible picture of the Trinity beyond that simply of its theological history and liturgical imagery. The integral approach reveals an internal structure and dynamic pattern of operation that is seen to be operational—not only throughout the entire cosmos, but also within the depths of each human brain, mind, psyche, and soul.

Following the integral methods pioneered by Aurobindo, Gebser, and Wilber, an integral view of the Trinity is explored, developed, superimposed, and interlinked in the next three chapters, which cover the following subject material:

1. metaphysical ideas from contemporary Christianity,
2. physical maps from quantum physics, and
3. fundamentals of Indian philosophy.

The resulting perspective is unlikely to be found in any single-sided historical, metaphysical, or theological approach. This superimposition of Christianity, Indian philosophy, and quantum physics leads to the dawning realization that *there must be a fundamental Trinitarian structure to the Whole.*

This vast Trinitarian foundation underlies, supports, and engages the universe that we know through all of our everyday activities, and even during our dreamtime at night. Reinforcing a multitude of traditional wisdom teachings handed down by every culture through the ages, it becomes more certain that through prayer and contemplative exercises, we have the capacity to *directly* touch, experience, and commune not only with one another, but also with that Whole which billions of living humans recognize as the Holy Trinity.

Six Metaphysical Concepts

Numerous concepts developed in the 20th century were not available to premodern metaphysical writers. Before delving more deeply into the physics and psychophysics of the Holy Trinity, six modern concepts, keys to approaching an integral understanding of the Trinity, are introduced here. Several of these concepts may be new to the general reader.

- Consciousness
- Nondualism
- Fourier Transform
- Holoflux
- Noosphere
- Omega Point

These terms are metaphysical in the sense that, with the exception of the Fourier Transform, they fall beyond the realm usually discussed by physicists with their near-exclusive focus upon concepts that can be directly related to a material science which tends to focus exclusively on data that is measurable in space-time.

Metaphysics itself, a term taken to indicate anything that is "beyond physics," first emerged as a distinction during the 1st century CE at the great library in Alexandria, when the librarians, while organizing the works of Aristotle along a shelf, chose to place scrolls dealing with physics and geometry first, and made up the word "metaphysics" μετά (meta) ("following after," or "beyond") for all other subject material on the shelf. Modern science has proceeded to follow this same pattern, distancing itself from observations deemed to fall outside the subjects of material science. This traditional separation, dividing physics from metaphysics, has grown so pervasive in our culture that opportunities to fully understanding the cosmos in a wider context have been greatly diminished. By contrast, the modern integral approach considers the entire shelf in an attempt to integrate and reconcile material from physics through and inclusive of metaphysics.

After a brief introduction to each of these six terms, they will be discussed in greater detail within the following three chapters which sketch the life work and metaphysical writings of Pierre Teilhard de Chardin, Sri Aurobindo, and David Bohm.

Consciousness

The term consciousness has taken on such a wide range of meanings that it is important to understand how it might be used in discussing the Holy Trinity. "Consciousness," the word itself, did not even exist until recently, as the neuropsychologist turned consciousness researcher Allan Combs explains:

> The word *consciousness* is of fairly recent origin, dating back only a few hundred years. Its Latin predecessor was the word *conscientia*, which all the

way back in Roman jurisprudence referred to the knowledge a witness has of the deeds of another person. The implication was that this knowledge was supposed to be "shared with" others, for example, in the court. Later the word was used by medieval Christian scholars to mean something very much like a *moral conscience.*[50]

In a medical setting, the frequently encountered phrase "the patient regained consciousness" would imply that consciousness is a binary condition: the patient is either "conscious" or "unconscious." In contrast, the approach taken in this book is similar to that which is described by Ken Wilber in his book, *The Spectrum of Consciousness*. There he discusses consciousness in terms of a spectrum, similar to radio waves considered to form a vast "electromagnetic spectrum" which spans a range of frequencies in wavelengths from the size of galaxies down to wavelengths many times smaller than the size of an electron. A diagram of "consciousness" drawn in the year 1619 can be viewed in Fig. 5.

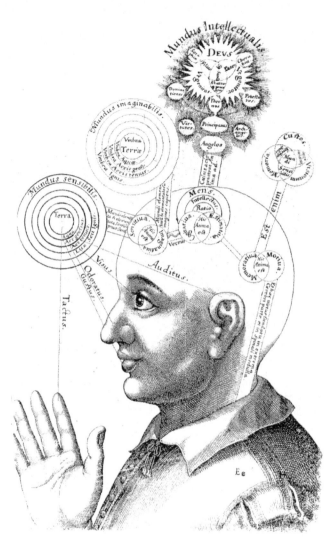

Figure 5. *Consciousness.*[51]

Nine hierarchies of angels can be seen in the region surrounding the Trinity at the top of the drawing. According to "Pseudo-Dionysius," a Christian theologian and philosopher of the late 5th century, angels of higher rank have greater power and authority over lower ranks. Each type has unique features, often with varying numbers of wings and faces. The hierarchies of angels seen communicating with human consciousness at the top of Fig. 5 are shown magnified in Fig. 6.

Figure 6. *Angelic Hierarchies Surrounding the Trinity.*

These nine angelic hierarchies are as said to be:

- Seraphim
- Cherubim
- Thrones
- Dominions or Lordships

- Virtues or Strongholds
- Powers or Authorities
- Principalities or Rulers
- Archangels
- Angels

Note that what are commonly called "angels," in Latin, "Angelos," are to be found at the bottom of the hierarchy, closest to the consciousness of the human being.

Nondualism

At the heart of much religious thinking, both East and West, is the assumption that *dualism* is at the foundation of all created structures within the universe, for example: light/dark, male/female, soul/body, heaven/Earth, human/God, good/bad, and so on.

Nondualism is in stark contrast to dualistic thinking. The term "nondualism," though frequently associated with Asian religious philosophies, is also found in many streams of thought in the West. Nondualism is a philosophical lens through which reality may be viewed as a unitary being, or as the physicist David Bohm would say, the "Whole."

In terms of consciousness, the psychologist William James described the situation of the relationship of finite, separate entities to the whole as follows: "The finite knowers, in spite of their apparent ignorance, are one with the knower of the all."[52] Fifty years later Carl Jung put forth the concept of the one (nondual) Self as the single center of consciousness

> The Self is not only the centre, but also the whole circumference which embraces both conscious and unconscious; it is the centre of this totality, just as the ego is the centre of each human consciousness.[53]

Issues of the Self—the center, the knower—and its origins were discussed by contemplative sages in northern India as far back as the 8th century BCE, and can be found in passages from the Chandogya Upanishad, which summarized the conclusions derived from generations of speculation over fundamental questions of existence:

—From what source did the universe come into existence?

—What was the nature of that source, *prior* to coming into existence?

—Was there just "a nothingness" or was there "a something?"

These arguments culminated in two possibilities:

1. In the beginning, at the source of creation, there was only *Sat* (Reality, Being) without-a-second.

2. In the beginning, at the source of creation, there was only *A-sat* (Nothingness, non-Being).

The majority of sages felt that it is difficult to accept that the universe was born from Nothingness or non-Being (a stance later adopted by Buddha's followers), and so they gravitated toward the first assumption, that at the beginning there must have been "one *Sat* only, without-a-second." Thus was established the metaphysical assumption that supports the modern philosophy of Vedanta. According to this view, the myriad of dualities (good/bad, light/dark, male/female etc.) are not seen to be fundamental, but are instead viewed as creative derivations, *subsets of the whole*, slices of the pie.

Christian Europeans, arriving in India, abhorred this idea and condemned this indigenous Indian belief that all of the created universe might be considered to be of the same substance as God. Western Christianity's view of God had become that of a transcendent Father figure, far beyond, above, and superior to nature and this obviously imperfect, sinful and transient universe. The Roman Catholic Church officially regarded pantheism as sinful and even heretical, and in 1600 condemned the monk Giordano Bruno to be burned at the stake for teaching that God was both immanent and infinite (Bruno also happened to be a mathematical cosmologist, who had extended the Copernican theory even further by theorizing that that stars were distant suns surrounded by exoplanets).

Now however, in the 21st century, *nondualism* has once again become a subject of significant interest among Christian contemplatives. In an essay on unitive consciousness, the contemplative Benedictine hermit monk, Fr. Bruno Barnhart (trained as a chemist, a modern Bruno!), in the first paragraph of his paper entitled "Purity of Heart and Contemplation," declares:

> This paper is an exploration of nonduality as the theological principle of a rebirth of sapiential (or "wisdom") Christianity in our time.[54]

Fr. Bruno goes on to identify the major contemporary problem in trying to reconcile philosophy, religion, and science:

> To put it very simply, the dominant rational-analytical consciousness of the past few centuries in the West has largely extinguished the participative and unitive modes of consciousness in the mainstream of Western thought—whether theological or secular.[55]

Bruno points out that over the past fifty years the growing impact of Asian metaphysical approaches to contemplation have recharged Western Christian monastic practice. During my first protracted retreats as a guest at Benedictine monasteries, in Italy as well as in California, I was astonished to find, in both monastery book stores, a large section of books on Asian philosophy, religion, and even yoga! In concluding his essay, Fr. Bruno directly equates Christian contemplation with nondual experience:

> The interpretation of Christian contemplation as nondual experience demands that we understand the phenomenon in terms of the whole person rather than as a fulfillment of one human faculty—be it even the contemplative intellect, the *nous* of Plato and Plotinus. . . . Let us summarize this conception of contemplation—in the Christian context but from our Eastern perspective. *Contemplation is **a direct, "nondual" experience of the inner self**.* It is, therefore, not merely an isolated phenomenon, but the momentary awareness of something that is present at every moment of our life. Contemplation is a direct experience of the ground of consciousness, of a depth from which we may live continually.[56]

The Fourier Transform

The Fourier Transform is a unique mathematical formula, discovered in 1798, that implies the existence of a dimension (or dimensions) outside of what we consider to be our normal world of space-time. The Fourier transform was initially discovered over two hundred years ago by Jean-Baptiste Joseph Fourier (1768–1830), a French physicist and mathematician who entered a Benedictine monastery at the age of nineteen, hoping to become a priest.

Several years later, due to his demonstrated ability to understand abstract mathematics, Fourier was asked by the abbot to leave the rural monastery to teach at a Jesuit school in Paris. He was soon caught up in the political fervor of the

French Revolution, and was briefly imprisoned during the Terror of 1795.

Upon release, Fourier, in his late 20s, not only solidified his reputation as a brilliant mathematician and physicist, but was soon recognized as a staunch defender of Napoleon and the newly established French Republic. Due to his increasingly public involvement with politicians and philosophers, he was soundly criticized by leading mathematicians of the time, among them the famous Pierre-Simon Laplace and Joseph-Louis LaGrange, whose own discoveries later found widespread applications in engineering.[57]

Early in 1798 Napoleon proposed a military expedition to seize and annex Egypt as a French colony, to thereby to bolster the influence of the young French Republic through undermining England's access to India. Napoleon chose the young Fourier to be his science advisor during the expedition.

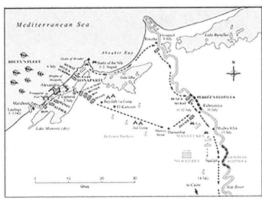

Napoleon's Campaign in Egypt, 1798

Figure 7. *Napoleon in Egypt.*

Napoleon's fleet docked at Alexandria and within days his troops had quickly routed the combined Egyptian and Ottoman armies, which lost more than 50,000 men in the French assault. Cairo soon fell, but while Napoleon was victorious on land, his armada of warships was ambushed by a British fleet under Admiral Nelson during a surprise attack. With its warships destroyed, the French army lost essential industrial equipment that it had relied upon for the manufacture, maintenance, and repair of field cannons and other artillery pieces.

At Napoleon's bidding, Fourier quickly set up an enormous workshop in Cairo to replace the missing technology, and in the process, he became fascinated by techniques of measuring and controlling the heat flow in the forging of cannons. Due to lack of a clear understanding of heat flow, forging a metallic cannon barrel was at the time more of an art than a science. Fourier's mathematical focus upon the physics of flowing heat radiation led him to discover a radically new and more accurate way of predicting thermal dynamics based upon a trigonometric series (later called the Fourier series).[58]

Here, in the first paragraph of his publication, *The Analytical Theory of Heat*, Fourier reveals how intertwined (integral) were his philosophical and scientific perspectives:

> Primary causes are unknown to us; but are subject to simple and constant laws, which may be discovered by observation, the study of them being the object of natural philosophy. *Heat, like gravity, penetrates every substance of the universe, its rays occupy all parts of space.* The object of our work is to put forth the mathematical laws which this element obeys. The theory of heat will hereafter form one of the most important branches of general physics.[59]

Two centuries later it is widely understood that electromagnetic fields, like gravity, penetrate every substance of the universe, and we now know that "heat" is a perceived effect of purely electromagnetic energy waves. Radio engineers and physicists use the Fourier transform in their work to analyze radiant energy phenomena and to design electromagnetic devices. The application of Fourier transform analysis is also foundational to understanding quantum mechanics, as the physicist David Bohm writes here in the first page of his 646-page textbook, *Quantum Theory*:

> It is not generally realized that the quantum theory represents a radical change, not only in the content of scientific knowledge, but also in the fundamental conceptual framework in terms of which such

knowledge can be expressed. . . . It is presupposed that the reader is moderately familiar with Fourier analysis.[60]

The power of analysis using the Fourier transform lies in its application for simplifying calculations in what is called "the frequency domain" that otherwise would be extremely difficult, if not impossible, to perform within the "space-time domain." The calculus required to solve problems and design circuits using space and time coordinates is extremely difficult due to non-linearity and turbulence encountered in even the simplest of spacetime relationships. Space is curved, as Einstein predicted and physics has confirmed, and time itself is dependent on the velocity of an energy waveform in space, making almost all calculations dealing with complex signal waveforms moving through space and time exceedingly difficult. However, through use of the Fourier transform, physicists are able to transform all coordinates *out from space-time* into what is called the *frequency domain*, a timeless, spaceless domain where the same exact frequency configurations can be manipulated using simple linear mathematical methods, and thus avoid the complex calculation problems associated with complex coordinates in time and space. Once the calculations have been made, a reverse Fourier transform is applied to bring the solution back into space and time, where the resulting answers can be used to solve problems inherent in designing workable signal circuitry, or predicting the thermal effects of casting molten metal in various geometries.

Fourier analysis was initially used only to solve heat flow problems; however in 1925, more than a century after Fourier's discovery, the MIT physicist Norbert Wiener (1894–1964), often referred to as the "father of cybernetics," published a book on the Fourier transform, indicating how it might be used to facilitate signal analysis and synthesis. Wiener highlighted the power of the Fourier transform for encoding signals and the communication of information in biological organisms, the human brain, and electromagnetic devices.[61]

Until recently, most engineers and physicists using the Fourier relationship assumed that the frequency domain described by the Fourier transform is not "real" in the sense that space and time are assumed to be "real" to human beings who experience being alive in space and time. Many who are familiar with the Fourier transform assume that it is just another abstract mathematical tool, and they never consider the ontological implications of the relationship between the two domains expressed by the Fourier transform.

Nevertheless, philosophers exploring the roots of science have posed such questions as: Why does pure mathematics seem to govern natural phenomena? Where might such mathematical principles come from? Are they eternal? Did mathematical relationships somehow exist when the universe began? Or are they timeless, somehow eternal? The Fourier transform itself assumes that there is a space-time dimension that exists and that signals in space-time can be transformed into an existing *frequency domain*, manipulated, and then transformed *out of* the frequency dimension back into what we know as space-time.

It may thus be inferred that deeper implications of the Fourier transform for our everyday reality are that the world consists of two domains or regions: 1. a physical space-time domain, and 2. a nondual otherworldly region known as the frequency domain, or as the physicist David Bohm called it, the "the implicate order," (introduced in the next section). In fact, while discussing the source of consciousness itself, Bohm has stated:

Consciousness is to be comprehended in terms of the implicate order, along with reality as a whole. . . . the implicate order *is also its primary and immediate actuality*.[62]

This basic grasp of the Fourier transform is important in our approach to understanding the Trinity. In terms of the Holy Trinity archetype, the relationship described by the Fourier transform implies a mathematical link or bridge between that hypostasis that is referred to as "the Father," in a timeless transcendental dimension, and the manifestation known as "the Son," which we understand to co-exist within the human dimensions of time and space in our material universe. To understand this mathematical equation in greater detail and how it was derived, the reader is referred to the section at the end of this book: "Appendix A: The Fourier Transform."

The Implicate Order and the Explicate Order

To the physicist, David Bohm (1917–1992), the larger universe, referred to as "the Whole," consists of two domains, an *implicate order* and an *explicate order*, linked by the two-way transformation process of energy mapped by the Fourier transform relationship. Bohm's *explicate order* is our everyday world of space and time, the familiar region sensed by human beings primarily through the qualia of vision and hearing. Space-time consists of four dimensions: three dimensions of space (height, width, and length) plus a single dimension of time.

Contemporary physics asserts, however, that there are *more than* these familiar four dimensions within which our sensory systems work. Einstein himself, in developing his general theory of relativity, demonstrated that it takes ten fields or dimensions to describe fully the mathematics of gravity.[63]

While classical Newtonian physics has focused solely within an exploration of the four dimensions of space-time (height, width, length, time), quantum physics has begun to seek data implicating additional dimensions outside of space-time. But where are such dimensions to be sought? Are they perhaps outside of, other than, or even *beyond* space and time? Fig. 8 maps the explicate and implicate order in relation to time, space, and the nonlocal frequency domain. In the center can be seen a mathematical depiction of the Fourier transform, which links and bridges the two orders.

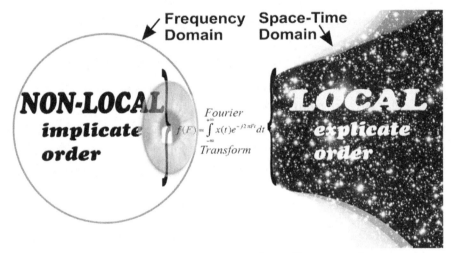

Figure 8. *The Implicate and Explicate Orders.*

In the diagram of Fig. 8, an iris-like lens at the Planck length aperture, between David Bohm's implicate order and the explicate order, mirrors Karl Pribram's 1991 conceptualization in *Brain and Perception*:

> These two domains characterize the input to and output from a lens that performs a Fourier transform. On one side of the transform lies the space–time order we ordinarily perceive. On the other side lies a distributed enfolded holographic-like order referred to as the frequency or spectral domain.[64]

It is the implicate order, located at the center, everywhere, that is the ground, base, or center out of which dynamically springs the space–time continuum itself, the explicate order. This will be developed and explained in great detail in Chapter IV, "Trinitarian Quantum Physics."

The Noosphere

The term noosphere was first used sometime in 1921 during informal conversations in Paris among three colleagues and close friends: Pierre Teilhard de Chardin (1872–1953, an anthropologist and geologist), Vladimir Ivanovich Vernadsky (1863–1945, a geologist and chemist), and one of Henri Bergson's closest academic disciples, Edouard Louis Emmanuel Julien Le Roy (1870–1954, a mathematician and philosopher).

Meeting regularly to discuss cutting-edge ideas in the physics of evolution (during the same period in which Einstein received his 1921 Nobel Prize) the three friends identified the *noosphere* as a term appropriate to refer to a vast *region of collective consciousness*. This noosphere they saw as an emerging region of the planet Earth, an evolving extension of consciousness interpenetrating yet distinct from the region identified by Vernadsky as the *biosphere* (a term Vernadsky he himself used as the title of his 1926 book). According to Vernadsky it was Le Roy who first used the term, but Le Roy credits his friend Pierre Teilhard de Chardin with coining the term *noosphere*.

Several years later, in his major work, *The Human Phenomenon*, Teilhard describes the arc of cosmic unfoldment on planet Earth, painting a picture of evolution through time as more than merely the physically observable panorama of measurable manifestations, but as an increasingly complex crystallization of distinctly beautiful form and conscious mentation. Having seemingly reached a zenith on Earth in *homo sapiens*, this evolutionary arc is pictured as moving steadily toward ever greater "complexity-consciousness"[65] or "internal centro-complexification"[66] through the process of centration[67] or centrogenesis,[68] all terms developed by Teilhard in essays collected in his posthumous publication *Activation of Energy*[69].

Where then might we see planetary geophysical features corresponding with Teilhard's vision of the noosphere? Like the invisible water in which all fish swim, we emerge into (and throughout our lives exist within) the geomagnetic field of the earth. Constantly bathed by this swirling vortex of geomagnetic radiation, we never see nor seldom think of the fact that directly below us, occupying half of the diameter of the planet, is a glowing vibrating source of geomagnetic radiant flux emanating from an enormous crystalline iron-nickel[70] core of glowing energy. Yet we have all seen magnetic compass needles line up with the magnetosphere and for centuries have relied upon that field to chart the course on land, sea, and air. And this is far from a static field as we can see in the swirling glow of the aurora borealis when these dynamically pulsing geomagnetic fields are lit up with ionized gasses in far latitudes.

The Omega Point

A term introduced by Teilhard de Chardin, the *Omega Point* concept has often been misinterpreted by modern theologians as a point of time *in the future*, known as the *parousia*. However, this reading ignores much of Teilhard's writing which indicates that the Omega Point is located within space itself now, at the Center, everywhere. Thus the Omega Point is *not* located in some far off future time, but is eternally present. It is here, now, within every center. In describing the evolution of consciousness, Teilhard tells us we are destined to break through into this "ultra-centre of unification and wholeness:"

> The curve of consciousness, pursuing its course of growing complexity, will break the material framework of Time and Space to escape somewhere toward an ultra-centre of unification and wholeness, where there will finally be assembled, and in detail, everything that is irreplaceable and incommunicable in the world.[71]

It will be demonstrated in this book that the Omega Point is to be found within each one of us, spatially *at the center* of our very being. In "The Heart of Matter," completed in Paris in 1950, Teilhard describes Omega in terms of what can only be seen as a culmination of his own direct personal experience (as a priest and mystic) of consciousness approaching Omega. He states clearly that the discovery of this Omega "brings to a close what I might call the natural branch of the inner trajectory I followed in my search for the ultimate consistence of the universe."[72] Teilhard goes on to define his vision of Omega as "the complex unit in which the organic sum of the reflective elements of the World becomes irreversible within a *transcendent Super-ego*."[73]

In a lecture delivered at the French embassy in Peking in 1946, Teilhard discusses the importance of the point Omega concept, its perceptual observation by mystics, and its function in the terraforming of a planetary consciousness:

> Let us suppose that from this universal centre, this Omega point, there constantly emanate radiations hitherto only perceptible to those persons whom we call "mystics."[74]

II.   Trinitarian Christianity

The themes upon which we are now touching are, without doubt, most delicate ones, which no one has the right to approach without reverent awe, deep humility and a sincere respect for tradition. Yet is it not precisely this respect for tradition, this awe and humility which oblige us to bring all our faith to bear upon an examination of them?

Raimundo Panikkar, *The Trinity*, 61.

Before exploring Trinitarian Christianity and Teilhard de Chardin's discoveries of the human experience of the Trinity from the vantage of human consciousness, it is important to go deeper into the meaning and implications of the word "contemplation."

The Latin word *contemplatio* (from the root *templum* or sacred place) was first used by Roman writers to translate the Greek word θεωρία (*theoria*). A dictionary definition of the word "contemplation" offers the following: "serious and quiet thought for a period of time."[75] In the Christian West during the Middle Ages, contemplation was often described as "gazing with love upon God," "the experience of union with God," or "a state of mystical awareness of God's being."[76]

Today, with the East-West convergence of traditions and cultures, *contemplation* can now be understood not only as a particular mode of religious practice, but also as an introspective approach to a highly complex participatory experience often described as "non-ordinary awareness," "nondualism," or "nondual consciousness."

Contemplation has come to be seen as consisting of a wide range of practices for exploring other dimensions of consciousness through a variety of means. The oceanic dimensions of consciousness itself have become the "final frontier," and those who venture to sail into the strange, sometimes terrifying, and often overwhelming oceans of consciousness are called contemplatives, mystics, saints, or psychonauts. In a more secular context, contemplation can be understood as the art and practice of discovering and exercising various faculties as necessary to arrive at a rich, direct, "nondual" experience of the vast inner (and outer) self–Jung's big Self, in contrast with the normal waking state, which has been called the "little ego-separated self."[77] In earlier cultures, contemplative techniques were the explicit domain of the monk or shaman, often in eremetical settings of silent forest or cave, far from the noise and bustle of village and city.

Unfortunately, the value of pursuing or even teaching the more contemplative dimensions of the religious experience seem to have been lost or discarded by modern Christian cultures. My own introduction to contemplation began fairly late in life, even though my religious instruction began when I was six years old, in a convent school near London. We were required to study what is called "the catechism," a collection of fundamental Christian truths, according to the Roman Catholic Church, in question and answer format. This catechism was published by Cardinal Bellarmine, an Italian Jesuit priest, in 1597, and it consisted of a series of questions and answers children and catechumens were asked to memorize. I still clearly recall the struggle to memorize the following:

Q. *Who made you?*
A. God made me.

Q. *Why did God make you?*
A. God made me to know, love, and serve Him in this world, and to be happy with Him forever in the next.

Unfortunately the catechism taught us nothing about any actual approaches to prayer, contemplation or meditation. In fact, I cannot recall ever hearing the words "contemplation" or "meditation" until well into my 20s. As children we simply learned that "to pray" encompassed the recitation of memorized prayers, aloud or silently, alone or in a group. To pray well was somehow to recite these prayers with what the nuns called "feeling" or "devotion." Years later, entering college to study science and engineering, I still had no concept of Christian mysticism, meditation, or contemplation.

Strangely enough, it was not the nuns or priests, but Dr. John Lilly, a medical doctor and researcher from Stanford, who first introduced me to the concept of contemplation and various techniques one might use for the experiential exploration of consciousness. In 1970, during my second year in New York, I came across an advertisement for a lecture to be given by Dr. Lilly on *Programming and Metaprogramming the Human Bio-Computer*, the title of a book he was about to publish.

Intrigued by the topic, I attended the lecture, which was presented to an audience of twenty or so in a small hotel room near Carnegie Hall on 56st street. His talk made an enormous impression on me, perhaps because I had been so recently immersed in studying computer languages, electromagnetic theories, and exploring first-hand the effects of psychotropic substances upon my own consciousness. His talk involved all three topics, and were central to several years of research that he had conducted in "interspecies communication." His theory was that the brain operates as a biocomputer, and that one can learn to program and reprogram the operations of the brain, and thus consciousness itself, through the practice of silent contemplative techniques in a soundproof, lightproof environment. In the late 1950s Lilly had established a research center called the Communications Research Institute on St.

Thomas in the U.S. Virgin Islands. There he conducted a series of experiments, condoned and financially supported by the National Institute of Mental Health. The experiments involved administering clinically pure LSD-25 to dolphins and their trainers and recording their audible and subaudible interactions as they floated in large indoor pools of water.[78]

Lilly's extensive knowledge of electronics and software made his ideas all the more fascinating, even more so when I discovered that, like myself, he had also become a licensed HAM radio operator at an early age. His obvious enthusiasm for exploring the psyche in every way possible, through science as well as by direct introspective experience, was contagious. I was particularly encouraged by his assertion that individuals with backgrounds in physics and electronics, having developed the capacity to focus for extended periods upon abstract concepts, would find considerable success in applying the esoteric techniques of contemplation. In the future, he said, scientists will fill the ranks of a new generation of mystics.

In 1970, shortly after meeting Lilly, I began my first attempts to practice meditation and contemplation, guided mostly by what I was able to find in my books on Taoism, Buddhism, and Hinduism. I also attended the occasional lecture by Swami Satchidananda at his Integral Yoga Institute in Lower Manhattan, or weekend satsangs (spiritual talks) held by Trungpa Rinpoche, a Tibetan holy man who often visited New York City to give talks at the Cathedral of St. John the Divine. But during that time, I had no idea that there might also be a Christian dimension to contemplative practice.

Many years later, living in Saudi Arabia and trying to introduce my young son and daughter to their Christian heritage, I discovered, almost by accident, books written by Christian saints describing their own experiences of meditation, contemplative states, and "interior prayer." Among the works I found in the company library were *The Cloud of Unknowing*, the *Interior Castles* by St. Teresa, the *Dark Night of the Soul* by the Spanish priest known as St. John of the Cross, and especially his amazing poem, "En Una Noche Oscura," which describes the mystical journey of contemplation. I later learned that an early president of the oil company ARAMCO had been a Roman Catholic, and while Islam is the only religious practice legally allowed in Saudi Arabia, he had been able to circumvent the prohibition within the American-run compound in eastern Saudi Arabia.

To my amazement, the 14th century text of *The Cloud of Unknowing* sounded much like the Asian writings on contemplative practices that I had devoured regularly years earlier. I soon found other Christian contemplative works, and was particularly surprised by a collection of four volumes called *The Philokalia*, written between the 4th and 15th centuries CE, consisting of essays for the guidance and instruction of monks in the art and practice of contemplation.[15]

For years I had felt like an "outsider," a contemplative without roots or tradition. Instead of being deeply focused within a single tradition (that of my ancestors), my private contemplative practice incorporated prayers from Christianity, Hinduism, and Buddhism, and I was guided by a mixture of teachings from Chinese, Japanese, and Tibetan sources. My spiritual life was thus "all over the map," and I seldom discussed these topics with strangers, nor even close family, yet I continued my daily silent contemplative period.

But it wasn't until 1990 that I made my first silent monastic retreat at a Christian monastery. While living with my

---

[15] The *Philokalia* is a collection of essays written between the 4th and 15th centuries by contemplative masters of the Orthodox Christian tradition and first published in Venice in 1782.

family in the eastern desert of Saudi Arabia, I had read Thomas Merton's autobiographical masterpiece, *The Seven Story Mountain*, and immediately wanted to experience an extended silent contemplative retreat with monks. I contacted a Franciscan priest who recommended the Benedictine monastery of New Camaldoli on the Big Sur coast of California, and I soon made arrangements to leave my family for a week of silent prayer and meditation.

It was during the second day of my retreat that I wandered into the small bookstore run by the monks for retreatants. To my absolute astonishment, here, in a Catholic monastery bookstore, were books on yoga, contemplation, and Asian religions, all subjects I had assumed would be taboo in such a deeply traditional Roman Catholic environment. It was a cathartic moment for me. Suddenly I felt much less isolated in my own enthusiasm for contemplation. On the shelf above the books on yoga I noticed a section on Russian Orthodox mysticism, and a four book set of the *Philokalia* translated into English from the Russian and Greek. Suddenly I felt at home!

The next year, shortly after living through the Gulf War with my family in Saudi Arabia, I was able to visit the mother house of this particular Benedictine order, the Camaldolese, near Arezzo in Tuscany. There I had a moving experience while visiting the small cell of the founder of the order, St. Romuald, in the chapel where he prayed. In 1992 I was accepted as a Benedictine Oblate of the Camaldolese, vowing to practice prayer and contemplation every day for the rest of my life, and to visit one of their monasteries for retreat from time to time. A year later I found myself traveling to southern India for a long retreat with Fr. Bede Griffiths, a Camaldolese priest and monk originally from Great Britain, who presided over a Catholic/Hindu retreat center known as the Saccidananda Ashram on the banks of the Kaveri River, known as the "Ganges of the South," and especially sacred to the Hindus. The name Saccidananda is a Sanskrit term equivalent to "Holy Trinity."[79]

During my week long retreat at Shantivanam (which means "Forest of Peace"), I spent a great deal of time with Father Griffiths, who presided over this Christian "ashram," originally founded in 1938 by a French priest, Jules Monchanin. There I was also able to live out my fantasy of sitting on my blanket on the banks of a holy river in India, practicing silent contemplation during the periods of dawn and dusk. All along the river bank can be found small temples dedicated to God and the holy spirit of the Kaveri River, the source of water for much of the often parched lands of South India. At dusk the silence was broken only by a strange slap, slap, slap sound which I soon discovered was made by local Indian women doing their daily washing by slapping their cotton saris on the water surface before hanging them on the bushes along the river to dry.

Temple on the Kaveri River, near Shantivanam.

Fr. Griffiths wrote extensively on contemplation, Eastern mysticism, and Christian faith. Educated at Oxford, the British-born priest left England in 1955 to spend the next forty years in

India, pioneering a Christian monastic presence in India that incorporated the customs of a Hindu ashram within a Benedictine Christian contemplative context. He welcomed people of different religious traditions to join him at Shantivanam, encouraging them to meet together in a monastic setting along the most sacred river in Tamil Nadu.

With his deep background in both Western theology and Indian metaphysics, Fr. Griffiths bridges both East/West and science/mysticism in his writing. In his book *A New Vision of Reality: Eastern Science, Eastern Mysticism and Christian Faith*, Fr. Griffiths tells us that we use the names in the Trinity "to point to a reality which is beyond everything we can describe," and explains that:

> The spirit of man is a capacity for God. It is not God. My *atman,* myself, is not God, but rather it is a capacity for God which can be filled by God and can be transformed into God and this is a gift of pure grace.[80]

Fr. Griffiths was a great proponent of ecumenism, an approach not fully appreciated by the local Catholic bishop who, though of Indian ancestry, did not readily approve of the ecumenical, transcultural approach to liturgy at Shantivanam, where elements of Hindu symbolism, including traditional hymns to the Trinity in the Tamil language, were regularly incorporated into the Roman Catholic mass. Fortunately the Bishop was not in a position to censure what transpired at Shantivanam, as monks in the Catholic church are relatively free from local ecclesiastical authority. Fr. Griffiths himself was actively interested in respecting and encourage local Indian cultural traditions, and sought to foster a healthy East/West dialogue. Here he explains his own view of ecumenism:

In genuine dialogue we open ourselves to one another while being perfectly true to our own faith, our own religion, our own understanding—but at the same time open to the understanding of the faith, the religion of the other. Then growth can take place. This I feel is the task for humanity in the future.[81]

Another common theme in his writing is the discussion of nondualism, or *advaita* in Sanskrit. He felt that traditional Hindu metaphysical approaches to the Trinity offered rich possibilities for deepening Christian theological understanding:

Every human being has the power to go beyond himself and to open to what is called the holy mystery. In the Hindu experience you go beyond your ego, your empirical self, the self by which you normally act, you touch the true Self which is the pure subjectivity beyond. . . What I am suggesting is that in each tradition there is an experience of transcendent reality, of the transcendent mystery, which is interpreted in terms of non-duality. It has different expressions in each tradition but basically they are the same. . . I seriously feel that this is the philosophy of the future and that we ought to be able to see how we can build our theology around this basic principle.[82]

Christian Nonduality and Sapiential Wisdom

Another Camaldolese Benedictine philosopher-monk, and a close friend of Fr. Griffiths, was the American priest Fr. Bruno Barnhart (1931–2015). Trained as a chemist, Fr. Barnhart entered the remote monastery of the Sacred Heart Hermitage (also called New Camaldoli) in California at the age of 29. In his published writings, Fr. Barnhart suggests that Western Christianity, since the Renaissance and Enlightenment, has been living "in a sapiential vacuum" in which the participative and unitive modes of consciousness have largely contracted to be replaced by the dominant rational-analytical approach. As a result, Western monasticism has become increasingly involved in pastoral, cultural, and educational activities, rather than in solitude, silence, and contemplative prayer. By contrast, he points out, Eastern Orthodox Christian churches have continued to focus on "a spirituality of interiority, of separation from the world, of asceticism and the quest for continual prayer."[83]

Fr. Barnhart calls for Western Christian churches to consider a new emphasis on "wisdom" which he terms "sapiential theology," and he views wisdom here as a form of participative consciousness, a *knowing* that surmounts the duality of subject and object. At the heart of this approach is what he called *nonduality* (the unitive principle which Indians would call *advaita*), that he points out is clearly expressed in the Gospel of John, where in the following passage (John 17:30-23) Jesus states the reason for which he is praying:

> That they may all be one; even as you, Father, are in me and I in you, that they also may be in us, so that the world may believe that you have sent me. The glory that you have given me I have given to them, that they may be one even as we are one, I in them and you in me, that they may become perfectly one.[84]

Here, according to Fr. Barnhart, the central theological principle of *divinization* emerges, and it is in this mystery of the *incarnation* that the nondual Absolute becomes present in humanity in a new way. Barnhart sees the multiple streams of Asian influence helpful to remind us of the importance of the efficacy of the practice of "contemplation, understood as nondual consciousness and experience." He tells us that while faith itself is a dark unitive knowledge, faith itself can lead to the beginning of contemplation, which he has found to be a "direct experience of the ground of consciousness, of a depth from which we may live continually."[85] Fr. Barnhart affirms that, from the nondual center outward, contemplation reveals the experience of a progressive *emergence of a person who is participating in a divine incarnation,* both individually and collectively. The problem of contemporary Western culture is that the individual and collective incarnation has not yet integrated.

> It is obvious today that the individual and collective progressions are not yet integrated. In the extreme individualism of the West—and the many-sided fragmentation of the modern Western world—we see an emergence of the individual person which has not yet been balanced by a growth of the collective person.[86]

Fr. Barnhart tell us that an antidote to this problem may be found through the contemplative cultivation of what is referred to, both in Orthodox Christianity as well as in Roman Catholicism, as *purity of Heart,* where the term *Heart* is conceived of "as the central point or axis of the person where body, psyche, mind, and spirit are present together," and he goes further, providing a concise definition of contemplation:

> Contemplation is a direct experience of the ground of consciousness, of a depth from which we may live continually.[87]

It is Fr. Barnhart's direct experiential approach to this "central point or axis" that is clearly mirrored in Pierre Teilhard de Chardin's concept of the Omega Point, a central element in the development of his *hyperphysics* of consciousness.

Teilhard de Chardin: Anthropologist, Priest, Mystic

> In spite of all the theoretical objections that would seek to discourage the belief, our minds remain invincibly persuaded that a certain very simple fundamental rule lies hidden beneath the overpowering multiplicity of events and beings: to discover and formulate this rule, we believe, would make the universe intelligible in the totality of its development.[88]

> −Pierre Teilhard de Chardin

Hyperphysics

Early in the twentieth century, Marie Joseph Pierre Teilhard de Chardin,[89] a geologist, paleontologist, and priest by training, developed a model of consciousness, that he referred to as "hyperphysics."[90] He conceived of this model in the context of his knowledge of physics, his keen observational skills as a geo-paleontologist, and his own specific introspective experience over a 40-year period of careful observation and consideration. In developing hyperphysics, Teilhard conducted an integral exploration of a region inclusive of and yet beyond the conceptual boundaries of physics or paleontology or the priesthood. His theories of consciousness, detailed in his many essays, are examined and interpreted here through the lens of the Pribram–Bohm holoflux theories examined previously. The objectives of this chapter are to interpret and extend Teilhard's theories of hyperphysics in general, and to discover how Teilhard's theories can be reconciled with holoflux theory.

In a letter to Henri de Lubac[91] dated 1934, Teilhard uses the word *hyperphysics*, describing it as a kind of metaphysics springing from the hard sciences, a metaphysics based upon science, yet "another sort of metaphysics which would really be a hyperphysics."[92] In the first sentence of the Author's Note to

The Human Phenomenon, Teilhard states that the nature of his theories of hyperphysics is scientific, "purely and simply":

> If this book is to be properly understood it must be read not as a work on metaphysics, still less as a sort of theological essay, but purely and simply as a scientific treatise . . . only take a closer look at it, and you will see that this "hyperphysics" is not a metaphysics. [93]

It can be assumed that, trained in the sciences of geology and paleontology, Teilhard would have been an astute observer, constantly seeking and discerning patterns in the natural world. His published professional papers led to significant recognition in the field of paleontology; when published in 1971, a collection of his scientific papers filled eleven volumes.[94] Yet, in spite of the time constraints of his dual career as priest and scientist, he was able to develop, through a long series of unpublished essays written over his lifetime, a coherent theory describing a general physics of consciousness. Fueled by a lifelong practice of introspective observation, often alone in the silence of nature, Teilhard elaborated his map of the dynamics of consciousness, hyperphysics.

It is likely that Teilhard never knew how his life work in hyperphysics and the evolution of consciousness would be judged by mainstream science; the English edition of *The Phenomenon of Man* was only published in 1959, four years after his death, and was received somewhat critically both by the philosophical and the scientific community, as can be seen in this 1965 review:

> Is his proposed "hyperphysics" science? . .There has been considerable confusion both in the United States and in Europe, where it appeared in French four years earlier, over what it is—physics, metaphysics, theology, mysticism, prophecy?[95]

Rarely has a scientist, formally trained and active in a demanding technical profession, found time and interest (under the tacit threat of ridicule or censure) to develop a theory of consciousness based upon the data of first-hand participatory experience and observation. Pierre Teilhard de Chardin was one of the few: a trained scientist, holding a doctorate in geological paleontology from the Sorbonne, who wrote regularly and extensively to produce a science-based model of the evolutionary dynamics of consciousness, an "ultraphysics of union."[96] For over 40 years, through direct experience, observation, and keen analysis, Teilhard laid down a foundation and a legacy that he hoped would forge a new science-based understanding of the dynamics of consciousness in an evolving cosmos.[97]

Teilhard's Integral Life Experience

It is easy to see how the region of his birth, Auvergne in south central France, instilled in Teilhard a passion for geology and nature (Fig. 9).

Figure 9. *Auvergne landscape.* Graphic by Romary (2006).[98]

The most volcanic, mineral-rich region of France, Auvergne is also home to the largest oak forest in Europe, and it was here, a few miles from the highest volcanic summit in the region, that Pierre Teilhard de Chardin was born on May 1, 1881, the fourth of 11 siblings, in his family chateau, Sarcenat.[99]

Teilhard was a direct descendent of Voltaire, on his mother's side, and his father, descended from a noble family, was one of the largest landowners in the province, affording him ample free time to "build up sizeable collections of regional insects, birds, stones, and plants."[100] It was into this rich environment that Teilhard was born, soon becoming entranced with nature; he embraced his father's passion for geology, and at an early age began collecting and classifying specimens. But it was his mother's influence that instilled in her young son a love of the spiritual life, and he was introduced to regular family prayer, and a contemplative practice, the prayer on the Sacred Heart of Jesus. Following family tradition, Teilhard was sent to a Jesuit boarding school at the age of 11.[101]

Of all the Catholic religious congregations, the Jesuit order is especially known for its emphasis on intellectual research and scholarship, and in this environment Teilhard excelled academically. But it was here, also, that Teilhard began his daily practice of sitting for an hour in silent contemplation:

> It was at the school that he became an ascetic who voluntarily rose at dawn every day and went to sit in the chapel, often in freezing temperatures before the rest of the students awoke. He would follow a similar habit throughout his life, wherever he might be: in an Asian desert, in a prehistoric cave, or aboard a ship in rough seas.[102]

In 1899, at the age of 17, he made the decision to join the Jesuit order, and was formally accepted as a Jesuit novice, a candidate for eventual priesthood. After completing Jesuit secondary school, as part of his training as a novice, he was assigned abroad to teach physics and chemistry for a three-year period. Teilhard was sent to a Jesuit-run school in Cairo, Egypt, and it was there that he first experienced the fascination of an exotic new culture, an attraction to the mystery of surrounding antiquities, and most of all, perhaps, in the experience of profound silence in the vastness of a desert.[103]

> It was immediately after I had experienced such sense of wonder in Egypt that there gradually grew in me, as a *presence* much more than as an abstract notion, the consciousness of a deep-running, ontological, total Current which embraced the whole Universe in which I moved; and this consciousness continued to grow until it filled the whole horizon of my inner being.[104]

Upon returning from Egypt, in 1909, Teilhard spent several years studying philosophy and theology at a Jesuit center in Hastings, on the coast of England, 60 miles southeast of London. It was during this time that he carefully read and reread *Creative Evolution*, a recently published work by the popular French philosopher Henri Bergson (1859–1941), a book the Vatican would soon place on its Index of Forbidden Books.[105] Previously, Teilhard had uncritically accepted the currently held theory of the *fixity* of species, and though he knew of Darwin's theories, they had seemed to him only an interesting hypothesis, one certainly suspect in the eyes of his Jesuit community. But after a careful reading of Bergson's *Creative Evolution*, Teilhard found himself suddenly a "convinced evolutionist," in strong agreement with Bergson's arguments for evolution, while yet disagreeing with Bergson's vision of a "pre-existing and obdurate matter" being operated upon by a life-force energy, which Bergson named *élan vital*. Teilhard himself felt that this life-force, referred to by Bergson, was never to be found remote from matter, but from inception is at the very heart of matter.[106]

The dynamics of evolution, according to Bergson, is powered by a "vital" force of energy that animates not only life but the unfolding of the cosmos, and that fundamentally connects consciousness and body, an idea in radical contrast to widely accepted belief in the *dualism* of matter and consciousness, set forth by the seventeenth century philosopher–scientist René Descartes.[107]

The young Teilhard was especially impressed with Bergson's emphasis on the importance of *intuition* and *immediate experience*, as these were Teilhard's own tools, developed and honed during his daily contemplative practices. Through immediate experience he was able to observe directly the structure and dynamics of his own inner space, his own complexity-consciousness in process, and he says that this has led to "a new intuition that totally alters the physiognomy of the universe in which we move, in other words, in an awakening."[108] Near the end of his life Teilhard comments on the early influence of Bergson's book:

> I can remember very clearly the avidity with which, at that time, I read Bergson's *Creative Evolution* . . . I can now see quite clearly that the effect that brilliant book had upon me was to provide fuel at just the right moment . . . for a fire that was already consuming my heart and mind. And that fire had been kindled.[109]

The effect of Bergson's ideas upon Teilhard's worldview was significant indeed. In 1930, Teilhard wrote of Bergson, in a letter to his close friend Leontine Zanta (the first French woman to receive a doctorate in philosophy), "I pray for that admirable man and venerate him as a kind of saint."[110] After reading *Creative Evolution*, according to Teilhard's biographer Ursula King:

The magic word "evolution" haunted his thoughts "like a tune"; it was to him "like an unsatisfied hunger, like a promise held out to me, like a summons to be answered." Evolution was vital. It was the necessary condition of all further scientific thought.[111]

In 1912, Teilhard began formal graduate studies in geology and paleontology, eventually leading to his doctorate, though interrupted by World War I; as a student, he also began working at the Museum of Natural History in Paris. In 1914 he was called up for service by the French Army and quickly trained as a medical orderly.[112] After serving for some time behind the lines, he volunteered to be reassigned to the Western Front, as a stretcher bearer rather than as an army chaplain, and on January 22, 1915, he was assigned to a regiment of Moroccan light infantry, where "on arrival Teilhard made himself look like an Arab by exchanging his field-service blue for the khaki colors of the African troops, and his kepi for a red fez."[113]

It was here, alongside members of this regiment of Algerian tribesmen that Teilhard served for over three years in the trenches of the front lines. Teilhard was the only Christian in his regiment, but by the end of the war he was referred to affectionately by the North African Muslim soldiers he lived with in the trenches as *"Sidi Marabout,"* an acknowledgement of his spiritual power as a man closely bound to God, protected from all injuries by divine grace."[114] After the war, at the request of his war-time regiment, Teilhard was awarded the French Legion of Honour for bravery.[115] His citation reads:

An outstanding stretcher-bearer, who during four years of active service was in every battle and engagement the regiment took part in, applying to remain in the ranks in order that he might be with the men whose dangers and hardships he constantly shared.[116]

Teilhard thus witnessed first-hand, for a protracted period of his life, the enormous suffering and destruction of human life that was the characteristic brutality of the war. Such experience was in sharp contrast to his academic life.

It was in Belgium that Teilhard experienced the true horror of World War I. When they arrived at Ypres, the troops found a town that had just been burned down. Hundreds of soldiers lay on the ground, dead or dying. And after the Germans were through with their conventional weapons strike, they attacked their enemy with poison gas.[117]

Yet the young scholar/priest seemed to display no fear, at least to his closest colleagues. One of his fellow soldiers at the time, Max Bégoüen, wrote the following, describing an event he witnessed on the Belgian front, in 1915:

> The North African sharpshooters of his regiment thought he was protected by his *baraka* (an Arabic word meaning "spiritual stature" or "supernatural quality"). The curtain of machine gun fire and the hail of bombardments both seemed to pass him by. During the attacks of September 2 at Artois, my brother was wounded, and, as he wandered on the battlefield, he saw a single stretcher bearer rising up in front of him, and he, for it was Teilhard, accomplished his mission quite imperturbably under terrible ire . . . "I thought I had seen the appearance of a messenger from God."
>
> I once asked Father Teilhard, "What do you do to keep this sense of calm during battle? It looks as if you do not see the danger and that fear does not touch you."
>
> He answered, with that serious but friendly smile which gave such a human warmth to his words, "If I am killed, I shall just change my state, that's all."[118]

For four years he served as an unarmed stretcher-bearer at Verdun, until 1917, and thereafter in the front trenches of Chateau Thierry in 1918, participating in action of such great ferocity that it took the lives of over nine million of his fellow soldiers. The accounts of his disregard of his own safety in order to rescue the wounded of all nationalities led eventually to being awarded the Chevalier de la Legion d'Honneur in 1921 for bravery in action.

We can only imagine the experiences this young man must have lived through, the sounds, the sights, the deprivations of weather and humanity, yet out of the intensity of this existential life "on the Front," Teilhard began to experience a new form of consciousness not only in his own but collectively, a "quasi-collective" participatory functioning flux becoming "fully conscious" as he describes in a letter written at the Front in 1917:

> I'm still in the same quiet billets. Our future continues to be pretty vague, both as to when and what it will be. What the future imposes on our present existence is not exactly a feeling of depression; it's rather a sort of seriousness, of detachment, of a broadening, too, of outlook. ... but it leads also to a sort of higher joy, ... I'd call it `Nostalgia for the Front'. The reasons, I believe, come down to this; the front cannot but attract us because it is, in one way, the extreme boundary between what one is already aware of, and what is still in process of formation. Not only does one see there things that you experience nowhere else, but *one also sees emerge from within one an underlying stream of clarity, energy, and freedom that is to be found hardly anywhere else in ordinary life - and the new form that the soul then takes on is that of the individual living the quasi-collective life of all* men, fulfilling a function far higher than that of the

individual, and becoming fully conscious of this new state. .... This exaltation is accompanied by a certain pain. Nevertheless it is indeed an exaltation. And that's why one likes the front in spite of everything, and misses it.[119]

During this time and under these conditions he began to experience, observe, and ultimately write about, his own direct awareness of nonordinary states of consciousness. For example, it was at the front that he began to perceive, directly, for the first time, a sense of collective consciousness over and above his own. In his 1917 essay "Nostalgia for the Front," Teilhard asks, "Is it not ridiculous to be so drawn into the magnetic field of the war . . . more than ever the Front casts its spell over me . . . . What is it, then, that I myself have seen at the front?"[120] And he answers himself, "it is above all something more, something more subtle and more substantial, I might define it as a superhuman state to which the soul is borne." Having left the front lines, he experiences a feeling of loss: "I have the feeling of having lost a soul, a soul greater than my own, which lives in the trenches and which I have left behind."[121]

It trying to understand the impact of these experiences on the young Teilhard, it is worthwhile to consider that at Verdun, where Teilhard served during one of the most protracted battles of the war, the single battle continued for over nine months, and the human losses approached apocalyptic proportion:

> A French estimate that is probably not excessive places the total French and German losses on the Verdun battlefield at 420,000 dead, and 800,000 gassed or wounded; nearly a million and a quarter in all.[122]

It was at Verdun, the night before the attack on Fort Douaumont, on October 14, 1916, that Teilhard experienced an extraordinary vision, which he recounted afterwards in the

81

short essay, "Christ in Matter."[123] Here, in the visual imagery alone, one can only imagine that Teilhard was experiencing a major psychotropic vision, perhaps brought on by fatigue, synesthesia from the constant bombardment, or from the stress of being continually at the front on the eve of a major offensive attack.

The Powerful Vision

The imagery of Teilhard's vision is so intense and specific here that one wonders, even, if he might have ingested ergot-infected rye bread (ergot mold on rye bread has been reported to induce LSD-like symptoms; in 1951 an entire French village became infected with the ergot alkaloid, experiencing hallucinations).[124] Here is Teilhard's description of this pivotal, altered-state experience that occurred in an abandoned chapel, at night, during the battle of Verdun:

> Suppose, I thought, that Christ should deign to appear here, in the flesh, before my very eyes—what would he look like? Most important of all, in what way would he fit himself into Matter and so be sensibly apprehended? . .Meanwhile, my eyes had unconsciously come to rest on a picture that represented Christ with his Heart offered to men. This picture was hanging in front of me, on the wall of a church into which I had gone to pray . . . I was still looking at the picture when the vision began. (Indeed, I cannot be certain exactly when it began, because it had already reached a certain pitch of intensity when I became aware of it.) All I know is that as I let my eyes roam over the outlines of the picture, I suddenly realized that they *were melting*. They were melting, but in a very special way that I find it difficult to describe.
> If I relaxed my visual concentration, the whole of Christ's outline, the folds of his robe, the bloom of

his skin, merged (though without disappearing) into all the rest . . . the edge which divided Christ from the surrounding World was changing into a layer of vibration in which all distinct delimitation was lost . . . I noticed that the vibrant atmosphere which formed a halo around Christ was not confined to a narrow strip encircling him, but radiated into Infinity. From time to time what seemed to be trails of phosphorescence streamed across it, in which could be seen a continuous pulsing surge which reached out to the furthest spheres of matter— forming a sort of crimson ganglion, or nervous network, running across every substance. *The whole Universe was vibrating* . . . . It was thus that the light and the colours of all the beauties we know shone, with an inexpressible iridescence . . . these countless modifications followed one another in succession, were transformed, melted into one another in a harmony that was utterly satisfying to me . . . I was completely at a loss. *I found it impossible to decipher* . . . . All I know is that, since that occasion, I believe I have seen a hint of it once, and that was in the eyes of a dying soldier.[125]

Decades later, Teilhard refers to this epiphanic experience, this "particular interior event" of 40 years prior.[126] He describes how it has been that, ever since this early revelation, he has had "the capacity to see two fundamental psychic movements or currents," which, when he first perceived them in his 1916 epiphany, "reacted endlessly upon one another in a flash of extraordinary brilliance, releasing . . . a light so intense that it transfigured for me the very depths of the World."[127] In his final essay, completed a month before his death, Teilhard stresses the *objective validity* of this initial evidence that had led directly to his new understanding of consciousness and the universe, evidence that had presented itself to him experientially in 1916:

What follows is not a mere speculative dissertation in which the main lines of some long-matured and cleverly constructed system are set out. It constitutes the evidence brought to bear, with complete objectivity, *upon a particular interior event, upon a particular personal experience* .... Today, after forty years of continuous thought, it is still exactly the same fundamental vision that I feel I must present, and enable others to share in its matured form—for the last time.[128]

It is this subsequent "forty years of continuous thought" that makes the uniqueness of his observations, expressed in his essays, so significant for the development of consciousness studies. Four sides of Teilhard's nature reinforced one another, integrally it would seem: scientific training, mystical vision, exceptional intelligence, and a passionate enthusiasm for discovery and understanding. While he was formally a scientist, highly trained and experienced in the observation, collection, classification, and written interpretation of geological and anthropological data, yet he was also a Jesuit priest, deeply immersed in observing the internal phenomena of spirit during his daily contemplative period. His was a quest to bring scientific reasoning and understanding to bear upon a direct vision, one that has been described by his biographer as:

a powerful vision linked to experiences of a deeply mystical, or what might be called pan-entheistic, character although he often simply called them "pantheistic." These experiences occurred over many years.[129]

Throughout his writing, one encounters passages that can only be seen to refer directly to personal experience of a sort of perception that he himself categorized as pantheism and mystical vision (which, along with his fascination with evolution, caused him enduring conflict with more conservative forces in the Vatican). Teilhard states that his perception, "as experience shows, is indeed the result . . . of a mystic absorbed in divine contemplation."[130] Elsewhere Teilhard regards this special psychic perception as a natural ability, but one that requires practice and cultivation in order to catalyze the required change of state in consciousness:

> This perception of a natural psychic unity higher than our "souls" requires, as I know from experience, a special quality and training in the observer . . . once we manage to affect this change of viewpoint then the earth, our little human earth, is draped in a splendor. Floating above the biosphere, whose layers no doubt gradually merge into it, the world of thought, the noosphere, begins to let its crown shine. The noosphere![131]

Teilhard's contemplative, mystical interests began at an early age, during which he searched to discern some "Absolute" in his experience of prayer with his large Catholic family, described here in, "My Universe," written on the battlefield of the Marne, three weeks after the beginning of a major attack by the Germans:

> However far back I go into my memories (even before the age of ten) I can distinguish in myself the presence of a strictly dominating passion: the passion for the Absolute. At that age, of course, I did not so describe the urgent concern I felt; but today I can put a name to it without any possible hesitation. Ever since my childhood, the need to lay hold of "some Absolute" in everything was the axis of my inner life.[132]

During 1926 and 1927 Teilhard wrote *The Divine Milieu* while working in China, where he had effectively been banished by the Jesuit authorities; it is in the middle of this essay that he describes what can be only understood as a personal experience of deep contemplation in which, through a process of increasing centro-complexity, he began to travel consciously toward an encounter with a heretofore unimagined depth of inner being:

> And so, for the first time in my life perhaps (although I am supposed to meditate every day!), I took the lamp and, leaving the zone of everyday occupations and relationships where everything seems clear, I went down into my inmost self, to the deep abyss whence I feel dimly that my power of action emanates. But as I moved further and further away from the conventional certainties by which social life is superficially illuminated, I became aware that I was losing contact with myself. At each step of the descent a new person was disclosed within me of whose name I was no longer sure, and who no longer obeyed me. And when I had to stop my exploration because the path faded from beneath my steps, I found a bottomless abyss at my feet, and out of it came—arising I know not from where—the current which I dare to call *my* life. What science will ever be able to reveal to man the origin, nature and character of that conscious power. . .? Stirred by my discovery, I then wanted to return to the light of day and forget the disturbing enigma in the comfortable surroundings of familiar things.[133]

In the development of Teilhard's mystical sense, the possibility cannot be ruled out that Teilhard in midlife had the occasion to experience consciousness-expanding drugs, that would have provided new material for development of his theories of consciousness. On an ocean passage from France to China in 1926, Teilhard had befriended a French couple with a homestead in East Africa, Henry de Monfried and his wife, Armgart.[134] Monfried has been variously described as "a pirate, a smuggler, and an arms dealer."[135] Nevertheless the three immediately developed strong bonds that lasted for decades, and Teilhard would often visit them in their East African home during his many voyages between Asia and France. As one of Teilhard's biographers comments:

> Teilhard was so attracted to this couple that, still aboard the *Angkor*, he confessed to Armgart, "I have full faith in Henry, in what he says about himself; but even more truly, I love you, you and him."

On a return voyage from China, three years later, Teilhard stopped in East Africa to join Henry and Armgart for a visit, with apparently no reservations at all concerning the use of opium: according to Teilhard's biographer, Jacques Arnould, "Teilhard brought Monfried opium from China—'for his personal use.'"[136] On another occasion, Teilhard saved Monfried from arrest by local authorities in China when Monfried was trying to pick up a shipment of hashish in Chinese Turkistan.[137] It should be noted that the use of hashish and opium was widespread in China during this time, and we can assume that the European enclave of intellectuals and artists in Peking in the "roaring 20s" may likely have experimented with psychotropics such as hashish and opium, particularly as the practice was not illegal during Teilhard's years in Peking:

> Ma Fuxiang [a Chinese warlord in the early 20th century] officially prohibited opium and made it illegal in Ningxia [included Peking], but the Guominjun reversed his policy; by 1933, people from every level of society were using the drug.[138]

In such an environment, during his decade long friendship with the American artist, Lucile Swan, it is not beyond consideration that Teilhard may have experienced the psychotropic effects of hashish and/or opium, which would have only provided rich psychic material for self-observation and development of his ideas concerning a hyperphysics of consciousness, noosphere, and the Omega point.

Our thesis holds that over his lifetime, it is Teilhard's mystical sense aligned with his rigorous scientifically trained skill in observation as a geologist and paleontologist, coupled with his Jesuit training in logic, clarity, and expressive writing that gave him the ability to record his ideas so prolifically; in addition to *11* volumes of scientific publications published during his lifetime, there now exist *13* volumes of speculative philosophy, all published after his death.[139] In 1951 he wrote a short essay entitled "Some Notes on the Mystical Sense: An Attempt at Clarification," which begins with the sentences:

> The mystical sense is essentially a feeling for, a presentiment of, the total and final unity of the world, beyond its present sensibly apprehended multiplicity: it is a cosmic sense of "oneness." It enables us to become one with all by co-extension "with the sphere": that is to say, by suppression of all internal and external determinants, to come together with a sort of common stuff which *underlies* the variety of concrete beings. It is access to Aldous Huxley's "common ground."[140]

It is clear that Teilhard as geologist/paleontologist was in an ideal position for observing, documenting, and interpreting the direct experiences of the inner life of Teilhard the contemplative priest. This integral configuration underlies the development of his "hyperphysics," his "physics of centration."[141]

After World War II, having just spent six years in relative isolation under the Japanese occupation, Teilhard gave a lecture at the French Embassy in Peking, in which he talks about the "growing importance with which leading thinkers of all denominations are beginning to attach to the phenomenon of mysticism."[142] He goes on to describe mysticism in the perception of the Omega point:

> Let us suppose that from this universal centre, this Omega point, there constantly emanate radiations hitherto only perceptible to those persons whom we call "mystics." Let us further imagine that, as the sensibility or response to mysticism of the human race increases with planetisation, the awareness of Omega becomes so widespread as to warm the earth psychically.[143]

It is my contention that Teilhard's hyperphysics emerged as a product of multiple factors: a deep contemplative mystical sense combined with extensive scientific training, intense experience, and high intelligence, acting together in Teilhard to provide a truly integral perspective. In Fig. 10 can be seen a symbolic diagram of the multiple factors that contributed significantly to Teilhard's unique Gebserian multiperspectival consciousness. Not only was Teilhard a highly educated geologist, but he was also a trained paleontologist, and leader of the small group who made the paradigm-breaking discovery of the Peking Man in China. He was also a deeply devout Jesuit priest who practiced daily prayer and silent contemplation, even during extended expeditions into the remote regions of outer Mongolia. And as a philosopher he had studied directly with Henri Bergson during his university days in Paris.

That Teilhard's understanding grew over the arc of his lifetime is evident in essays striving to express his vision, beginning in World War I and continuing until his death in 1955. In all of his essays can be detected his motivated energy to express as clearly as possible in words the framework of his understanding, and to relate what he experienced directly:

It seems to me that a whole lifetime of continual hard work would be as nothing to me, if only I could, just for one moment, give a true picture of what I see.[144]

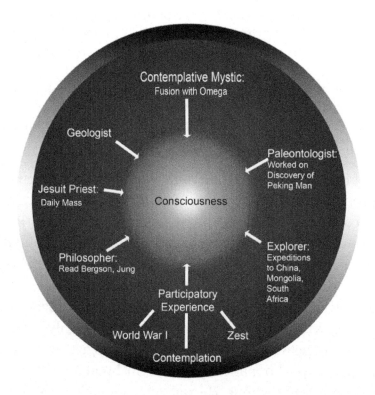

Figure 10. *Teilhard's multiperspectival consciousness.*

In 1922 Teilhard was awarded his doctorate, defending his thesis on mammals of the Lower Eocene (56 to 33.9 million years ago) in France.[145] According to a biographer, "The board of examiners had no hesitation in conferring on him the title of doctor, with distinction."[146] In that same year, the British psychologist Conway Lloyd Morgan (1852–1936) presented a series of radical new ideas at speaker at the Gifford Lectures, in which he extended the ideas of Henri Bergson.[147] Morgan described how an observed increase of complexity in the evolutionary process often results in discontinuous leaps with the past, rather than through a more gradual, steady process, as had been predicted by the theory of Darwinian natural selection.[148] Lloyd Morgan's theory can be seen as a precursor to an expression of the dynamics of complexity-consciousness in Teilhard's own hyperphysics. The direct effect of centro-complexification, according to Teilhard, catalyzes transformation in the organization and functioning of consciousness, causing a phase shift, as when water crystallizes into ice, or transforms into steam. It is this principle of centro-complexity that drives, that initiates this catalysis.

Unfortunately, essays such as "Centrology," that develops the theory of centro-complexity in detail, were never published in Teilhard's lifetime. Conservative elements in the Catholic hierarchy made it difficult if not impossible for him to publish much of his work, in great part because the Church had not yet reconciled the science of evolution with doctrinal Catholicism, and Teilhard's essays and lectures soared unchecked on a wave of evolutionary ideas.

Though Teilhard was forbidden to teach, lecture, or publish outside of a narrow range of scientific material, yet his strictly scientific publications fill 11 volumes, indicating the extent of his output and providing an indication of his professional stature as a world-class paleontologist. Teilhard's books and essays on speculative philosophy and the evolution of consciousness, on the other hand, though published between 1955 and 1976, only after his death, fill another 13 volumes.[149]

Certainly being forbidden to publish had its effect on Teilhard. To keep him out of Paris, where the Church saw his ideas as attracting too much enthusiasm among young seminarians, he was virtually banished from Paris, ordered to an assignment in China early in his career, and then banished again, to America, after the war and near the end of his life.[150]

These challenges (some might say affronts) to the expression of his richest ideas, coupled perhaps with the horror and suffering he had experienced at first hand during two world wars, all must have taken a toll on his emotional side, and must surely have contributed to his frequent bouts of despondence and depression. Pierre Leroy, his friend and colleague throughout their years of confinement in Peking, who, at 20 years Teilhard's junior, had first met Teilhard in 1928 in Paris, writes of Teilhard's bouts of depression:

> Many have rightly been struck by Pere Teilhard's great optimism. He was indeed an optimist, in his attribution to the universe of a sense of direction in spite of the existence of evil and in spite of appearances . . . but how often in intimate conversation have I found him depressed and with almost no heart to carry on . . . . During that period he was at times prostrated by fits of weeping, and he appeared to be on the verge of despair . . . . Six years thus went by in the dispiriting atmosphere of China occupied by the Japanese and cut off from the rest of the world.[151]

Yet when Teilhard was finally able to leave China, at the war's end, he wrote, during the sea passage on his return to France, "These seven years have made me quite grey, but they have toughened me—not hardened me, I hope—interiorly."[152] He retained the passion and motivation to write extensively, particularly in his later years, and he continued the development of his observations and conclusions regarding consciousness and the dynamics of energy in an evolving universe. He himself would likely have characterized the gift of this persevering energy with the term "zest," which he defines here a 1950 essay:

By "zest for living" or "zest for life," I mean here, to put it very approximately, that spiritual disposition, at once intellectual and affective, in virtue of which life, the world, and action seem to us, on the whole, luminous—interesting—appetizing.[153]

It is almost as if the restriction placed upon him by the Church against publication gave him free rein to explore his ideas in essays that were freely distributed among his closest friends and many acquaintances. In spite of the censorship of the Church, many unofficial copies of his writings were made, and most have been published in posthumous collections.[154] One of his most profound essays, "Centrology: An Essay in a Dialectic of Union," discussed in detail later in this chapter, was written in his period of isolation in Peking during Japanese wartime occupation.[155] Soon after emerging from his seclusion in China, Teilhard was deeply disappointed when the Vatican forbade him to publish what he considered to be his major work, *The Human Phenomenon*, while simultaneously refusing him permission to accept the offer of a prestigious teaching Chair at the College de France. Yet in spite of such opposition to his visionary understanding of the energy of consciousness, it has been noted that, "he wrote *more* religious and philosophical essays in the years 1946–1955 than during any other period of his life—his bibliography lists over ninety titles for this time."[156]

Energy: Axial and Tangential

Energy is the central element in Teilhard's technical modeling of the cosmos. He says that while "in metaphysics the notion of being can be defined with a precision that is geometric," things are not so clear in physics, where the notion of energy is "still open to all sorts of possible corrections or improvements."[157] Teilhard's essays on the energy of consciousness, spanning four decades, systematically introduce a coherent range of such corrections and improvements. In the last page of his essay, "Activation of Energy," Teilhard states, "there are two different energies one axial, increasing, and irreversible, and the other peripheral or tangential, constant, and reversible: and these two energies are linked together in 'arrangement.'"[158] Thus Teilhard's hyperphysics posits two modes, domains, or dimensions of energy, not only of a *tangential component* of energy that operates within space–time dimensions, and which is measured and explored by modern physics, but also a *radial* or *axial component* of energy. It is this axial energy, providing the direct link with the center which Teilhard termed Omega, that guides, informs, and maintains the evolutionary process throughout the space–time cosmos.[159] He describes this radial component of energy as "a new dimensional zone" that brings with it "new properties," and he describes how increasing centration along the radial component leads to increasing states of "complexity-consciousness." [160] As Teilhard says here:

> Science in its present reconstructions of the world fails to grasp an essential factor, or, to be more exact, an entire dimension of the universe . . . all we need to do is to take the inside of things into account at the same time as the outside.[161]

Energy, for Teilhard, is not simply regarded as a mathematical abstraction. He views energy as the matrix of consciousness, the driver of evolution, and as a living, communicating radiation or flux. For Teilhard energy is "a true 'transcosmic' radiation for which the organisms . . . would seem to be precisely the naturally provided receivers."[162]

Teilhard is critical of the one-dimensional approach to energy taken by contemporary research. He asks, "What is the relationship between this interior energy . . . and the goddess of energy worshipped by physicists?"[163] His answer is that there are two fundamental categories or modes of energy, and implies that physicists deal with but one mode. In his own words, "We still persist in regarding the physical as constituting the 'true' phenomenon in the universe, and the psychic as a sort of epiphenomenon."[164]

He also describes these two components of energy in physical and the psychic terms: "*physical energy* being no more than *materialized psychic energy*,"[165] but he is not able to posit a mathematical or physical relationship between these two dimensions, other than to express the hope that "there must surely be some hidden relationship which links them together in their development."[166]

A Thinking Earth: The Noosphere

Despite clerical resistance to his ideas, Teilhard continued to be fascinated by what he saw as the emerging evolution of a collective human consciousness upon the planet Earth, the emergence of a "thinking Earth," a phenomenon that he had directly intuited in his intense experiences at the Front in 1917. He continued his dual work in the fields of paleontology and speculative philosophy; for example in January 1923 he finished an essay on speculative theology, "Pantheism and Christianity," only to publish two months later the scientific essay, "Paleontology and the Appearance of Man."[167]

Intense life experiences led Teilhard to the perception of an emerging planetary consciousness, an awakening into a new mode of consciousness that he termed the *noosphere*.[168] His term for this phenomenon, after his death, has been conceptualized as "*an ultimate and inevitable sphere of evolution* . . . a scientific approach with a bridge to religion."[169]

During the war, Teilhard had given the name "The Great Monad" to his conception and experience of an emerging consciousness.[170] But by 1920, during his doctoral studies, he was using the term "Anthroposphere" in referring to this thinking sphere of the planet.[171] In Paris in 1921, drawn together by similar interests, Édouard Le Roy (1870–1954) and Teilhard de Chardin met and became friends. A mathematician and philosopher by training, Le Roy immediately found in Teilhard an intellectual equal, and the two began a lifetime relationship, leading with the year to the exploration of a new concept, the noosphere.[172] Le Roy had studied with Henri Bergson, and had become known as his protégé; subsequently he had been appointed successor to Bergson at the College de France.[173] Though 10 years Teilhard's senior, the two soon began a series of informal weekly discussions:

> Punctually, at 8:30 p.m., on Wednesday evenings Teilhard would call at Le Roy's apartment in the Rue Cassette, and it was not long before the two men were thinking and speaking with a single mind.[174]

Though Le Roy was a decade older than Teilhard, their relationship appears to have been considerably more than simple mentorship; Teilhard says in a letter,

> I loved him like a father, and owed him a very great debt . . . he gave me confidence, enlarged my mind, and served as a spokesman for my ideas, then taking shape, on 'hominization' and the "noosphere."[175]

Over their many months of frequent discussion, the two grew so close in their philosophical thought that Le Roy would later say in one of his books:

I have so often and for so long talked over with Pere Teilhard the views expressed here that neither of us can any longer pick out his own contribution.[176]

Their meetings soon included a mutual acquaintance, the brilliant writer Vladimir Ivanovich Vernadsky (1863–1945), a distinguished Russian geologist from St. Petersburg, who eventually founded the field known as biogeochemistry. Vernadsky popularized his term "the biosphere" in a series of lectures at the Sorbonne during 1922–1923, frequently attended by Le Roy and Teilhard.[177]

Vernadsky viewed the phenomenon of life as a natural and integral part of the cosmos, and not merely some epiphenomenon. Accordingly, he professed that universal physical laws, discovered by science over a wide range of seemingly disparate fields, would eventually find continuation with fundamental principles that are the ground of life.[178]

Not widely acknowledged in the West, Vernadsky was the first to recognize the importance of life as a geological force, an idea that predates the more recent Gaia hypothesis:

> James E. Lovelock, the British inventor and the other major scientific contributor to the concept of an integrated biosphere in this century, remained unaware of Vernadsky's work until well after Lovelock framed his own Gaia hypothesis. Whereas Vernadsky's work emphasized life as a geological force, Lovelock has shown that earth has a physiology: the temperature, alkalinity, acidity, and reactive gases are modulated by life.[179]

Teilhard left Paris for China on April 6, 1923, booking inexpensive shipping routes that gave him opportunity to spend time exploring the Suez, Ceylon, Sumatra, Saigon, and Hong Kong, before arriving in Shanghai. During his time at sea, he had ample hours to think about and to observe the biosphere:

Teilhard spent his time aboard ship reading, writing, and observing nature. He liked to look at the stars at night—so clear and bright when seen from a ship far from the intruding lights of terra firma—and by day observe the state of the ocean, calm at times and stormy at others.[180]

On May 6, 1923, barely a month after departing from Marseille, Teilhard completed a remarkable essay, later called "Hominization," that sets forth his first extended exploration of the "Noosphere" concept, and may be considered an outgrowth of recent discussions with Vernadsky and Le Roy in Paris."[181] In the essay, Teilhard begins by making a subtle shift from the usual Cartesian linear approach to paleontological classification toward a more spherical, three-dimensional metaphysical geometry: "We begin to understand that the most natural division of the elements of the earth would be by zones, by circles, by *spheres*."[182] In the last half of the essay, Teilhard develops his understanding of the "Noosphere" concept, and in one section, "The Psychic Essence of Evolution," Teilhard says:

> It has appeared as a possible element in a sort of higher organism which might form itself . . .or else something (someone) exists, in which each element gradually finds, by reunion with the whole, the completion of all the savable elements that have been formed in its individuality.[183]

In this "reunion with the whole" can be seen a foreshadowing of the main theme of one of his final essays, written thirty-two years later, "The Death-Barrier and Co-Reflection," in which is described a process whereby each individual human, at least the "savable elements," transcends the physical death barrier, merging with the Noosphere due to "the principles of the conservation of consciousness. . .

conceived as the luminous attainment of *a new psychological stage.*"[184]

Barely a week before his own death, Teilhard concludes his "breaking the death-barrier" essay with the statement that "the interior equilibrium of what we have called the Noosphere requires the presence *perceived by individuals* of a higher pole or centre that directs, sustains and assembles the whole sheaf of our efforts."[185] The emphasis that Teilhard places on the words "perceived by individuals" can be seen here to underscore the experiential, participatory dimension of his quest to explore and to understand the dynamics of the planet Earth, considering it, certainly from Vernadsky's biospheric view, as an evolving organism at every level.

But in 1924, thirty-two years before his final essay, Teilhard found himself in a state of withdrawal as he arrived in China, a somewhat banished intellectual from Paris. A friend commenting about Teilhard's state of mind at that time, wrote, "his friends noticed that he seemed to be abstracted and withdrawn."[186] Teilhard himself writes, shortly after his arrival in China, "I feel very much as though I had reached the limit of my powers: I seem somehow unable to keep things in my mind. I have the continual feeling that as far as my own life goes, the day is drawing to a close."[187]

Arriving in the Chinese city of Tientsin (today's industrial port city of Tianjin) he joined the French 'Paleontological Mission in China' founded by his fellow priest Fr. Licent (whom Teilhard soon discovered to be the sole other member of the 'Paleontological Mission'). After a two week stay in Tientsin he found himself departing on his first expedition into upper Mongolia and the mountainous Ordos desert with his fellow priest, Licent, who himself had been exploring Mongolia for the past nine years. They were travelling to an area where Licent had discovered fossil deposit sites from which he had previously shipped to Teilhard in Paris specimens from the Tertiary Period (65 million to 2.6 million years ago).

The two priests traveled and camped for over a year in this vast silence of an area of Mongolia. Even today, in the 21st century, Inner Mongolia, Gansu, Xinjiang is considered an isolated area of China. But in an early 1924 letter Teilhard writes, "I looked over the steppes where gazelles still run about as they did in the Tertiary period, or visited the yurts where the Mongols still live as they lived a thousand years ago."[188]

It was here, during this extended period of solitude in the Mongolian high desert plains, on some silent bright day or crystalline night under the canopy of stars, that Teilhard experienced a new realization, a new communion with God and the universe. And if we read carefully we can even pick out expressions of these particular moments, as recorded in *The Divine Milieu* (1927), when a young priest begins to establish this connection consciously, becoming one with the energies of the divine being in the surrounding landscape:

> On some given day a man suddenly becomes conscious that he is alive to a particular perception of the divine spread everywhere about him. . . . It began with a particular and unique resonance which swelled each harmony, with a diffused radiance . . . And then, contrary to all expectation and all probability, I began to feel what was ineffably common to all things. The unity communicated itself to me by giving me the gift of grasping it. I had in fact acquired a new sense, *the sense of a new quality* or *of a new dimension*. Deeper still: a transformation had taken place for me in *the very perception of being*."[189]

The result of this transformation was a new level of written communication and communion, as his friend Pierre Leroy recounts: "It was during this expedition, in the stillness of the vast solitude of the Ordos desert, that one Easter Sunday he finished the mystical and philosophical poem, *Mass upon the altar of the World.*"

As to how Teilhard attained to this "new sense in the very perception of being," precisely what occurred to establish the connection to this "hidden power stirring in the heart of matter, glowing centre," he does not give a clue, but he personalizes it and gives it a name "the *divine milieu*," characterizing it as a sound, a single note, an "ineffably simple vibration:"

> Just as, at the center of the divine *milieu*, all the sounds of created being are fused, without being confused, *in a single note* which dominates and sustains them (that seraphic note, no doubt, which bewitched St. Francis), so all the powers of the soul begin to resound in response to its call; and these multiple tones, in their turn, compose themselves into a single, *ineffably simple vibration* in which all the spiritual nuances . . . shine forth . . . inexpressible and unique.[190]

And Teilhard assures us that this new sense arises from a profound interior vision: "One thing at least appears certain, that God never reveals himself to us from outside, by intrusion, but from within, by stimulation, elevation and enrichment of the human psychic current."[191]

In 1927 under the heading "The Growth of the Divine Milieu" he writes:

> Let us therefore concentrate upon a better understanding *of the process by which the holy presence is born and grows within us.* In order to foster its progress more intelligently let us observe the birth and growth of the divine milieu, first in ourselves and then in the world that begins with us.[192]

Being a Catholic priest, Teilhard easily associated the cosmic Christ with the Omega Point, and saw this confluence as being a harmonious solution to the problem of bringing his vision into alignment with his faith (and with his employer, the Vatican, who nevertheless at that time censored in toto his speculative essays). In a 1945 essay Teilhard writes, "Just suppose that we identify the cosmic Christ of faith with the Omega Point of science: then everything in our outlook is clarified and broadened, and falls into harmony."[193]

In 1955, almost thirty years after his early experiences of the *Milieu* in the trenches at Verdun and in the vast Mongolian desert, and just two weeks before his death on an Easter Sunday in New York, Teilhard completed "The Christic."[194] Only twenty pages long, this final essay describes his mature vision, integrating science and religion, and recapturing his earlier first experiences of the psychic movements or currents.

In the first section of the essay, "The Amorization of the Universe," we find a summary of Teilhard's many years of experiencing "the two fundamental psychic movements or currents." These two fundamental currents can be seen to reflect his distinct vision of energy as having two mutually perpendicular components (like the Cross) or movements, a tangential flow in space and time that fills the cosmos with the creative electrical radiance of resonant matter, and a second current, a magnetic radial inflow of energy resonance, of spirit returning to the source, the process of centration, of noogenesis, of Christification leading toward Omega.

"On the one side," says Teilhard, is "the irresistible convergence of my individual thought with every other thinking being on earth," and "a flux, at once physical and psychic."[195] This is the tangential seen here as the very flux of collective thought on the planet Earth, an experience of the matrix-like web of human consciousness active in the biosphere.

And on the other side, . . . a centration of my own small ego . . . a sort of Other who could be even more I than I am myself . . . a Presence so intimate that it could not satisfy itself or satisfy me, without being by nature universal. [196]

Here is expressed the magnetically radial component of consciousness, the energy of centration, pulling inwardly toward a center that, perhaps beyond the event horizon of time-space, is also the universal Center, the Omega, the ultimate personalization of human cosmogenesis, fully personalized, and identified by Teilhard the Catholic priest as "the Christic."

Upon returning to Paris, after having spent 18 months in his extended expedition to Mongolia, Teilhard resumed teaching classes at the Institut Catholique, from which he had taken a leave of absence.[197]

Teilhard gave four lectures on evolution during the winter months of 1925; and at the same time continued to develop his theory of the noosphere—a kind of cosmic envelope created by the reflection of the mind. The word was his own invention—it had come to him during the war—but the word and the idea were both adopted later by Le Roy and the Russian geologist Vernadsky, who was in Paris at the time.[198]

One of the earliest discussions of the "nous" or "noos" may be found in the writings of the Pre-Socratic Greek philosopher who introduced philosophy to Athens, Anaxagoras (500–428 BCE).[199] In developing his philosophy of the infinite interconnectedness of an infinite multitude of imperishable small parts, Anaxagoras concluded the following:

A single overarching principle is needed to provide unity to the whole system. This principle is *nous* . . . . *"Nous"* is more related to the concept of mind in the sense of the human mind or reason (though distinct from "logos," which is also sometimes translated as reason). It represents, furthermore, a kind of unity of thought a "thinking thing" in some sense.[200]

The Neoplatonists developed the concept of the *nous* even further 800 years later, and this can be found particularly in Plotinus.[201] According to Plotinus, writing in the third century CE, the original Being, the One, emanates the *nous*, the archetype of all manifestations in the visible world of time and space.[202]

> Plotinus presents a philosophy of Unity: unity as unfathomable and transcendent, and unity as omnipresent and immanent.[203]

This Neoplatonist *nous* is accessible to the human mind under certain conditions, and it is what the Neoplatonists termed the *anima mundi*, or "world soul" that bridges the *nous* with the material world of time and space.[204]

The noosphere for Teilhard, as expressed in his numerous essays, corresponds more with the Neoplatonist *anima mundi*, rather than the Anaxagoras *nous*, which appears to be more like Bohm's implicate–explicate "wholeness."[205] Teilhard's concept of the noosphere is indeed part of the phenomenal world while maintaining links to the transcendent; but it is specifically associated with the planets in general, and the Earth in particular, with human consciousness evolving within a planetary sphere. Teilhard goes so far as to discuss the possibility of multiple, numerous noospheres, associated with distant planets, and speculates that there may indeed be communication between these multiple noospheres.[206]

Though there had been some controversy over the origin of the word "noosphere," shortly before his own death Teilhard confirmed that the word was his own in a letter referring to the recent demise of his friend Édouard Le Roy. In the letter, Teilhard writes:

> I believe, so far as one can ever tell, that the word 'noosphere' was my invention; but it was he [Le Roy] who launched it.[207]

In a 1951 essay, almost 30 years after first using the term, Teilhard elaborates his mature understanding of the noosphere:

> It is an amazing thing—in less than a million years the human "species" has succeeded in covering the earth: and not only spatially—on this surface that is now completely encircled mankind has completed the construction of a close network of planetary links, so successfully that a special envelope now stretches over the old biosphere. Every day this new integument grows in strength; it can be clearly recognized and distinguished in every quarter; it is provided with its own system of internal connections and communications—and for this I have for a long time proposed the name of *noosphere*.[208]

In a collection of essays, *The Biosphere and Noosphere Reader*, the editors begin their Preface by characterizing the search for the noosphere:

> The noosphere lies at an intersection where science and philosophy meet . . . an interdisciplinary domain of wide interest and high relevance that remains outside the purview of most specialists, but is of major significance for the future of humankind.[209]

The authors of *The Biosphere and Noosphere Reader* take four distinct approaches to Teilhard's concept:

1. The *noosphere* is a product of the biosphere as transformed by human knowledge and action.

2. The *noosphere* represents an ultimate and inevitable sphere of evolution.

3. The *noosphere* is a manifestation of global mind.

4. The *noosphere* is the mental sphere in which change and creativity are inherent although essentially unpredictable.[210]

Locating the Noosphere

At this point we speculate as to where in the physical space–time universe the noosphere might be found. To find the noosphere let us try a thought experiment and build a likely image of the noosphere. Picture in your mind the geometry of the planet Earth. Imagine the heat, approximately 7200° C in the central core.[211] Place your consciousness at the absolute geometric-gravitational central point of the planetary core. Now begin to move (or to rise) along a radial line slowly outward, toward the cold of space, noting the temperature drop as you move along the line away from the center of the planet, and stop at the moment you arrive at the temperature 98.2° F, the average human core temperature.

Repeating the above procedure multiple times, with many different radii moving away at different angular separation from the core, a three-dimensional surface mapping, like a mathematical brane, or Teilhard's isosphere, will begin to emerge, an infrared energy isosphere to which each human being is linked through an identical resonance frequency.[212]

The shape of this isosphere will likely be highly organic and fractal in appearance, sometimes hovering above the ground on thermoclimes where the "ambient temperature" reaches 98.2° F, while in arctic regions and below the oceans it will be located hundreds of feet the surface of ice or water.

But the noosphere is more than simply a dynamic location on the surface of an isosphere at or above or below the rocky surface of the earth. It is energy at the same frequency band as the human body, that has been said to generate, with each heartbeat, approximately 1.3 watts of radiant power.[213] While we normally think of each heartbeat as simply a pushing of blood through the arteries, it is also radiantly generating infrared electromagnetic energy (the infrared being a range of the spectrum that we often hear simply described, dismissively, as "heat").

How might this information be used to substantiate Teilhard's passionate vision of the reality of a noosphere that would manifest in some planetary energy of consciousness. In the Table below, three values of energy output are compared.

Table 1

Radiant Energy Outputs, Compared

Source of energy	Power Output
Most powerful radio frequency transmitter on planet[214]	1,000,000 watts
Maximum output of Three Mile Island nuclear reactor[215]	873,000,000 watts
Combined electromagnetic output of human heartbeats[216]	9,100,000,000 watts

A chart of global population growth (Fig. 11) indicates that there are currently approximately 7 billion human beings living on the planet.

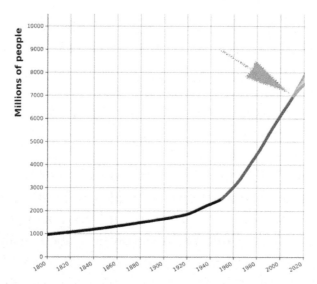

Figure 11. *Human population of the Earth since 1800.*
Graphic by Aetheling (2012).[217]

Accordingly, we multiplying 7 billion humans by the average of 1.3 watts of radiation per human to find the current amount of energy being broadcast by all human hearts as over nine gigawatts (9,100,000,000 watts), as shown previously, at the bottom of Table 6. In the table, this can be seen dwarfing the output power of the most powerful radio transmitter in the world at 1,000,000 watts (one megawatt), and even of the maximum energy output of the Three Mile Island nuclear power plant, that occasionally operated at its maximum output of 873,000,000 watts.

It is possible that the nine gigawatts of electromagnetic energy being continuously broadcast by our collective heartbeats may be taking part in a vast energetic interactive resonance with Gaia. Our own collective energy transmits in the far infrared in the 10-micron wavelength range (predicted by Wien's Law for our body temperature range) is the part of the geomagnetosphere that is us, the noosphere (the "us" sphere).

Evidence of direct interaction of the electromagnetic energy of the geomagnetosphere with human consciousness can be viewed in Fig. 12.

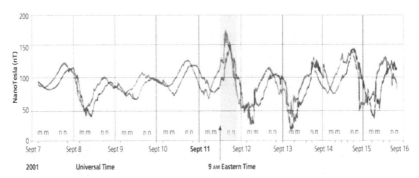

Figure 12. *Evidence of a coherent planetary standing wave.*[218] Image from McCraty, Deyhle, and Childre,"The Global Coherence Initiative," 75, fig. 10. Reprinted with permission from HeartMath Institute.

This is a chart recording daily data from Geostationary Operational Environmental Satellites and weather satellites in geosynchronous orbit over the United States in the days before, during, and after the September 11, 2001, terrorist attacks on the United States. Continuous readings show a marked peak on September 11, 2001 followed by several days of marked disruption in the observed diurnal rhythm of the geomagnetosphere.[219]

In the conclusion of the paper, the authors state: "The study . . . supports the hypothesis that humanity is connected via a global field."[220] Perhaps the same hypothetical "global field" of radiation can be seen in the one Teilhard describes in a 1953 essay, "A Sequel to the Problem of Human Origins":

Our minds cannot resist the inevitable conclusion that were we, by chance, to possess plates that were sensitive to the specific radiation of the "noospheres" scattered throughout space, it would be *practically certain* that what we saw registered on them would be a cloud of thinking stars.[221]

In early summer of 1923, Teilhard found himself travelling for the first time on an expedition into the Ordos Desert of Outer Mongolia.[222] It is here that he has another major vision, a peak experience later recounted in "The Mass on the World," and of which he comments:

> I see the same thing as I saw long ago at the "front" (which from the human point of view, was the most alive region that existed): one single operation is in process of happening in the world, and it alone can justify our action.[223]

After 18 months in China, Teilhard returned to Paris, only to discover that his earlier essay on "original sin" had been discovered by a Jesuit colleague in one of his desk drawers at the Institut Catholique, and subsequently forwarded to the Vatican, "where the Holy Office and the Jesuit headquarters already held a file on Teilhard."[224] Reproaching him for having dared to discuss new ways of understanding original sin, the Church authorities (1) insisted that he "sign a pledge to keep silent in the future," (2) permanently revoked his license to teach at the Institut Catholique, where he had been an Assistant Professor in geology, and (3) asked him to leave Paris.[225] Teilhard's return to China in 1926 seems to have been at a low point in his career:

> His departure had something of the aspect of a disgrace. He had been removed from Paris by the prudence of his superiors, to whom he had been denounced for propagating dubious ideas, and who feared a censure that would be equally prejudicial to the career of the young scientist and the good name of the Order. Thus he was leaving France under a

cloud for an indefinite time, and he saw the momentum of his influence broken just as it was beginning to prove fruitful.[226]

Problems with a previous essay only aggravated the situation, one of his earliest essays, "Cosmic Life," a 56-page essay written at Dunkirk on the front during Easter week, April 24, 1916. When he sent it for publishing to the editors of a Jesuit periodical in Paris, *Etudes,* it was rejected for including such sentences as "The life of Christ mingles with the life-blood of evolution."[227] In the rejection letter, one of the editors explained:

> Your thesis is *exciting* [he used the English word, in the midst of French] and interesting to a high degree . . . . It is a rich canvas, full of beautiful images. But it is not at all suited for our peaceful readers.[228]

The essay had then been brought to the attention of officials at the Vatican by Teilhard's Jesuit supervisor, Father Claude Chanteur, who expressed strong reservations about giving Teilhard formal admission into the Jesuit Order, but who eventually, perhaps reluctantly, allowed the 37-year-old Teilhard to take his solemn vows, on May 26, 1918.[229]

Upon his return to China in 1926, Teilhard made the best of his virtual exile, involving himself deeply in running the Jesuit museum there, and accompanying Father Licent on extensive paleontological expeditions into the vast interior of Eastern Mongolia.[230] During the next 20 years, Teilhard travelled extensively between China and Paris, but during the years from 1940 to 1946 he found himself in Peking under the Japanese occupation, unable to travel. Instead, he devoted himself to perhaps his most challenging essays on the dynamics of consciousness, including "Centrology," discussed in the following section.

In May of 1946, at the end of World War II, Teilhard returned to Paris, where he tried unsuccessfully to obtain permission to publish a major work he had completed in China over a period of several years, *The Human Phenomenon*. While in Paris awaiting a reply, Teilhard began giving lectures on his latest philosophical ideas after a hiatus of 22 years, and soon he began to attract the interest of young Jesuit students, as well as a more secular public that had become less conservative as a result of the war. While Teilhard scrupulously avoided large venues (he had been henceforth forbidden in 1923 to give large public addresses), he soon fell into a hectic activity alternating between intimate private conversations and semipublic discussions. During one such series of monthly discussions with several Jesuit intellectuals, Teilhard set forth two fundamental points in his philosophy, as recorded by one of the attending priests, Fr. Lejay:[231]

- God acts globally on the whole of evolution and consequently utilizes, in selective fashion, all the possibilities offered by secondary causes.

- Evil is a by-product of evolution, for there is no evolution without groping, without the intervention of chance; consequently, checks and mistakes are always possible.[232]

After the war in Europe, the topic of evil was of great interest, not only among intellectuals, but also among the general public.[233] Teilhard's characterization of evil as a part of the process of an evolutionary energy did not set well with conservative Church authorities, nor did his growing popularity among intellectual Jesuits and the public. He was offered a Chair at the College de France, but received word from the Vatican in 1950 that he was not permitted to accept the position. That same year even his close friends and sympathetic colleagues were censured: "Jesuit academics who had espoused Teilhard's ideas, among them his friend Henri de Lubac, were ordered by the Vatican to leave their positions."[234] Teilhard decided that he could no longer reside in Paris, and after securing a position in New York, Teilhard left Paris to travel, and eventually, in virtual exile, to spend the rest of his life in North America.

In 1954 Teilhard mentioned in a letter to a nephew that when he died, he wished that it might be on Easter Sunday, the quintessential day, as a Catholic, for celebrating resurrection transformation into eternal life.[235] Perhaps this can be seen as an example of real psychic precognition, for the next year, on April 10, 1955, Teilhard attended Easter services at St. Patrick's Cathedral and enjoyed the Sunday afternoon in company of his close friend Rhoda de Terra and her daughter.[236] Pierre Teilhard de Chardin died while drinking a cup of tea in the front room: "Suddenly, while standing at her window, he fell full length to the floor like a stricken tree."[237] Only a few friends attended his funeral, and only two people accompanied his body on the journey to the cemetery, 60 miles north of New York City, along the banks of the Hudson River to the Jesuit novitiate of St. Andrews-on-the-Hudson.[238]

> Only Pére Leroy and another priest accompanied Teilhard on his last journey. The coffin had to be laid in a temporary vault because the earth was still too frozen for a grave.[239]

Teilhard is buried near the east bank of the Hudson River, under a simple stone inscribed only with his name, dates, and "R. I. P." The small grave remains, but the seminary was sold in 1970 and is now the headquarters of the Culinary Institute of America.[240]

Teilhard's Hyperphysics

Teilhard sees the current human phenomenon of consciousness to be in the early stages of what he terms a "noogenesis," a change of state in human consciousness into a more powerful union, a "joining with other centres of cosmic life to resume the work of universal synthesis on a higher scale."[241] The dynamics of this change and the architecture of consciousness itself is the subject of Teilhard's hyperphysics. Teilhard's ideas are clear, his writing style is straightforward and his logic transparent. But appreciation of his more detailed observations on the dynamics of an energy of consciousness requires careful examination of his more technical writing. Teilhard was fascinated by the phenomenon of "change of state," such as when water changes state to become ice, and, in particular, of evolutionary changes of state, such as when matter changes state to become life. But his greatest interest can be seen in potential imminent changes of state in consciousness itself, both human and cosmic, as he observed here in 1937 (note in the quote that Teilhard often uses the words "spirit" and "consciousness" interchangeably):

> The phenomenon of spirit [consciousness] is not therefore a sort of brief flash in the night; it reveals a gradual and systematic passage from the unconscious to the conscious, and from the conscious to the self-conscious. It is a *cosmic change of state*.[242]

Teilhard here describes three critical points in the evolutionary arc of Earth consciousness, three changes of state:

- "First the appearance of life whence emerged the biosphere."

- "Then, the emergence of thought which produced the noosphere."

- "Finally, a further metamorphosis: the coming to consciousness of an Omega in the heart of the noosphere."[243]

In his numerous essays Teilhard constructs the picture of a panoramic evolutionary arc: The Earth, having experienced a change of state at the moment when life appeared, experienced another change of state as life erupted into self-reflection (thought) in the biological zenith of *homo sapiens*. Teilhard predicts that this evolutionary arc is now moving toward yet another change of state, and is in the process of transforming human consciousness, collectively, into an even greater "complexity-consciousness,"[244] an "internal centro-complexification,"[245] both in the individual as well as the species, through the process of "centration"[246] or "centrogenesis."[247] These terms have all been constructed and developed by Teilhard to articulate and support his theory, and can be regarded as specific to his theory of hyperphysics. We will examine and clarify these terms by focusing on three essays in which his physics of consciousness, hyperphysics, is set forth: two written in 1937, the third and most technical written in 1944, near the end of Teilhard's long seclusion in Peking under Japanese occupation:

- "The Phenomenon of Spirit" (1937), written during an ocean voyage

- "Human Energy" (1937), written in Peking

- "Centrology" (1944), written in Peking

While major components of Teilhard's hyperphysics are presented in these three essays, additional insights into the same concepts can be found throughout his many other writings, both published and unpublished.

"The Phenomenon of Spirituality" (1937)

In 1937 Teilhard made the long Pacific voyage from Shanghai to the United States, where he had been invited to receive the Mendel Medal in recognition of his work in paleontology, specifically as one of the discoverers of Peking Man.[248] During this voyage he completed an essay, "The Phenomenon of Spirituality," in which he not only discusses evolution, consciousness, and morality, but begins to articulate details of a hyperphysics of consciousness.[249] In this essay he joins with panpsychist philosopher–scientists from Plato to William James in affirming that it is impossible to deny that consciousness is a part of the natural universe.[250] He also introduces his concept of *centrology,* a basic building block of hyperphysics, and a seed from which, nine years later, emerged the cornerstone of Teilhard's hyperphysics, the essay "Centrology: An Essay in a Dialectic of Union," written in Peking in 1944.[251] The richness and diversity of ideas developed in "The Phenomenon of Spirituality" are stunning and wide-ranging. The topics move from evolutionary cosmology to consciousness, morality, and future research, and at the conclusion of the essay, he speaks of the possibility of seeking scientific proof of consciousness as a *centre* of energy:

> Regarding the possibility of proof obtained by direct observation . . . there must be a means . . . of recognizing . . . some psychic effect (radiation or attraction) specifically connected with the operation of this centre.[252]

In approaching Teilhard's essay, it is important at the outset to consider his frequent use of the terms "spirituality" and "spirit," as opposed to the term "consciousness." As a Jesuit Catholic priest, Teilhard's free use of the words "spirit" and "spirituality" may be easily understood, though the words are colored with religious overtones. Teilhard often seems to interchange the words "spirit" and "consciousness" in his essays, and often one assumes the terms may be synonymous, but the following passage in another essay, also written in 1937, offers a distinction between "spirit" and "consciousness":

> Human energy presents itself to our view as the term of a vast process in which the whole mass of the universe is involved. In us the evolution of the world towards the spirit becomes conscious.[253]

This tells us that Teilhard, like Bohm, views the universe as a "process" and as a "whole."[254] Teilhard also sees our human state as one in which the "evolution of the world" is becoming "conscious," and in which our human consciousness itself is evolving "towards the spirit." The relationship of spirit to consciousness for Teilhard is reminiscent of the metaphor from alchemy, of the ouroboros snake chasing its tail (Fig. 13).

Figure 13. *The Ouroboros. Graphic by Pelekanos (1478).*[255]

However, Teilhard often uses the word "spirit" when "consciousness" would appear to be more appropriate, and henceforth in quoting passages from Teilhard we will provide an alternate reading of "consciousness" via angle brackets, where deemed appropriate, as in "the phenomenon of spirit [consciousness] . . . is the thing we know best in the world since we are itself."[256]

In the opening of his essay, "The Phenomenon of Spirituality," Teilhard argues that consciousness, whether a force or an energy, should be regarded as a natural, real phenomenon in the universe, worthy of study alongside other equally "real" phenomena that are taken as objects of interest in science (e.g., light, heat, electromagnetism, gravity, etc.):

> Around us, bodies present various qualities: they are warm, colored, electrified, heavy. But also in certain cases they are living, conscious. Beside the phenomena of heat, light and the rest studied by physics, there is, just as real and *natural*, the *phenomenon of spirituality*.[257]

Teilhard finds it surprising that humans have never truly come to understand this spirit/consciousness in which we are all glaringly immersed:

> The phenomenon of spirit [consciousness] has rightly attracted human attention more than any other. We are coincidental with it. We feel it from within. It is the very thread of which the other phenomena are woven for us. *It is the thing we know best in the world since we are itself,* and it is for us everything. And yet we never come to an understanding concerning the nature of this fundamental element.[258]

Teilhard describes the two most conventional approaches traditionally taken in regarding the elusive phenomenon of consciousness:

1. Religious traditions regard consciousness [spirit], in general, to be of a transcendent nature, not of this physical, space–time world, while by contrast, and

2. Modern science regards consciousness as an epiphenomenon, a unique accident in the recent evolutionary history of the planet.

Teilhard tells us that in this essay he will propose and develop an alternative to these two approaches:

> I propose in these pages to develop a third viewpoint towards which a new physical science and a new philosophy seem to be converging in the present day: that is to say that spirit [consciousness] is neither super-imposed nor accessory to the cosmos, but that it quite simply represents the higher state assumed in and around us by the primal and indefinable thing that we call, for want of another name, the "stuff of the universe."[259]

Teilhard tells us that the phenomenon of consciousness has been overlooked as an object of study within physical science because, at first sight, the "consciousness portion of the world presents itself in the form of discontinuous, tiny and ephemeral fragments: a bright dust of individualities," while in truth the dimensions of this consciousness ought to be taken as "the dimensions of the universe itself."[260]

But in order to see this, says Teilhard, we need to develop a new form of perception, a new sense with which we may "educate our eyes to perceiving collective realities." Teilhard predicts the development not only of a new form of "direct vision," but the emergence of a previously unsuspected psychic ability, a new sensory mode:

> Men have for long been seeking a means of immediately influencing the bodies and souls around

them by their will, and of penetrating them by *a direct vision* . . . . Nothing seems to me more vital, from the point of view of human energy, than the spontaneous appearance and, eventually, the systematic cultivation of such a "cosmic sense."[261]

Teilhard has sensed evolutionary transformations both through his direct inner vision, as well as through his outer vision, he has critically observed both an internal as well as an external nature. Evolution, claims Teilhard, is often accompanied by sudden changes of state, as in water that is seen to become ice, or a solution in crystallization, change of state in "not only molecular or atomic complexity, but interiorization."[262] Teilhard perceives, both internally and externally, that in consciousness change of state follows a process of centration or compression. This can be compared with and contrasted to entropy, the movement of expansion, diffusion, and dissipation, and together they can be seen as "two fundamental cosmic movements . . . which we can grasp experientially."[263] He describes these two contrary movements as the concurrent movement of energy in two directions, the "vitalization" and the "dissipation" of energy and says that they "are merely the opposite poles of a single cosmic event."[264] Fig. 14 contrasts the two movements of entropy and centration.

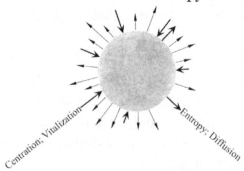

Figure 14. *Entropy and centration.*

In words that parallel David Bohm's description of an ongoing process of enfolding and unfolding between an implicate and an explicate order, Teilhard describes "the inward furling from which consciousness is born . . . around a centre . . . the All becoming self-reflective upon a single consciousness."[265]

At this point he brings up a theme that will arise repeatedly in his later essays, the transcendence of death by the individual personality.[266] Teilhard says, "to become super-conscious the fragmented building blocks of man must unite itself with others,"[267] but without losing personalities previously acquired, without losing information. Recall that Teilhard had sensed this phenomenon as a totalization of multiple centres[268] of consciousness, in 1916 at the Front.

He goes on to state that humans in general seem to have lost the "faculty of totalization," with the exception of a few mystics, who have been able to experience union by dissolution, much as salt in the ocean. But it is union by differentiation that interest Teilhard, not union by dissolution.

> We can see a justification ahead for our hope of a personal immortality . . . without becoming confused with one another . . . to complete ourselves we must pass into a greater than ourselves . . . . In this convergent universe, all the lower centres unite, but by inclusion in a more powerful centre. Therefore they are all preserved and completed by joining together.[269]

Teilhard now turns to the implications of such a theory for morality, in a section he calls "Moral Applications." He describes two categories of morality, the "Morality of Balance," and the "Morality of Movement."[270]

Morality of Balance vs. Morality of Movement

Here Teilhard describes two types of morality, the morality of balance, and the morality of movement. The old morality is the morality of balance, an attempt at homeostasis, a "morality that arose largely as an empirical defense of the individual and society."[271] Teilhard goes on to say, "Morality has till now been principally understood as a fixed system of rights and duties intended to establish a static equilibrium."[272] However in light of the modern discovery of the evolutionary nature of everything in the universe, the human being must be seen as "an element destined to complete himself cosmically in a higher consciousness in process of formation," and thus the need for a new morality, a morality of growth (movement), one that will foster and catalyze evolutionary change, a growth into a new formation of being. Teilhard says that new times and a new understanding of the trajectory of life and consciousness implies that while the "moralist was up to now a jurist, or a tight-rope walker," the moralist of the future must "become the technician and engineer of the spiritual [consciousness] energies of the world."[273] He says that for those who see the development of consciousness "as *the* essential phenomenon of nature . . . morality is consequently nothing less than the higher development of mechanics and biology. The world is ultimately constructed by moral forces."[274] Having argued the urgent requirement for a new morality, a morality of growth, Teilhard sets forth "three rules that clearly modify or complete the idea we have of goodness and perfection:"[275]

- Good "is what makes for the growth of spirit [consciousness]."

- Good is everything that brings "growth of consciousness to the world."

- "Finally, best is what assures their highest development to the spiritual powers [consciousness] of the earth."[276]

Teilhard summarizes, "many things seemed to be forbidden by the morality of balance which become virtually permitted or even obligatory by the morality of movement." For example, in following a morality of balance, as long as we follow society's rules, we are permitted to waste our lives in any frivolous pursuit (i.e., in sheer entertainment); whereas under a morality of movement such things as research through experimentation with psychotropic drugs and participatory exploration of multiple religions would likely be permissible. With disregard of likely disapproval by Vatican censors, Teilhard urges a new human morality of growth (see Table 2) that "will forbid a neutral and 'inoffensive' existence, and compel him strenuously to free his *autonomy* and *personality* to the utmost," and he urges us "to try everything and to force everything in the direction of the greatest consciousness."[277]

Table 2
Morality of Balance versus Morality of Growth[278]

Morality of balance	Morality of growth
Homeostasis; closed.	Evolutionary movement; open.
Fixed rules, rights, and duties to sustain the present.	Whatever fosters growth of consciousness for the future.
Love is subordinate to procreation.	Love gives incalculable spiritual power.
The old moralities of balance are static, powerless to govern the earth.	What is needed is a new morality of movement, of growth.

One can see in Table 2 why the more conservative Church authorities might have had problem with these ideas, but Teilhard is an unapologetic explorer (and a mystic), who states unequivocally:

> The boldest mariners of tomorrow will set out to explore and humanize the mysterious ocean of moral energies . . . our goal is to try everything and to force everything in the direction of the greatest consciousness . . . ever since its beginnings life has been a groping, an adventure, a risk, and general and highest law of morality: to limit force is sin.[279]

At the conclusion of his essay, Teilhard urges us "situate the stuff of the universe in consciousness . . . and to see nature as the development of this same consciousness." He regards the idea of a cosmos as "a moving towards personality," and he concludes with a statement that, once more would likely win him no affection among more conservative elements in the Vatican:

> This is the origin of the present crisis in morality . . . a powerlessness of (old) moralities of balance to govern the earth. It is necessary for the religions to change themselves . . . what we are all more or less lacking at this moment is a new definition of holiness.[280]

Holoflux Theory and Teilhard's "Spirit"

At the heart of this essay, Teilhard introduces a major hypothesis in a key paragraph that is essential to understanding his hyperphysics, and that accords well with Bohm's model in ontological quantum physics, in which the cosmos is seen both as simultaneously unfolding and enfolding:

> Everything that happens in the world, we would say, suggests that the unique centre of consciousness

around which the universe is furling could only be formed gradually, through a series of diminishing concentric spheres, each of which engenders the next; each sphere being moreover formed of elementary centres charged with a consciousness that increases as their radius diminishes. By means of this mechanism each newly appearing sphere is charged in its turn with the consciousness developed in the preceding spheres, carries it to a degree higher in each of the elementary centres that compose it, and transmits it a little further on toward the centre of total convergence.[281]

This description can be seen as congruent with the theory of holospheres, in which smaller dimensions converge to the limit found at the Planck holosphere, at which point begins the implicate order, discussed more fully in Chapter IV, "Trinitarian Quantum Physics."

Teilhard concludes this section by telling us that "the final centre of the whole system appears at the end both as the final sphere and as the centre of all the centres spread over this final sphere."[282] This "centre of all centres" can be understood as Bohm's implicate order, transcending space–time. Teilhard also refers to this centre as "a quantum of consciousness," and tells us that each degree of consciousness at a given moment only exists as "an introduction to a higher consciousness," and that this general process is irresistible and irreversible.[283]

If we accept this hypothetical model, says Teilhard, then we are led to two conclusions for the present and for the future:

1. The source of all our difficulties in understanding matter is that it is habitually regarded as inanimate.[284]

2. We are moving towards a higher state of general consciousness . . . other spheres must exist in the future and, inevitably, there exists a supreme

centre in which all the personal energy represented by human consciousness must be gathered and "super-personalized."[285]

How might we understand Teilhard's use of the term "spirit" in terms of holoflux theory? It is evident that Teilhard's "spirit" appears to be equivalent to holoflux energy as it manifests within Bohm's implicate order. In the holoflux theory, spirit has a nonlocal locus embedded within a Planck-length spherical center in space–time, everywhere. Conversely, what is termed consciousness is localized in space–time, manifesting as expanding flux in detectable fields of electromagnetic waves, illustrated in Fig. 15.

SPIRIT **CONSCIOUSNESS**

NON-LOCAL   LOCAL

Figure 15. *Nonlocal spirit versus local consciousness.*

Yet they are in relationship, they both exist as part of Bohm's "Wholeness," and there exists a direct connection between spirit and consciousness through the phenomenon of frequency resonance operating through Fourier transform-like mathematical processes.

It is useful to go topologically further into the holoflux analogy. Imagine the communal locus of Teilhard's "spirit" as it is found within, at the very center of every "point" within space–time. The holoflux process *is* the implicate order, is *one with* the implicate order; "spirit," as implicate order holoflux, has the advantage of being self-superpositioned, fully interconnected, transcending the limits of time and space and can be identified in electrical engineering terms as the frequency domain.

Let us now move outward in scale, bridging the transition zone, the isospheric shell that divides the implicate order from the explicate order. Here we see holoflux emerging from the implicate order as it transforms into space–time energy, flaring forth as waves of spherically vibrating electromagnetic energy. These waves of energy emerge everywhere into space–time from a holoplenum of Planck diameter isospheres. Each isosphere can be seen to encapsulate the entire implicate order, within which the infinity of frequencies from all time and all space are eternally enfolding into a hyper-harmonic flux.

In terms of Bohmian holoflux theory, the first approach to consciousness, the religious, is focused almost exclusively upon an implicate domain, energy as a transcendent flux, and a focus which generally ignores or rejects as unreal the space–time explicate domain; conversely, in the second approach to consciousness, the modern scientific, the focus is upon space–time explicate mode phenomena, completely ignoring the possible reality of a non-space–time domain.

Teilhard proposes an alternative to these two, seemingly mutually exclusive, approaches:

> I propose in these pages to develop a third viewpoint towards which a new physical science and a new philosophy seem to be converging at the present day: that is to say that spirit is neither super-imposed nor accessory to the cosmos, but that it quite simply represents the higher state assumed in and around us by the primal and indefinable thing that we call, for want of a better name, the "stuff of the universe." Nothing more; and also nothing less. Spirit is neither a meta-phenomenon nor an epi-phenomenon; it is *the* phenomenon.[286]

Evidence of Teilhard's "spirit," or "*the phenomenon*," can be seen in the "Holy Spirit," from Teilhard's Catholic teaching of the Holy Trinity. to It is in accord with the sub-quantum holoflux model that views the Whole as one single energy, processing within and between two primary domains, a space–time domain, and a spectral domain.

Fig. 16 presents a Planck diagram of the Holy Trinity highlighting Teilhard's distinction between *tangential consciousness* and *axial consciousness* mapped by Bohm's distinction between an nonlocal (implicate) order, and a local (explicate) order in space and time.

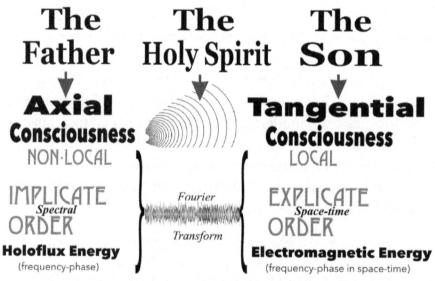

Figure 16. *A Planck Diagram of the Holy Trinity.*

The identifies "spirit" in the center, bridging the nonlocal implicate order and the local explicate order. Between the two orders that make up the Whole we see the energy process of the Fourier Transform as the Holy Spirit, possibly the mysterious "dark energy" being sought by physicists.[287] Conversely, "consciousness" can be seen on the right, in the space–time region, manifesting as the energy of consciousness in time and in space (i.e., a Cosmic Christ consciousness) and also identified here as electromagnetic energy.

A Christian approach to the diagram would consider God the Father as hypostasis of the Non-Local Implicate Order, the Holy Spirit as hypostasis of continuous two-way Fourier transforms, and the Son as physically-manifest consciousness within space and time.

"Human Energy" (1937)

It is in an essay written in Peking that same year, "Human Energy," Teilhard describes three forms of energy, and implies that modern science only considers the first two, ignoring the third; these three he identifies as:

- Incorporated energy,

- Controlled energy, and

- Spiritualized [conscious] energy.

Incorporated energy manifests in rocks, crystals, neurons, etc. Controlled energy is that generated by humans and used to power human devices thermodynamically and electrically. Energy of the third kind, Teilhard's "spiritualized energy," or we would say, the "energy of consciousness," is the primary subject of his essay, "Human Energy."[288]

In this essay Teilhard proposes that each human "represents a cosmic nucleus . . . radiating around it waves of organization and excitation within matter."[289] Teilhard immediately proposes, based it seems upon his own experience, that these radiations can be perceived by human beings, and he makes reference to the need for development of a special psychic mode of perception:

> This perception of a natural psychic unity higher than our "souls" requires, *as I know from experience*, a special quality and training in the observer. Like all

broad scientific perspectives it is the product of a prolonged reflexion, leading to the discovery of *a deep cosmic sense.*[290]

Teilhard warns that it is a matter of perception, of tuning, of intent. He says that we are like a cell that can see nothing but other cells, but that there are more complex configurations of being if we only can learn how to join with them. He says that "the thoughts of individuals . . . form from the linked multiplicity, a single spirit of the earth," and that he sees humanity continuing to evolve "in the direction of a decisive expansion of our ancient powers reinforced by the acquisition of certain new faculties of consciousness."[291] Teilhard emphasizes that this growth is not a walk of random chance, but that it unfolds within a universe that is alive with an energy that is also synonymous with the mystery we call love or allurement:

> Love by the boundless possibilities of intuition and communication it contains, penetrates the unknown; it will take its place in the mysterious future, with the group of new faculties and consciousnesses that is awaiting us.[292]

Here he expresses a consideration missing in most physical descriptions of energy, the category of "love," something that Teilhard includes as perhaps the most real, fundamental manifestation of energy in his hyperphysical theories. As early as 1931, in "The Spirit of the Earth," Teilhard had referred to an energy of consciousness, of sensation, of love, as manifesting in a spectrum (much as Jung, in 1946, used the imagery of the spectrum to characterize the energy of the psyche).[293] Teilhard says that, "Love is a sacred reserve of energy; it is the blood of spiritual evolution."[294]

> Hominized love is distinct from all other love, because the "spectrum" of its warm and penetrating

light is marvelously enriched. No longer only a unique and periodic attraction for purposes of material fertility; but an unbounded and continuous possibility of contact between minds rather than bodies; the play of countless subtle antennae seeking one another.[295]

Teilhard sees this organic love-consciousness energy growing more complex and changing through some natural evolutionary process, currently unknown, but he is confident that there will be an eventual mastery and understanding of this same phenomenon (conscious love) in terms of physics.

Accordingly, he stresses the importance of those engaged in scientific research to turn their focus upon the human phenomenon of consciousness.

He is hopeful, telling us with conviction that "physics will surely isolate and master the secret that lies at the heart of metaphysics," and will accelerate this evolution toward the emergence of a new cosmic sense:

Nothing seems to me more vital, from the point of view of human energy, than the spontaneous appearance and, eventually, the systematic cultivation of such a "cosmic sense."[296]

One in Many: The Noosphere

In a section entitled "Organization of Total Human Energy: The Common Human Soul," Teilhard discusses his concept of the noosphere, and sees in the process of "raising men to the explicit perception of their 'molecular' nature" that the possibility opens for them to "cease to be closed individuals, to become parts . . . to be integrated in the total energy of the noosphere."[297] But Teilhard is at pains to reassure the reader that this does not imply the loss of individuality, and he points out that individual human souls (the quanta of consciousness)

131

are not like gas molecules, "anonymous and interchangeable corpuscles," but that the formation of the noosphere requires, on the contrary, a "maximum of personality" to be manifest through each human individual sub contribution:

> "The utility of each nucleus of human energy in relation to the whole depends on what is unique . . . in the achievement of each."[298]

Assuming that consciousness is evolving and the material universe is evolving, Teilhard wonders where might the energy come from that guides the coalescing centro-complexity into such exquisite configurations, and he wonders what might be the nature of energy within this evolution (i.e., what is "informing" and "powering" this evolutionary process)? His answer can be found in a section he calls, "The Maintenance of Human Energy and 'The Cosmic Point Omega.'" He explains that such energy is axial, that it "is found to be fed by a particular current" flowing from the center, the Omega point, that he calls a "tension of consciousness."[299] The same phenomenon in holoflux theory, this "particular current" flowing from the center, can be seen in Bohm's quantum potential wavefunction, Q, that according to Bohm is also driving the patternings of evolution.

Here Teilhard makes a diversion into a subject he repeatedly brings up, the continuation of the centres of personality after physical death. He says that

> Reflective action and the expectation of total disappearance are *cosmically incompatible* . . . death leaves some part of ourselves in some way, to which we can turn with devotion and interest, as to a portion of the absolute . . . as *imperishable*.[300]

He points out that cosmic evolution is a work of *"personal nature,"* and that we are each a unique "centre of personal stuff totalizing, in itself, the essence of our personalities . . . the universal centre of attraction"; at this point he begins to discuss the "centre of psychic convergence," the noosphere, and brings up the image of the sphere.[301]

> "The totality of a sphere is just as present in its centre, which takes the form of a point, as spread over its whole surface."[302]

What are the implications in Teilhard's statement, "the totality of a sphere is just as present in its center?" We could say that it implies a sharing of information storage between the isosphere in space–time and the implicate order at the center (Wheeler's qubits of conscious information spread over the surface of a sphere, would be seen here be in resonance with the implicate center). Next Teilhard poses a question whose solution appears to corroborate the concept of an implicate order within the quantum holosophere, and he concludes with his famous dictum, "union differentiates":

> Now why should it be strange for the universe to have a centre, that is to say to collect itself to the same degree in a single consciousness, if its totality is already partially reflected in each of our particular consciousnesses? . .Union, the true upward union in the spirit [consciousness], ends by establishing the elements it dominates in their own perfection. *Union differentiates.*[303]

But not only are each of the centres of consciousness preserved in their union, they are *evolutionarily enhanced*; the n centres join, but in that joining, although they retain their own personalities, an additional personality, $n + 1$, is formed, and *"since there is no fusion or dissolution of the elementary* personalities, the centre in which they join *must necessarily be distinct from them, that is to say have its own personality.*"[304]

It is at this point in his essay that Teilhard introduces the term Omega, describing it as the cosmic point of total synthesis without which "the world would not function," and describing its relationship to the noosphere:

> The noosphere in fact *physically* requires, for its maintenance and functioning . . . the unifying influence of a *distinct* center of super-personality . . . a centre different from all the other centres which it "super-centres" by assimilation: a personality distinct from all the personalities it perfects by uniting with them . . . . Consideration of this Omega will allow us to define more completely . . . the hidden nature of what we have till now called, vaguely enough, "human energy."[305]

The Omega Point

Central to the architecture of Teilhard de Chardin's hyperphysics is the concept of Omega or the Omega point. According to his close friend Henri de Lubac, Teilhard's first use of the term can be found in one of his earliest essays:

> In the first essay that was entitled *Mon Univers* (1916) he carefully distinguishes, in order to study their relationships, "Omicron, the natural term of human and cosmic progress," from "Omega, the supernatural term of the Kingdom of God" or "Plenitude of Christ." Later, he was to abandon this particular terminology, but he retained the distinction it expressed.[306]

Twenty years later Teilhard was using the term in a more secular, scientific context, as seen here at the close of a lecture delivered at the French Embassy in Peking on March 10, 1945.[307]

134

Ahead of, or rather in the heart of, a universe prolonged along its axis of complexity, there exists a . . . centre of convergence . . . let us call it the *point Omega*.[308]

Teilhard devotes an entire section to "The Attributes of the Omega Point," in his book, *The Human Phenomenon*, begun in Paris in 1939 and completed in China during World War II. In a section that in his first draft had been called, "Spirit and Entropy," Teilhard says of Omega:

Expressed in terms of internal energy, the cosmic function of Omega consists in initiating and maintaining the unanimity of the world's reflective particles under its radiation. But how could it carry out this action if it were not somehow already . . . *right here and now*? . .Autonomy, actuality, irreversibility and finally, transcendence are the four attributes of Omega . . . Omega is the principle we needed to explain both the steady advance of things toward more consciousness and the paradoxical solidity of what is most fragile . . . . Something in the cosmos, therefore, escapes entropy—and does so more and more.[309]

An important element of Teilhard's model of human energy lies in his understanding that consciousness can be expressed in thermodynamic terms. In the essay "Human Energy," in a section with the title, "V. THE MAINTENANCE OF HUMAN ENERGY AND 'THE COSMIC POINT OMEGA,'" Teilhard describes how an axial form of this heat energy powers the current of conscious human energy. Teilhard describes the generation of this current:

Considered in its organic material zones, human energy obeys the laws of physics and draws quite naturally on the reserves of heat available in nature.

But studied in its axial, spiritualized form, it is found to be fed by a particular current (of which thermodynamics might well be, after all, no more than a statistical echo), which, for want of a better name, we will call "tension of consciousness."[310]

Teilhard here once again links thermodynamics to the phenomenon of consciousness, and he goes on to refute the widespread scientific paradigm of consciousness as a mere epiphenomenon of the material universe:

We still persist in regarding the physical as constituting the "true" phenomenon in the universe, and the psychic as a sort of epiphenomenon . . . we should consider the whole of thermodynamics as an unstable and ephemeral by-effect of the concentration on itself of what we call "consciousness."[311]

In one of his last essays, "The Nature of the Point Omega," Teilhard states that it is in the noosphere that all is truly preserved, for it is here that all experience is gathered and saved eternally:

In convergent cosmogenesis, as I have said, everything happens as if the preservable contents of the world were gathered and consolidated, by evolution, at the centre of the sphere representing the universe . . . a cosmic convergence . . . to bind objectively to the real and already existing centre.[312]

This image of the "centre of the sphere," Teilhard's description of "Point Omega," is equivalent to a Planck diameter black hole or "Planck holosophere," discussed later in this chapter. Here again can be seen a congruence between Teilhard's process viewed as a convergent cosmogenesis, and

Bohm's process seen as an enfolding of the explicate into an implicate domain.

Teilhard concludes the essay "Human Energy" with a highly optimistic observation revealing once again his lifelong fascination with the concept of the human personality's mode of survival beyond biological death:

> The principle of the conservation of personality signifies that each individual nucleus of personality, once formed, is forever constituted as "itself"; so that, in the supreme personality that is the crown of the universe, all elementary personalities that have appeared in the course of evolution must be present again in a distinct (though super-personalized) state . . . each elementary person contains something *unique and untransmittable* in his essence.[313]

"Centrology: Dialectics of Union" (1944)

During the occupation of China by the Japanese, Teilhard's anthropological work was severely curtailed, and he found himself with time to go deeply into the development of his more abstract ideas, which he expressed systematically and in great detail in his 1944 essay, "Centrology," written under somewhat stark wartime conditions during his Peking confinement. At the beginning of his essay he boldly states what he considers to be the scientific nature of this essay: "It is not an abstract metaphysics, but a realist ultraphysics of union."[314]

Teilhard opens his essay with an immediate discussion of "Centres and Centro-Complexity," describing how in living elements of the biosphere we find a continuation of the "granular (atomic molecular)" structure of the universe, and that, in fact, the human body "is simply a 'super-molecule.'"[315] However, unlike conventional physicists, who see cosmic particles as sources or centers of radiation and then map that radiation in the space–time domain, Teilhard places the focus of his inquiry on the "within" of each so-called particle. According to Teilhard, the space–time particles are not only centers of origination of radiation but each one of them also "has" a within, and "is" a within, a within that is a mode of consciousness, a psychic centre:

> They are psychic centres, infinitesimal psychic centres of the universe . . . in other words, consciousness is a universal molecular property.[316]

Teilhard goes further to claim that an increase in consciousness can be found associated with an increase in "centro-complexity," and he defines "the coefficient of centro-complexity" as "the true absolute measure of being in the beings that surround us."[317] Teilhard describes biology as "simply the physics of very large complexes."[318]

He points out that the atomic complexity of a virus is of the order of 10^5 atomic particles, and this complexity increases dramatically by the time we reach the size of a cell at 10^{10}, but in the brains of large mammals, has reached the great complexity of 10^{20} particles.[319]

Teilhard states that "if the universe is observed in its true and essential movement through time, it represents a system that is in a process of internal centro-complexification," and asserts a definition of evolution to be "a transition from a lower to a higher state of centro-complexity."[320]

In his essay, "Man's Place in the Universe," Teilhard had argued that existence entails three infinities: the infinite large, the infinite small, and the infinite complex, and he illustrates this with the chart reproduced in Fig. 17.[321]

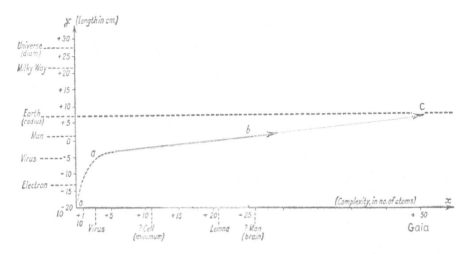

Figure 17. *Teilhard's natural curve of complexities.*[322]

Using data from objects in nature Teilhard plots a curve with two axes: a vertical y-axis scaled in Size (length in centimeters), and a horizontal x-axis on which is measured increases in Complexity (total number of atoms per object). Note that both scales are calibrated in base 10 logarithms. The curve plots size vs. complexity for various natural entities, named on both axes.

Points "a" and "b" on the plot indicate where Teilhard believes "state changes of consciousness" have occurred. Point "a" marks the emergence of life, and point "b" indicates the emergence of reflective consciousness (i.e., thought, being able to think about thinking).

While Teilhard does not discuss the arrow extending the curve to the right, the implication is clear if we mentally plot the value for the *Complexity* of Earth, that has been estimated to consist of 1.33×10^{50} atoms.[323] Accordingly we have increased the width of Teilhard's horizontal axis scale, that in his own notebook stops at the human brain's +25 atoms, and have doubled the x range, to the Earth's +50 atoms. At +50 the curve in Fig. 17 has been extrapolated to intersect Teilhard's

139

converging curve at point "c," marking a planetary change of state, a state described here by Teilhard as an awakening of a consciousness common to the whole earth:

> We can see it only as a *state of unanimity*: such a state, however, that in it each grain of thought, now taken to the extreme limit of its individual consciousness, will simply be the incommunicable, partial, elementary expression of a total consciousness which is common to the whole earth, and specific to the earth: *a spirit* [consciousness] *of the earth*.[324]

Elsewhere Teilhard has described the importance of the concept of reflection (alternately translated into English as reflexion), and this is associated with point "b" on the complexity chart, the concept also applies to a projected point "c" which would be a change of state for the consciousness of the planet, a noospheric "reflection":

> "Reflection," as the word itself indicates, is the power acquired by a consciousness of turning in on itself and taking possession of itself *as an object* endowed with its own particular consistency and value: no longer only to know something but to know *itself*; no longer only to know, but to know that it knows.[325]

Teilhard's chart thus supports the first general conclusion in his essay on "Centrology," that the universe is in a state of internal "centro-complexification," and that in this "transition from a lower to a higher state of centro-complexity," we see a concomitant increase in complexity-consciousness, in a process that Teilhard terms cosmogenesis through centrogenesis.[326]

Form his earliest essays, Teilhard sees the planet itself as an evolving, larger entity, out of which humanity has sprung and to which humanity is adding new capabilities. Teilhard presents geological and zoological evidence of the planet Earth as an evolving lifeform,[327] a global being in the transitional process of awakening into a planetary state of reflective self-consciousness. He identifies a distinct axis of successive forms, layers of increasing complexity and centrification running from geogenesis through biogenesis and beyond, into psychogenesis; this axis, he insists, can be seen continuing in the present noetic awakening that it is life itself that is engendering the birth of a new mode of planetary consciousness, comprising an entity that he himself has named, the noosphere.[328]

He speculates that eventually "life might use its ingenuity to force the gates of its terrestrial prison . . . by establishing a connection psyche to psyche with other focal points of consciousness across space," and "the possibility of 'centre-to-centre' contacts between perfect centres."[329]

But it is not only the planet itself that is evolving for Teilhard, he also views consciousness in humanity as evolving and thus sees the human species accelerating toward an evolutionary threshold, where it will experience the nature of energy and self-reflection in ever newer ways, while feeling itself drawn magnetically toward new states of greater cohesion and complexity, not only of radiant physical energy, that he terms "the tangential component," but of an increasingly conscious, psychic flow, the spiritual or "radial component" of energy.[330] He even senses an imminent transformation in the biophysical gateway, the human brain, in which he foresees form and function itself complexifying past the point of isolated self-reflection:

> Is there not in fact, beyond the isolated brain, a still higher possible complex: by that I mean a sort of "brain" of associated brains? . . . . From this point of view, the natural evolution of the biosphere is not only continued in what I have called Noosphere, but

assumes in it a strictly convergent form which, towards its peak, produces a point of maturation (or of collective reflection).[331]

Another term used by Teilhard in describing this process is "convergence." He states that, "In the organo-psychic field of centro-complexity, the world is convergent; the isospheres are simply a system of waves which as time goes on (and it is they which measure time) close up around Omega point"; the world, according to Teilhard, is moving continuously in "a transition from a lower to a higher state of centro-complexity."[332]

Centrogenesis

Teilhard coins a new term, "centrogenesis," to encapsulate this process. In "Centrology," Teilhard begins his discussion of centrogenesis by claiming that the universe is made up of psychic nuclei, similar to the theory of monads developed by Gottfried Wilhelm Leibniz; monads were described by Leibniz as being the most basic, fundamental entities of which the cosmos is constructed (an idea seen here as a precursor to the model of holospheres in the holoplenum), however in his theory the monads are completely independent of one another, though in complete harmony.[333] Unlike the monads of Leibniz, Teilhard's nuclei are interconnected in three simultaneous ways.[334] These relationships are as follows:

- Tangentially—"on the surface of an isosphere"

- Radially—"through nuclei of lower centro-complexity" (n^1, n^2, etc.)

- Radially—"inwardly, creating an isosphere of a higher order" ($n + 1$)

Teilhard describes these elementary cosmic centres as "partially themselves," and "partially the same thing." In Fig. 18 can be seen four drawings presented by Teilhard at the beginning of his essay on "Centrology."

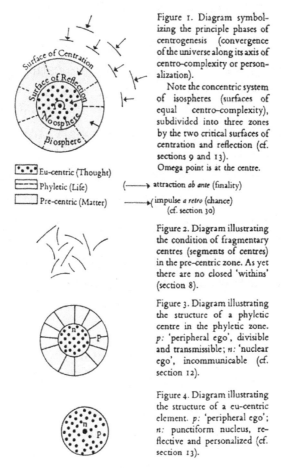

Figure 1. Diagram symbolizing the principle phases of centrogenesis (convergence of the universe along its axis of centro-complexity or personalization).

Note the concentric system of isospheres (surfaces of equal centro-complexity), subdivided into three zones by the two critical surfaces of centration and reflection (cf. sections 9 and 13). Omega point is at the centre.

Eu-centric (Thought)
Phyletic (Life)
Pre-centric (Matter)

attraction *ab ante* (finality)

impulse *a retro* (chance) (cf. section 30)

Figure 2. Diagram illustrating the condition of fragmentary centres (segments of centres) in the pre-centric zone. As yet there are no closed 'withins' (section 8).

Figure 3. Diagram illustrating the structure of a phyletic centre in the phyletic zone. *p:* 'peripheral ego', divisible and transmissible; *n:* 'nuclear ego', incommunicable (cf. section 12).

Figure 4. Diagram illustrating the structure of a eu-centric element. *p:* 'peripheral ego'; *n:* punctiform nucleus, reflective and personalized (cf. section 13).

Figure 18. *Teilhard's Figures 1 through 4 in "Centrology."*[335]

Teilhard's images in the Figure above depict the distinct stages of centrogenesis. Here we can see the condition of "fragmentary centres (segments of centres)," not yet enclosed in isospheric configurations, and still devoid of what Teilhard calls "personality." These are elements that he terms "pre-centric" fragments, having no "withins."[336]

More evolved is the second image from the bottom, that reveals *phyletic centricity*, a change of state brought about by the self-closing of numerous fragmentary centers, which he defines as "life," and that manifest as phylum.[337] In regarding this state, Teilhard brings up two questions: (1) He asks, "how can we conceive the passage and communication of a 'within' from mother-cell to daughter-cell?", and (2) "Under what conditions is the phylum provided the greatest possible richness and variety for the evolutionary transmission of successful properties?"[338]

To answer the first question, Teilhard observes that there are "two sorts of ego in each phyletic centre, a nuclear ego . . . and a peripheral ego."[339] The *peripheral ego* is incompletely individualized, separate, and according to Teilhard, it is therefore divisible and can be shared through replication or association. Teilhard's then explains how the second ego, the *nuclear ego*, communicates:

> It is in virtue of the arrival at zero of its centric diameter that the living centre, in its turn, attains the condition and dignity of a 'grain of thought."[340]

Thus the particular phyletic centre (consisting of a peripheral ego and a nuclear ego) retains access to all of the information ever associated with the particular phylum through resonance among phyletic isospheres (nuclear egos).

This is in agreement with both Sheldrake's theory of morphic resonance and Bohm's quantum cosmology as it provides a mechanism whereby speciation information may be shared through resonance, transferred into the explicate domain via the implicate domain, and vice versa.[341] Since the implicate order of the nuclear ego is nondual (outside of the space–time domain), it has random access to information generated in *all time* and *all space* and is thereby able to apply total information in its processing. Reflective consciousness is also a characteristic of this phyletic center, and the typical human personality can be here identified with Teilhard's "peripheral ego," while Omega provides a guiding force via centrogenesis (Bohm's quantum potential function, Q).

To answer his second question, (how does the phylum provided the greatest possible richness and variety for evolutionary growth?), Teilhard identifies a "two-fold complexity," one spatial, and the other temporal. Spatial complexity refers to the spread of the phylum over the surface of its isosphere, the creation of a population of phyletic centres that gather experience and mutate in the ever-changing environment. At the same time, the action of temporal complexity provides the vast number of "trials" over the myriads of generations of which the phylum's ancestors represent the total sum.[342]

At the bottom of Fig. 18 (Teilhard's Figure 4), we see Teilhard's final figure, the "structure of a eu-centric element," as a major, and perhaps ultimate, "change of state" in the emerging process, a reflection of consciousness in the noosphere, a reflective connection with Omega.[343] In the typical human grain of thought "reflection" has not yet reached a resonance with Omega. However it is possible to effect, in the individual, as Teilhard says, a "eu-centered, 'point-like' focus . . . and this is enough to allow the appearance of a series of new phenomena in the later advances of centrogenesis."[344] It is not difficult to assume that the "point-like focus" recommended here by Teilhard is a reference to his own direct experience in effectuating such a focus, his own participatory experience of consciousness.

Teilhard laments that while humans are generally reflective, only a few have yet been able to integrally connect with the punctiform nucleus, Omega; but those able to connect for any duration find that they now "possess the sense of irreversibility," a conviction that makes "an escape from total death . . . possible for a personalized being."[345] At this point, says Teilhard, "Welded together in this way, the noosphere, *taken as a whole*, begins to behave tangentially, like a single megacentre . . . ontogenesis of collective consciousness and human memory."[346] Here, Teilhard makes a prediction, stating that the evolution of human society on the planet will eventually lead to the following:

> the accelerated impetus of an earth in which preoccupation with production for the sake of well-being will have given way to the passion for the discovery for the sake of fuller being—the super-personalization of a super-humanity that has become super-conscious of itself in Omega.[347]

In a psychically convergent universe, the process of a reflective connection of the peripheral, phyletic ego with the central, eu-centric ego leads ultimately to a "final concentration upon itself of the noosphere," Omega.

> Omega appears to us fundamentally as the centre which is defined by the final concentration upon itself of the noosphere—and indirectly, of all the isospheres that precede it.[348]

"All the isospheres that precede it" in time and space, of course, are the isospheres that are ourselves, our ancestors, and other centers of phyletic centro-complexity. When a locus of fragmentary centers closes, joining together to form a phyletic center, the newly formed noosphere experiences a state change and awakens. From that point, moving forward in space and time, the phyletic noosphere evolves through a series of internal noospheres, growing higher in energy and complexity, until it reaches its ultimate "final concentration" at Omega, as Teilhard states, "In Omega then, a *maximum complexity*, cosmic in extent, coincides with a *maximum cosmic centricity*."[349] In other words, at the heart of matter, at the Omega point, Teilhard tells us that maximum complexity equals maximum centricity.

Teilhard refers to the centre as "a quantum of consciousness," and tells us that each degree of consciousness at a given moment only exists as "an introduction to a higher consciousness." [350] He says that this general process is irresistible and irreversible.[351]

> The initial quantum of consciousness contained in our terrestrial world is not formed merely of an aggregate of particles caught fortuitously in the same net. It represents a correlated mass of infinitesimal centres structurally bound together by the conditions of their origin and development.[352]

Moving forward in his essay on centrology, Teilhard goes on to describe four attributes of Omega as:

- Personal

- Individual

- Already partially actual (space–time energy)

- Partially transcendent (implicate order holoflux energy)[353]

It is personal "since it is centricity that makes beings personal," and, "Omega is supremely centred."[354] It is individual because it is "distinct from (which does not mean cut

147

off from) *the lower personal centres* which it super-centres."[355] These lower centres are the various phyletic, peripheral egos, each of which is uniquely individual, yet can join with Omega without losing their individuated personality; in fact it is in the relationship, the resonance with Omega, that the very uniqueness of the individual is highlighted (i.e., "union differentiates").

Omega is both "partially actual" and partially transcendent." The relationship is one Teilhard characterizes as, "a 'bi-polar' union" of the emerged and the emergent. It is partially transcendent beyond the very center of space–time, within the Bohmian implicate order. There, all is "partially transcendent of the evolution that culminates in it." And it is there that all space–time experience is gathered, in the partially transcendent, in continuous communication via a mathematically dynamic process. Otherwise, Teilhard tell us, there would not "be the basis for the hopes of irreversibility."[356]

And it is Omega that provides the momentum for centrogenesis.

> Drawn by its magnetism and formed in its image, the elementary cosmic centres are constituted and grow deeper in the matrix of their complexity. Moreover, gathered up by Omega, these same centres enter into immortality from the very moment when they become eu-centric and so structurally capable of entering into contact, centre to centre.[357]

Centrology and Complexity: Being and Union

At this point in his essay, Teilhard inserts what he calls "A Note on the 'Formal Effect' of Complexity" in which he examines the underlying roots of his assertion that consciousness *increases* with complexity in union (centro-complexity), and he states that an understanding of this phenomenon has come to him "experientially."[358] Teilhard sets forth, in two Latin propositions, the fundamental ontological relationship between being and union:

1. The one passive:
   "*Plus esse est a* (or *ex*) *pluribus uniri.*"

2. The other active:
   "*Plus esse est plus plura unire.*"

Plus esse can be translated as "more being," "growth in being," or "being increases," but from the context of this essay the phrase *plus esse* might be translated as "consciousness increases."[359] Thus Teilhard describes a bi-modal process of an increasing conscious in the universe: actively and passively.

In the first proposition, the verb *uniri* is in the passive voice, "be united," and in context can be translated, "become one, become a center." The *a/ex* prepositions, often used interchangeably in Latin, indicate "out of" and "from." Thus *a pluribus* can be translated "out of many, from many," and accordingly, the first proposition may be translated as, "A new conscious center grows by many being joined."

In the second proposition, however, the verb *unire* is in the active voice, (i.e., "unite"), which in context can be translated "make a centered unity" of *plura* (literally, "more/many things"). Thus the second proposition can be translated as "A new consciousness center grows by many uniting." Teilhard next applies these two propositions to the following stages of centro-complex evolution:

1. The appearance of life through association of fragments of centres.

2. The deepening of phyletic centres.

3. The emergence of reflective centres.

In the first instance, for a state change occurring in the domain of pre-life, Teilhard again formulates a metaphysical axiom in Latin: *Centrum ex elementis centri*, which translates as, "The Center out of elements of the center." In this domain Centres are "built up additively, through the fitting together and gradual fusing of 'segments' of centres."[360] This is a passive growth.

In the second stage, Teilhard says, "being born from an egg (*centrum a centro*) complexifies upon itself by cellular multiplication." Here, each centre complexifies itself by increasing its own depth of complexity.[361] Here the active growth emerges, a growth in part directed by the centre. A similar pattern can be seen in Bohm's quantum potential function, a guiding energy from within the implicate order, within Teilhard's Omega point.

Finally, it is in the eu-centric that this quantum potential metaphysical process becomes super-active, and as Teilhard says, it is from "the noospheric centre, Omega," that there emerges *"Centrum super centra,"* translated as "a new Centre emerges from an old centre."[362] Teilhard is saying here that Omega is not simply the sum of components, but something *new*, a unique entity bursting forth:

> In the eu-centric domain, the noospheric centre Omega, is not born from the confluence of human "egos," but emerges from their organic totality, like a spark that leaps the gap between the transcendent side of Omega and the "point" of a perfectly centered universe.[363]

Teilhard describes how, for individual human phyletic "egos," it may be possible to go beyond the present general evolutionary stage of consciousness, developed through the general societal drift of hominization through time. Teilhard explains how such an evolutionary leap might be accomplished:

> This can be envisaged in two ways, either by *connecting up neurones* that are already ready to function but have not yet been brought into service (as though held in reserve), in certain already located areas of the brain, where it is simply a matter of arousing them to activity; or, who can say?, by direct (mechanical, chemical or biological) stimulation of new arrangements.[364]

In his phrase, "direct stimulation," we can imagine a range of approaches which might be used to catalyze the evolutionary growth and transformation of consciousness within an individual, who would then experience what Teilhard terms, an "Ultra-hominization," of reflective consciousness, evolutionarily beyond that of the currently conventional ranges of human experience.

His first suggestion, "connecting up neurones that are already ready to function," might be seen as a catalysis by birth (genetic predisposition), accidental circumstances (serendipitous encounters with the sublime), or specific psycho-physical techniques (e.g., prayer, yoga, physical exercises, special diets, fasting, sweat lodges, etc.); but Teilhard goes even further to suggest that the evolutionary process might be boosted within the individual human personality "by direct (mechanical, chemical, or biological) stimulation," and here we are reminded of exploration and critical experimentation with psychotropic drugs (psilocybin mushrooms, LSD, cannabis, ayahuasca, etc.), or through direct energy-stimulation devices as can be seen in the recent technologies of transcranial magnetic stimulation, or transcranial direct current stimulation.[365]

Similarly, but moving from neuronal to human level, Teilhard forecast's the connecting up of a network of individual consciousness via "a direct tuning:"

> In nascent super-humanity . . . the thousands of millions of single-minded individuals function in a nuclear way, by a direct tuning and resonance of their consciousness.[366]

At the close of "Centrology," Teilhard sets forth his "Corollaries and Conclusions." He begins by summarizing, in a sequence of five stages, the evolution of consciousness, and defining five points on the arc of centro-complexity at which occur categorically distinct evolutionary changes of state:

1. The appearance of life through association of fragments of centres.

2. The deepening of phyletic centres.

3. The emergence of reflective centres.

4. The birth of mankind (and reflective thought).

5. The dawn of Omega.[367]

In each of these five steps can be seen the effect of an increase in union, the creative energy of union causing changes of state, not simply due to some rearrangement or summation of parts, but, as Teilhard says, "doing so under the influence of the radiation of Omega."[368] The holoflux theory analog of Teilhard's "radiation," of course, is Bohm's quantum potential function, "Q," radiating from the implicate order to emerge within space–time. Teilhard's "Omega point" can thus be viewed as a spherical portal, an analog of Bohm's "implicate order."

In discussing the transition from Stage 4 to Stage 5, the change of state from the "birth of thought" to the "dawn of Omega," Teilhard insists that there should be *no* concern that such a change of state would mean a loss of personality, or a death of our uniquely distinct egos; on the contrary, says Teilhard, the noosphere is comprised of an effective *re-union* of all individual "savable elements" of each personality. Even more, it serves to effect an even higher, more complete integration of *each* individual experience, a heightening of individual personality, "a cosmic personalization, the fruit of centrogenesis."[369] It is, stresses Teilhard, through each sub personality center-to-center contact *within* the noosphere (through the centre), that each individual personality is "super-personalized."[370] This center-to-center contact, Teilhard tells us, is a perceptual condition of each individual center merging into the noosphere, and it *is not an epiphenomenon* of such a union, but that it is a *requirement* for reaching full integral personalization:

> Something (someone) exists, in which each element gradually finds, by reunion with the whole, the completion of all the savable elements that have been formed in its individuality; thus the interior equilibrium of what we have called the Noosphere requires the presence *perceived by individuals* of a higher polar centre that directs, sustains and assembles the whole sheaf of our efforts.[371]

This process can be seen as a cybernetic feedback loop: the "higher polar centre" receives input from all of the "savable elements" of each "individuality," and, working with this information, the higher personality ("polar center") "sustain and assembles the whole sheaf of our efforts." In this way evolution proceeds through a continuous cyclic process of individual centres developing in space–time, merging into their respective centres through the directional "drift" of centro-complexity, *but not being lost* in the merger.

> To the extent that the grain of consciousness is *personalized*, it becomes released from its material support in the phylum . . . detached from the matrix of complexity, and meets the ultimate pole of all convergence.[372]

Finally, the fifth stage in the process of centro-complexity, "the dawn of Omega," occurs at the point where *thought* transforms into omni-contact with all other centres, as well as with the "higher" (n+1) center of personality, at which point there is a flaring forth into a categorically new mode of reflective consciousness, effecting a major change in state. Teilhard concludes that, "Far from tending to be confused together, the reflective centres intensify their *ego* the more they concentrate together."[373]

Isospheres

A key concept developed in "Centrology" is Teilhard's model of "isospheres," which he defines as "surfaces of equal centro-complexity."[374] He sees evolution catalyzed on these isospheres when "a maximum density of particles with a corresponding maximum of tentative gropings is produced on each isosphere." Listed in Table 3 are "isospheres" which have been defined for the planet earth, arranged in radial order.

These various regions of the planet each have their own unique and identifiable physical characteristics (temperature, density, etc.), and each might be considered as an isosphere of the planet.

The smallest possible isosphere in space would be Bohm's *Planck holosphere*, a geometrical holosphere with diameter of one Planck length (the smallest unit of space at 10^{-35} cm) below which space has no meaning (discussed fully in Chapter IV). Our thesis is that Teilhard's Omega Point and the Planck holosphere are one and the same phenomenon.

Table 3

Isospheres of Planet Earth

Scientific designation	Above/below sea level (miles)
Exosphere	310–620 mi.
Ionosphere or Plasmasphere	37–271 mi.
Thermosphere	56–311 mi.
Mesosphere	31–53 mi.
Stratosphere	10–30 mi.
Troposphere	4–12 mi.
Hydrosphere	0 to -5 mi.
Lithosphere or "rocky crust" (upper layer, crustal rocks) (0°–870° C.)	-275 mi.
Mantle (870°–3700° C) Upper Mantle (870° C) Asthenosphere (100–250 km deep)	-21 to -1793 mi.
Inner Mantle (semi rigid, 870°–3700° C)	
Outer Core (molten, 3700°–5000° C, 1370 miles thick)	-1800 mi.
Inner Core (Crystalline iron/nickel) (5000°–7200° C, 750 mile sphere)	-2170 mi.

Note. Data from Tarbuck and Lutgens, *Earth Science*, 6-71.

Teilhard's use of the word "isosphere" is focused less upon the physics of geology, and more upon the physics of metaphysics, a topology of consciousness, as he states in "Centrology":

> Thus there emerges the pattern of a *centered universe*—elements of equal complexity (and hence

of equal centricity) being spread out over what we may call isospheres of consciousness.[375]

Fig. 19 depicts a holoflux topology of nested isospheres surrounding Teilhard's Omega. According to Teilhard, these isospheres of consciousness are concentric, "the radius of each sphere diminishing as the complexity increases."[376]

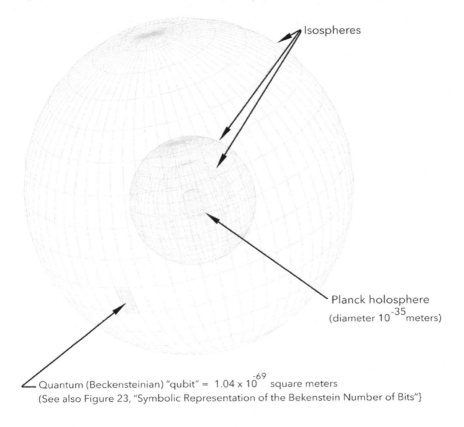

Isospheres

Planck holosphere
(diameter 10^{-35} meters)

Quantum (Beckensteinian) "qubit" = 1.04×10^{-69} square meters
(See also Figure 23, "Symbolic Representation of the Bekenstein Number of Bits")

Figure 19. *Isospheres surrounding Planck holosphere.*

Here Teilhard has clearly indicated the direction in which he sees increased consciousness: toward the centre, in the direction of Omega. According to holoflux theory, the radial distance between any two nested isospheres may be no less than the Planck length, and this leads us to visualize an enormous yet finite series of isospheres in space–time, nested like Russian dolls, or perhaps like separate capacitor plates in in an electronic circuit, beginning at the boundary of the Planck holosphere (enclosing Omega, the implicate order), and reaching an outer limit at the current (continuously expanding) diameter of the universe.

In this cosmological topology of nested three-dimensional isospheres, electrons would not travel in planar, two-dimensional, circular orbits, as depicted in Bohr's model; in the holoflux model, electron movements are seen as tangential flowing processes over three-dimensional shells, spherical movements over the surface regions of isosphere.377

As we move outward from the central Planck holosophere into isospheres of higher radial dimensions, each holosophere must be separated, minimally, by one Planck length. The manifestation of these isospheres in space–time would provide the geometric capacity for storing multiple qubits of information, as previously developed by John Wheeler in considering the event horizon of a black hole. Thus we may envision quantum states in a series of holospheric shells extending from the central Planck holosophere to the current boundary of the universe, spheres rather than rings. The universe here can be seen to consist of an almost infinite holoplenum of intersecting concentric shells of implicate order holospheres throughout space–time.

As seen in Bohr's model, to move from one shell to another shell, the electron cannot move *continuously* through some intervening space–time gap, but instead is seen to execute a quantum leap to another level, possibly moving from one isospheric shell to another during a single Planck time cycles of 5×10^{-44} seconds, to appear at the next holosphere shell at a "clock-speed" of light, yet not moving *in* space–time as normally understood, but moving in and out of the explicate and implicate orders.

Viewed from the perspective of holoflux theory, a transformation of information flowing into the implicate order (frequency domain) occurs, cycling feedback "radiation" (Bohm's quantum potential function, "Q") into space–time, nudging every centre in an ever-so-slightly new direction in their evolutionary arcs in space–time.

Such a transformation might also be identified with Jean Gebser's "mutation of consciousness," the evolutionary mutation into what Gebser calls "integral consciousness."[378] In full agreement with Teilhard's assertion that evolution precludes loss of experienced personality, Gebser assures us that in evolving structures of consciousness, previous properties and potentialities do indeed survive:

> In contrast to biological mutations, these mutations of consciousness do not assume or require the disappearance of previous potentialities and properties, which, in this case, are immediately integrated into the new structure.[379]

Like Gebser, Teilhard observes that all personalities are incomplete, that they are continually evolving, however slowly, and compares our individual personalities to the fragments of centres that seek for one another in the pre-living zones of matter, reminding us that, "at our level of evolution we are still no more than rough drafts."[380] Teilhard here states with emphasis, *"the personal—considered quantitatively no less than qualitatively—is continually on the upgrade in the universe."*[381]

It is clear that in his writings Pierre Teilhard de Chardin, the trained anthropologist, regarded his theories of hyperphysics not as philosophy or metaphysics, but as an extension of physical science. He argues for a convergence of physics and metaphysics, but not a union, and in a topological, geodesic-like metaphor, defends his hyperphysics as being distinct yet parallel to existing categories of inquiry:

> Just like meridians as they approach the pole, so science, philosophy, and religion necessarily converge in the vicinity of the whole. They converge, I repeat, but without merging, and never ceasing to attack the real from different angles and levels right to the end . . . . It is impossible to attempt a general scientific interpretation of the universe without *seeming* to intend to explain it right to the end. But only take a closer look at it, and you will see that this hyperphysics still is not metaphysics.[382]

Breaking Teilhard's "Death-Barrier"

One of Teilhard de Chardin's mature conclusions is that our entire consciousness is *not* snuffed out when our material bodies die. If consciousness manifests as some mode of holoflux energy, then following Einstein's observation, that "Energy cannot be created or destroyed, it can only be changed from one form to another," any energy of consciousness must follow the same pattern.[383] While there may be a transformation of energy, there can be no absolute destruction, energy (even modulated energy) cannot suddenly vanish.

"The Death-Barrier and Co-Reflection"

By the very logic of evolution, in order for the species to learn, adapt, and preserve experiences gathered in the space–time domain, evolution at the human stage must break the "Death-Barrier," a term Teilhard develops in one of his final essays, "The Death-Barrier and Co-Reflection," completed January 1, 1955, three months before his own death, on Easter Sunday, April 10, 1955:

When biological evolution has reached its *reflective* stage ("self-evolution") it can continue to function only in so far as man comes to realize that there is some *prima facie* evidence that the death-barrier *can* be broken.[384]

Teilhard had written previously of his own participatory experiences supporting his belief in an immortality of consciousness in a letter to his paleontologist colleague and friend, Helmut de Terra:

> My visible actions and influence count for very little beside my secret self. My real treasure is, *par excellence*, that part of my being which the centre, where all the sublimated wealth of the universe converges, cannot allow to escape. The reality, which is the culminating point of the universe, can only develop in partnership with ourselves by keeping us within the supreme personality: we cannot help finding ourselves personally immortal.[385]

Teilhard assumes that if there is a part, or region, or mode, or domain of our consciousness, that continues beyond our bodies, beyond the death of our bodies, as he says in "Breaking the Death-Barrier," then should we not then be motivated to know and even to explore that domain? That is the real treasure he is sharing with us: once specific memories are gone, the personality lives on, "keeping us within the supreme personality," within the implicate order, at the center, everywhere. But this "personality of the transcendent" can be seen, by mystics at least, even before the approach of the Death-Barrier.[386]

Not only does Teilhard categorically reject the majority of contemporary humankind's tacit assumption that death is "the end" (i.e., the end of individual consciousness), but he worries that such an erroneous stance might delay what he saw as the natural emergence of a noosphere, cultivated and powered by human conscious energy, a collective holoflux of homo sapiens.[387]

Summary of Teilhard de Chardin's Trinity

The Omega Point ->   God the Father, the Logos
Centro-Complexity ->   The Cosmic Christ
Energy ->   The Holy Spirit

III. Trinitarian Vedanta

The concept of the Holy Trinity is not exclusive to Christianity, but can be found as one of the expressions and visions of an organizing structure to the manifest universe as recorded in some of the most ancient cultural records in existence. In India, the *Atharvaveda*, emerging at the end of the 2nd millennium BCE, speaks of Agni, the King of the Gods, as 'one energy whose process is threefold.'[388] Centuries later, during the Puranic period (c. CE 300-1200) arose the visual concept of the Trimūrti (literally "the three forms," or "three faces," see Figure 20), the widespread acceptance in India of the manifestation of the supreme God in three forms of Brahmā, Viṣṇu, and Śiva. A correspondence can be easily seen in the Christian Trinity as "God the Father," "God the Son," and "God the Holy Spirit." Note that Brahmā in the Figure is shown with three heads, reminding us that he acts as a sort of "Trinity within the Trinity," in alignment with the metaphysical teachings of Śaṅkarācārya (early 8th century CE), a monist who saw the universe as one connected Whole created by the One which underlies it all in every dimension.[389]

The belief that God the Father also transcends all three in some mysterious nondual form is in accord with the monism, or One God belief that underlies most religions. In one forms of Hinduism, called Shaktidharma, the three are female gendered, and tripartite sculptures are called Tridevi (literally "the three goddesses").

Figure 20. *Trimūrti at Ellora, 5th-7th CE.*

While the earliest Christian acceptance of God as Trinity is documented in the Nicene Creed, a prayer still recited by many Christians today, the wording of the creed was agreed upon only during the first "Ecumenical Council of Christianity held in 325 CE., one year after the transfer of the government of the Roman Empire to the ancient Greek outpost of Byzantium on the Bosporus strait, a narrow, defensible isthmus of land that separates what is now Europe from Asia. To Raimundo Panikkar, whose mother was Roman Catholic and father was Hindu Indian, it is clear that "the symbol of the Trinity is not a Christian monopoly, but in fact is common in many other traditions."[390] If, as Panikkar says, this is "reality itself that discloses itself as Trinity," then we should be able to find this same Trinitarian reality disclosing itself in the realms of modern science.

Sankara's Vedantic View of the Trinity

The philosophy of Vedanta emerged as a philosophical system in the 8th century CE with the great sage Sankara's assertion that the ultimate reality is perfect and without duality, and that both the creating entity, Brahman, and Brahman's projected universe of manifestation, are not separate entities, but that they interpenetrate everywhere and are "One."[391] This view is precisely that taken by modern quantum physics as developed by David Bohm, who insists that the universe is one "Whole" divided into two regions, what he terms an "implicate order" and an "explicate order," but much more about that later.[392]

For Sankara, the world should not be seen as completely unreal, but that it should be understood as being "real in a certain sense." To Sankara the world is not the entire reality, in fact it is the issue, the creation, of an even more comprehensive reality, which in Sanskrit is called *Brahman*. This Brahman happens to have three hypostatic attributes or essences which Shankara calls Sat, Cit, and Ānanda, or all three elided together, pronounced as "Saccidānanda," which can be loosely translated Being, Consciousness, and Bliss.

Let us now leap ahead 1200 years from Sankara to the 20th century writings of Sri Aurobindo and explore the nature of Saccidānanda as developed in his essays on Vedanta and the *Upanishads*.

Sri Aurobindo: Philosopher and Mystic

In any discussion of Indian philosophy, the concept of the Holy Trinity is encapsulated in the single word Saccidānanda, itself a combination of three Sanskrit terms: "Sat" (Being), "Cit"

(Consciousness), and "Ananda" (Bliss).[393] Early in the 20th century, Sri Aurobindo wrote, "However Monistic may be our intellectual conception of the highest truth of things, in practice we are compelled to accept this omnipresent Trinity."[394]

In this section we explore fundamentals of Indian philosophy to expand the range of our understanding into the possible geometries and metaphysics of this Trinitarian mystery, which has been intuited throughout recorded history and described by both Hindu and Christian contemplatives. Beneath everything there must be, after all, only *one reality*, though it has been perceived and expressed in multiple ways by mystics and saints of widely different cultures.

The Trinitarian metaphysics discussed here are based upon a series of brilliant English language essays on classical Vedantic philosophy interpreted by the scholar and mystic Aravinda Ghose. Later in his life Aravinda was universally referred to as Sri Aurobindo. ("Sri" is a Sanskrit word denoting "that which glows with radiance," and is an honorific title often encountered within Indian culture, reserved for the most highly revered individuals, heavenly beings, or holy scriptures). Aurobindo's interpretation of Vedantic philosophy was expressed in detail over a seven year period in a series of articles for *The Arya*, a monthly journal published between 1914 and 1921. The journal was meant to be "a review of pure philosophy" by its founder, the French theologian and lawyer Paul Richard, but for the forty-two year old Aurobindo, emerging from four years of intensive yoga and meditative withdrawal, writing for *The Arya* was "in its most fundamental sense, an effort or an uprising and overcoming" in the sense that he was forcing himself to move out of isolation into the public sphere of writing and publishing once more.

I knew precious little about philosophy before I did the Yoga and came to Pondicherry — I was a poet and a politician, not a philosopher! How I managed to do it? First, because Richard proposed to me to co-operate in a philosophical review — and as my theory was that a Yogi ought to be able to turn his hand to anything, I could not very well refuse.[395]

Before exploring Aurobindo's rich metaphysical ideas, it is useful to review the intellectual foundation upon which he was able to draw in order to translate and to express clearly in English so many of the deep metaphysical ideas set forth in the ancient Sanskrit texts of the *Vedas* (Sanskrit for "knowledge," estimated to have emerged circa 1700 BCE) and the more recent *Upanishads* (700 to 600 BCE). Sri Aurobindo was one of those rare individuals who was a polyglot:

> By the turn of the century he knew at least twelve languages: English, French, and Bengali to speak, read, and write; Latin, Greek, and Sanskrit to read and write; Gujarati, Marathi, and Hindi to speak and read; and Italian, German, and Spanish to read.[396]

This knowledge of twelve languages must certainly have aided Aurobindo in choosing the words to convey abstract metaphysical concepts based upon his deep introspective experiences. In addition, his Cambridge education exposed him not only to Greek and Latin classics and major European philosophers, but also to new theories of evolution being discussed by his contemporary, Charles Darwin.

In 1878 at the age of six, Aurobindo and his two brothers were taken to England by his pro-Raj and British-educated Indian father where, when his parents returned to India, the brothers became part of the household of an Anglican minister in Manchester, the thirty-nine year old Reverend William Drewett. Nine years earlier, Sri Aurobindo's father had been trained in England as a surgeon and become an Anglican, and throughout his life he maintained an unquestioning admiration and respect for all things British, as did many British-educated Indians at the time, rejecting to a large extent his own cultural background, and not wanting his three sons to be in any way influenced by their ancestral culture back in India, at least until they were fully educated in the classic British tradition.

Aurobindo and his brothers spent five years in Manchester with the Drewett family, however the Reverend had a calling to evangelism and made plans to move to Australia to teach the aborigines. The three boys were left to continue their British education under the care of Drewett's elderly mother, who lived in London. Shortly after his twelfth birthday, Aurobindo and his two brothers left Manchester for London, where the boys were enrolled in a St. Paul's School for young men, a school founded by a friend of Thomas More in 1509 to help introduce the "new learning" of the Renaissance into England.[397] But after three years of relative stability, disaster struck in 1887 when his father suffered a serious financial setback in India. Soon after, the fifteen year-old Aurobindo and his brothers were asked to leave Mrs. Drewett's house to find cheaper lodging, and thus began their most difficult year. As Aurobindo's biographer Peter Heehs described the situation:

> During a whole year [1888– 89] a slice or two of sandwich bread and butter and a cup of tea in the morning and in the evening a penny sausage formed the only food." For growing teenagers, this was almost a starvation diet. Aurobindo and his brother had no wood for the fire and no overcoats to wear in what turned out to be the coldest winter in memory. As time went by, the boys at St. Paul's noticed that Aurobindo's clothing "grew more and more dirty and unkempt" and that he himself "looked more and more unhealthy and neglected."[398]

Somehow the sixteen-year-old endured these stark and exceedingly difficult living conditions in London while at the same time diligently pursuing his studies at St. Paul's School, hoping to absorb enough additional knowledge and to develop his writing skills sufficiently to make possible his one dream, a scholarship to King's College in Cambridge. In spite of his poor diet and lack of heat in his living quarters, he undertook an unusually heavy load of study at St. Paul's School, and was not only able to improve his ability for ad hoc translation of classical Greek, but won a prize for "knowledge of English literature, especially Shakespeare."[399] Shortly after his seventeenth birthday, in December 1889, Aurobindo travelled to Cambridge to undertake the rigorous three day scholarship examination given by King's College.

> Morning and evening he wrote translations from English into Latin and Greek and from Latin and Greek into English. There were also questions on classical grammar and history and an essay in English. On December 19, back in London, he learned that he had stood first. He later was told that he had "passed an extraordinarily high examination" with the best papers that the examiner had ever seen.[400]

During his two years at Cambridge, Aurobindo studied Western philosophy, Greek and Latin classics, usually read in the original languages. These included works by Homer, Plato, Epictetus, Aeschylus, Catullus, Virgil, and Dante, and as he had dreams of writing great English poetry, he also read widely from Shakespeare and Milton.[401] But above all, he had a passion for English Romantic poetry, an read everything he could find published by William Wordsworth, Lord Byron, Shelley, and John Keats. According to one professor, Aurobindo possessed "a knowledge of English Literature far beyond the average of undergraduates" and "wrote a much better English style than most young Englishmen."[402]

When he was nineteen he left King's College and sat for a series of qualifying examinations for the Indian Civil Service, a goal that his father had set for him years earlier, even though Aurobindo himself had little interest in such a career. He passed most of the examinations but near the end of the process he continued to postpone the requisite equestrian test. Although his heart was not in returning to India, he departed England for India as a young man at the age of twenty, and sadly while en route, his father died.

After several years as a college professor and administrator for the powerful Maharaja of Baroda in the western state of Gujurat, Aurobindo became passionately involved with a small group of Bengalis intent on working to overthrow the British Raj and establish a free sovereign nation in India. In 1908 he and a friend began publishing a weekly newspaper in Calcutta called "Bande Mataram" or "Victory to the Mother [Mother India]." (Fig. 21).

Figure 21. Aurobindo cover of *Bande Mataram*, 1907.

Aurobindo was the primary editor, contributing numerous highly articulate but incendiary articles to the newspaper, and became caught up in the organizing and encouragement of several groups of young revolutionaries. This ultimately led to an assassination attempt on a British Chief Magistrate, Douglas F. Kingsford, who was playing bridge at a British club in Calcutta. Unfortunately, the two bombers ran up to the wrong carriage, which had left the club that night shortly before the one carrying Kingsford. Instead of killing the Magistrate, the bomb landed in the carriage of a British mother and her daughter, killing both occupants. Although no evidence was discovered to directly implicate Aurobindo in the bombing, he was swept up by the police along with a dozen of his colleagues in the independence movement and sent to prison. He himself was put in isolation in a stone cell, five feet wide by five feet long, in the Alipore jail (Fig. 22) south of Calcutta. Such enforced isolation of an individual is not always a setback in the life of a great spirit, however, and in Aurobindo's case we are reminded of the effect of enforced imprisonment upon the lives of such notables as Ghandi and Nelson Mandela.

Sri Aurobindo in the Alipore Jail

Figure 22. *Aurobindo's "mug shot" at the Alipore jail, 1909.*

During many months of isolation in his cell in Alipore, while awaiting trial, Aurobindo began a daily practice of meditation, contemplation, and fasting. Within several months he began to have what he thought to be direct experiences of what he later termed the "silent, spaceless, and timeless Brahman." He took up deep breathing exercises of *pranayama*, which he had learned earlier during his days as a professor in Baroda, but here he had adequate time to practice in a sustained manner. At one point after a prolonged fast, he experienced such a flood of inner energy that he felt no need to eat, which was convenient as the food was somewhat repulsive, and he "decided to throw it in his privy basket." During the same period he did not require much sleep, and later told a friend that he only needed to sleep one night out of three. During the day he would often meditate while gazing at a large tree outside his jail cell window, and one day, to his astonishment, the tree assumed the spirit of Sri Krishna. Years later he wrote of his entry into confinement and its eventual result:

> Friday, May 1, 1908 . . . I did not know that day would mean an end of a chapter in my life, and that there stretched before me a year's imprisonment during which period all my human relations would cease, that for a whole year I would have to live, beyond the pale of society, like an animal in a cage. And when I would re-enter the world of activity, it would not be the old familiar Aurobindo Ghose. . . . I have spoken of a year's imprisonment. It would have been more appropriate to speak of a year's living in an ashram or a hermitage. . . . The only result of the wrath of the British Government was that I found God.[403]

After much delay and a long drawn out trial, Aurobindo was released from jail soon after his 37th birthday. Several of his co-conspirators had been banished to a brutal penal colony near Siam, but the court, presided over by a British judge who had been a classmate of Aurobindo's at Cambridge, ruled that there was insufficient evidence against the young professor and charges were dropped. Immediately Aurobindo began once more to write and to give public speeches to crowds of admirers. Now, however, his message was less political, and leaned more in the direction of promoting an ideal of cultural unity among all mankind, something far beyond the divisive nationalism which had formerly driven his thought and expression.

Unfortunately, the British authorities did not notice this change in Aurobindo's direction, but only saw that he continued to attract attention and a growing following. They decided that he was still a danger to British rule, and after what they saw as several months of "stirring up the public," the local police made plans to arrest Aurobindo Ghose and to banish him to the

British penal colony in the Andaman Islands, 800 miles to the west of India (Fig. 23).

Figure 23. *British penal colony, Andaman Islands.*

Up the Hooghly River to Freedom

Hearing that he was about to be jailed once more, Aurobindo and three friends fled at once by wooden boat up the Hooghly River to Chandernagore, a small town eighty miles north of Calcutta, where he all but vanished from view. There he spent long hours in silent yoga and meditation in the back room of a young revolutionary sympathizer's home. From this point forward he virtually abandoned politics in favor of exploring consciousness through reading, writing, and deep and prolonged periods of contemplative practice. However, he did manage to publish an amusing message to his followers in a regular column of his in the *Karmayogin*, a Calcutta newspaper:

We are greatly astonished to learn from the local Press that Aurobindo Ghose has disappeared from Calcutta and is now interviewing the Mahatmas in Tibet. We are ourselves unaware of this mysterious disappearance.[404]

The following month, while still managing to elude the British, who wanted to arrest and banish him to the penal colony, Aurobindo, with the help of his close friends, managed to evade the authorities and travel surreptitiously by boat a thousand miles south of Bengal to the French port of Pondicherry on the Bay of Bengal.

When the French authorities in the sleepy town of Pondicherry were eventually informed by the British of His political nationalist background, they put him under surveillance. However, Aurobindo was no longer interested in external social or political activities, and instead he moved ever more deeply into an exploration of inner consciousness.

Eventually he began writing of his experiences in monthly publications of a new philosophical review begun in 1914, called *The Arya*, founded by Aurobindo and his French friend, Paul Richard. It was Richard's wife, Mirra Alfassa, who was soon to grow close to Aurobindo in his spiritual quest, and was to become known, many years later, as "The Mother" at Sri Aurobindo Ashram (Fig. 24).

Figure 24. *Mirra Alfassa and Paul Richard Tokyo, 1918.*

Sri Aurobindo's explication of Vedanta, and in particular the Trinitarian metaphysics of Saccidānanda is discussed in his series of articles in *The Arya*, beginning with its first publication in 1914.[405] A number of these articles, including His own translations from Sanskrit, were collected and published later in *The Philosophy of the Upanishads*.[406] The widespread intuition of a metaphysical Trinity acting to generate and sustain the universe is here seen through the eyes of the 20th century scholar and mystic, Aurobindo Ghose.

Difficulties in Reading Sri Aurobindo's Writing

Perhaps unfortunately for the modern reader, Sri Aurobindo's writings are in a rather high Victorian-Edwardian style of English. When at the age of eighteen, Aurobindo had entered Kings College at Cambridge University, he mastered Greek, Latin, French, German, and Italian, was introduced to Darwin's theories of evolution, and began to publish long passages of poetry. Modern readers, acclimated to sound bites in the media, and even shorter Twitter texts, may find His Victorian language style at best imposing, with sentences often stretching into entire paragraphs and long subordinate clauses with the grammatical complexity of Latin. The breadth of his rich Edwardian vocabulary can leave many modern readers challenged, (e.g. in the first three pages of a major essay here discussed the reader encounters words such as "gurges," "illation," and "irrefragable"). Thus, even his mid-20th century publications, including the collected and edited versions of the 1914–21 *Arya*, present an obstacle to many modern readers. It is hoped the following discussion will overcome these difficulties in translation, and in so doing may serve as an introduction to Aurobindo's deep thinking and classical style.

The Search for the Absolute

Sri Aurobindo begins with the earliest history of thought of the Rishis[407] in India, who intuited the possibility of a unity and transcendental Oneness (or Absolute) behind the ever-shifting flux of change that manifests to human perception. He says that to discover this unity directly must have been the consummate goal of such early experiential exploration, and that one of the very first conclusions arrived at was that "the *sum* of all this change and motion is absolutely *stable, fixed* and *unvarying*,"[408] as must be the psychophysical relationships that operate at the most fundamental levels. While the goal of these ancient scientists of the introspective psyche was to determine these laws, their first conclusion was that "All this heterogeneous multitude of animate and inanimate things are fundamentally homogeneous and one."[409]

Aurobindo comments that while modern materialist science is realizing this same fact about the universe "slowly but surely," the Rishis began exploring the vast domain of consciousness over two millennia ago, using tools and techniques developed out of and from within their own consciousness. Their collective discoveries were handed down and refined over innumerable generations, and came at last to the following conclusion:

> Within the flux of things and concealed by it is an indefinable, immutable Something, at once the substratum and sum of all, which Time cannot touch, motion perturb, nor variation increase or diminish, and that this substratum and sum has been from all eternity and will be for all eternity.[410]

With regard to humanity and life itself, the Rishis discovered not just that "death itself is not a reality but a seeming, for what appears to be destruction, is merely transformation," but also that "life itself is a seeming," for beyond life and death there lies a condition which is "more permanent than either."[411]

These ancient explorers of mind eventually found ways to connect with a Oneness to which they could then focus their attention. As they explored, further questions arose. Was the Oneness intelligent or was it non-intelligent? Was it a God or was it a mechanical, insentient nature? Endless exploration and speculation by these early Aryan Rishis as to what was experienced resulted eventually in the following six diverging questions regarding the nature of this Oneness:

1. Is this Oneness simply the thing we call "time" that underlies all and everything?

2. Or is it *svabhāva*, an archetypal "essential nature" of things, taking various forms?

3. Or is it chance, blind mechanical interaction producing things by infinite permutation?

4. Or is it fate, predestined causative formation, fixed laws by which this world evolves itself in a preordained procession of phenomena and from which it cannot deviate?

5. Or is it a mother matrix that molded the original elements of the universe, the womb of the universe?

6. Or is it simply pure illusion projected by a myriad of separate "Egos"?

To make sense of all these speculations the sages tried the method of enumeration, called Sāṃkhya, developed by the early sage Kapila (6th century BCE). Their work led them to conclude that this Oneness about which sages had been speculating, "was the great principle of Prakriti, the single eternal indestructible principle and origin of Matter which by perpetual evolution rolls out through aeons and aeons the unending panorama of things."[412] And yet *behind* this Prakriti, or *before* this manifestation of material things in space-time, is its other half, which they labeled Purusha, loosely translated as spirit. Prakriti and Purusha can be seen as a duality within the Trinity, while the third element or hypostasis, that which unites and transcends both of them, is consciousness, designated by the word Cit (pronounced "chit") in Sanskrit. Thus the Egos, beings made of matter, exhibit *consciousness* both in their on-going activity and in the very act of their creation. Aurobindo here paraphrases Kapila to answer the question of just why have these seemingly separate egos of consciousness been created:

> Those conscious, thinking and knowing *Egos* of living beings, of whom knowledge and thought seem to be the essential selves and without whom this world of perceivable and knowable things could not be perceived and known, and if not perceived and known, might it not be that without them it could not even exist?[413]

By why? And for whose benefit? Aurobindo answers: "Surely for those conscious, knowing, and perceiving Egos, the army of witnesses, who, each in his private space of reasoning and perceiving Mind partitioned off by an enveloping medium of gross matter, sit for ever as spectators in the theatre of the Universe!"[414]

It must be remembered that Kapila's cosmological model of the Whole was published three hundred years before the birth of Socrates, and over the intervening centuries between Kapila and Aurobindo other major philosophical streams have branched from the initial Sāṃkhya structure:

1. Some saw that the army of Ego witnesses must be resolved into an ultimate single pre-existing and post-existing Witness, and thus arrived at various conceptions of Duality:

   a. God vs. Nature
   b. Purusha vs. Prakriti
   c. Spirit vs. Matter
   d. Ego vs. Non-Ego

2. Others, more radical, perceived Prakriti as the "shadow creation" of Purusha, so that "God alone remained" as the Real.

3. Still others believed that each ego is "only a series of successive shocks of consciousness and that the persistent sense of identity is no more than an illusion due to the unbroken continuity of the shocks."[415]

According to this last viewpoint, consciousness is only a subset of Prakriti, merely an illusion or at best one of its many sub-aspects, "so that Prakriti alone remains as the one reality, the material or real factor eliminating by inclusion the spiritual or ideal."[416] We can see in this argument a parallel to the modern widespread materialist paradigm held by the majority of neuroscientists that consciousness is a derivative, emergent, *byproduct* of the firing of neurons in the brain. If this were true, it would preclude the notion that consciousness might be co-extensive with a panpsychic universe of Prakriti.

But, Aurobindo points out, it is by this denial that Prakriti is seen as an "ultimate part of reality apart from the perceptions of Purushas." This leads to "the position of the old Indian Nihilists" which led directly to Buddhism, often accused of having a goal of trying to escape from pleasure and pain into a void of nothingness.[417] However, Aurobindo tells us that they were only trying to escape from a "limited pleasure which involves pain," and to escape from "pain which is nothing but the limitation of pleasure."[418] In actuality, he says, both approaches are really seeking an *absolute absence of limitation*, which is not a negative condition, but a positive infinity. Their so-called escape from individuality does not lead them into a void of nothingness at all, but into a state of experienced infinite existence, absolute consciousness, a transcendental awareness not necessarily limited by space or time.

In addition to such numerous interpretations of experiential reality by these sages, passed down through history in their attempts to articulate verbal, rational understanding to the results of their Yogic explorations of consciousness, there remains, however, another view that led "to the very threshold of Vedanta." This view was the "speculation that Prakriti and Purusha might **both** be quite real, and yet not ultimately different aspects, or sides, of each other and so, after all, of a Oneness higher than either."[419] Prakriti was seen to be real by close analysis of the phenomenal world, and Purusha was acknowledged to be real by the sense of identity consciousness and "by the necessity of a perceiving cause for the activity of Prakriti."[420] In light of this dawning Vedantic view, the Rishis held that they themselves must be real, that "they were the receptive and contemplative Egos" viewing Prakriti itself from outside Prakriti, as observers viewing space-time from a region outside of space-time.[421] It was as if each one of us were a single unique avatar of the one Purusha peering out into space-time from within a single transcendent center.

Over many generations of searching, investigating, and experiencing, the Seers of India developed a toolkit of incisive techniques required for any serious introspective first-person participatory investigation of the realities behind being, consciousness, and causality. These tools are the methods of *yoga*, codified in writing by Patañjali as early as the 4th century C.E. Through exploring consciousness with the tolls of *yoga* they discovered three "crowning realizations" in their search:

1. *Being* was determined to be real; Absolute Brahman; the true Self; absolute and transcendent, out of time; it must transcend time and space;" **nityo-nityānām**.

2. Puruṣa was determined to be real; "This then was the second realization through Yoga, **cetana-ścetanānām**, the One Consciousness in many Consciousness."[422]

3. Finally was the all-important realization that the Transcendent Self, the *puruṣa* in individual man, is not separate from the Transcendent Self, the *Puruṣa* of the Universe, that they are contiguous in being and share the same essence.

But here is the paradox. The customary non-Yogic sense of separate individuality is absolutely required by and is the key to the creation and maintenance of the universe itself. It is this illusory sense of separate individuality, which is, as Aurobindo says, "one of the fundamental *seemings* on which the manifestation of phenomenal existence perpetually depends." It is through this third realization that "the Absolute which would otherwise be beyond knowledge, becomes knowable."[423] The connection between *puruṣa* and *Puruṣa* will be seen as the key to accessing the riches of participation in *Saccidānanda*.

In actuality, Aurobindo tells us, the entire metaphysics of the Upanishads rests upon four Mahāvākyas (see Table 3):

Based upon these four grand truths, **Nityo-nityānām, Cetana-ścetanānām, So'ham,** and **Aham brahma asmi,** as upon four mighty pillars the lofty philosophy of the Upanishads raised its front among the distant stars.[424]

Sanskrit from the Upanishads	Sri Aurobindo's Translation
Nityo-nityānām	The One Eternal in many transient.
Cetana-ścetanānām	The One Consciousness within many Consciousnesses.
So'ham	He am I.
Aham brahma asmi	I am Brahman, the Eternal.

Table 3. The Four "Great Sayings" of the *Upanishads*

The Nature of the Absolute Brahman

The *Upanishads* can be viewed as a great collection of metaphysical data, of "observations and spiritual experiences with conclusions and generalizations from those observations and experiences," and, as Aurobindo states, "they have a scientific rather than a logical consistency."[425]

However if the *Upanishads* are critiqued primarily for logical inconsistency, an approach European scholars have often taken, their coherency seems to fall apart. They are seen to base themselves on an initial fundamental inconsistency, for in the Upanishads "it is distinctly stated that neither mind nor senses can reach the Brahman and that words return baffled from the attempt to describe It."[426]

Here we note the irony of the situation, that Brahman, while clearly not definable, and not intellectually knowable, remains yet the one true object of knowledge. In fact, the whole Upanishad seems to be, paradoxically, an attempt to describe Brahman with great detail.

Aurobindo addresses this irony by pointing out that the Brahman as ultimate reality is transcendent, absolute, and infinite, whereas the human senses and intellect are definitely finite. Thus the absolute reality of the Brahman is unknowable to and uncontainable by the intellect and the senses. This is perhaps due to their limited range, and perhaps because they are even focused in the wrong direction, looking outward rather than inward. It is accordingly beyond the powers of speech to describe Brahman because experience of the Brahman lies outside of the ranges of speech as we know it.

Nevertheless, aspects of the Brahman in its manifesting "shadows of light" in time, space, causality, and consciousness can indeed by perceived by mystics, shamans, yogis, and psychonauts through the means of *yoga vidya*, the science of "knowledge of union." While modern scientists only reluctantly admit that there may be some great ultimate reality "unknown and probably unknowable" to humanity, the *Upanishads* assert on the contrary that the ultimate Brahman does indeed exist in an absolutely real sense.

Although such existence is inexpressible in terms of any delimiting finite verbal expression or syntax, it is *immediately realizable* and attainable through special modes of direct experience. How this occurs is explained by the various yogic and contemplative means that have been discovered by noetic explorers and handed down through the ages in texts such as the *Upanishads*, first recorded in Sanskrit in the early part of the Axial Age, sometime between 800 to 500 BCE.

But while the material scientist searches for knowledge only in the limited, measurable and recordable phenomena of gross matter in space and in time, the Vedantic scientist has not limited himself to the field of space-time, but has ranged farther and farther into dimensions not even considered by the scientist of physical matter. In numerous instances, these psychonauts have brought back reports that they have "discovered a universe of subtle matter penetrating and surrounding the gross." It is into this dimension of "subtle matter" that the spirit moves during normal human sleep. In fact, says Aurobindo, this universe of subtle matter "is the source whence all psychic processes draw their origin."[427]

But even beyond these two dimensions, the *gross* and the *subtle*, experienced and named by Vedantic explorers, Aurobindo describes their discovery of an additional domain, the *causal*:

> There is yet a third universe of *causal matter* penetrating and surrounding both the *subtle* and the *gross*, and that this universe to which the spirit withdraws in the deepest and most abysmal states of sleep and trance and also in a remote condition beyond the state of man after death, is the source whence all phenomena take their rise.[428]

Aurobindo says that it is upon this Trinitarian scheme (of *gross, subtle, and causal*) that the whole structure of the Vedanta is built. Brahman manifests in each of three domains as shown in Table 4.

Domains of Brahman	Sri Aurobindo's Characterizations of these Domains
Causal Domain	**"Absolute Self"** -> Prajña, The Wise One
Subtle Domain	**"The Creator"** -> Golden Embryo birthing life and form
Gross Domain	**"Cosmic Ruler"** -> Helper, The Shining One (Deva)

Table 4. Sri Aurobindo's Three Domains of Brahman

He then goes on to declare an amazing possibility, that in each of these three manifestations, "He (Brahman) can be known and realized by the spirit of man."[429] Here by "spirit of man" Aurobindo is referring to the individual self, *puruṣa* (with a small "p"), only one of trillions upon trillions of the metaphorically tiny droplets of self that make up the vast ocean of the big Self, *Puruṣa* (with a capital "P"), named in the *Upanishads* as the Parabrahman, Absolute Brahman, the great Self, or God.

> The position has already been quite definitely taken that the transcendent Self in man is identically the same as the transcendent Self in the Universe and that this identity is the one great key to the knowledge of the Absolute Brahman.[430]

Because of this ultimate identity of the individual, seemingly separate *puruṣa* from the Brahman (the "big *Puruṣa*"), human knowledge of the Brahman is possible, "for this identity is a fact in the reality of things" states Aurobindo.[431]

Thus, all phenomena are nothing but "seemings" which only *appear to be* differences between the individual and Brahman, but the illusion is so convincing and pervasive "that it is almost always impossible for the material sensual being to conceive of the Supreme Soul as having any point of contact with his own soul, and *it is only by a long process of evolution* that an individual finally arrives at the illumination in which some kind of identity becomes to him conceivable."[432]

Knowledge of Brahman in the Material Domain

We have seen how Vedanta arrives at the conclusion that Brahman can be known and realized, perhaps separately, in *each* of the Gross, Subtle, and Causal domains (described in Table 2). Accordingly, while it seems a remote possibility to the vast majority of humans, Aurobindo assures us that Brahman *can be known directly* in our everyday material encounter in the Gross domain of material existence in space-time.

But how is it possible for us to know Brahman in the Gross material realm? How do we recognize such daily intimate contact, and how can it be felt, and if so, how? Aurobindo says "it can be felt, by the supreme sympathy of *love* and *faith*, either through love of humanity and of all other fellow-beings, or directly through the love of God."[433]

But, Aurobindo cautions that these feelings alone are not the fullest knowledge of Brahman. Each of the religions that stress love and faith alone are seen also to experience only a limited, perhaps one-sided, knowledge of the Absolute. It is only knowledge of all three hypostases of the Holy Trinity that offers the possibility of the complete experience of God. Thus it is imminently practical to acquire knowledge of the Trinity in every domain, and it is our contention that this is mirrored in the approach to the Vedantic knowledge of Brahman.

Knowledge of Brahman in the Subtle Domain

Those who are able to move beyond the *gross* material phenomenal dimension through discovery and practice of various psychophysical techniques such as found in yoga, drugs, shamanism, contemplative prayer, etc., find themselves beyond the *gross* domain, and discover "an entry into the universe of *subtle* phenomena."[434]

The *subtle* domain is the domain of energy, of radiant plasmoids, electromagnetic energy fields experienced in Christianity as a "descent of the flames of the Holy Spirit" upon the Apostles, where, as William Blake observed, "Energy is Eternal Delight." This experience is that of the very radiance of the oceans of emf fields filling an otherwise dark empty shadow of empty space, a flickering awareness, lightening flashing at the boundaries of dark energy.

Knowledge of Brahman in the Causal Domain

Knowledge of the Subtle Domain of energy in space-time is only the beginning for the psychonautic explorer sailing toward Brahman. "From the subtle Universe the individual rises in its evolution until it is able to enter the universe of *causal* matter, where it stands near to the fountain-head."435 This is the "Causal universe," an equivalent to the pure transcendent eternal atemporal non-spatial domain in which the multiple *puruṣa* resonates with the One *Puruṣa*, where:

> the difference between the individual and the Supreme Self is greatly attenuated . . . He is moreover, on the other side of phenomena and can see the Universe at will without him or within him; but he has still not necessarily realized the supreme as utterly himself, although this perfect realization is now for the first time in his grasp.436

This, says Aurobindo, is "Monism with a difference," but also a monism437 that can be ultimately grasped by the formerly separate *puruṣa*, and the question then becomes, what then happens to the individual Self, to the separate, unique yet isolated *puruṣa?* His answer is clear:

> Then the individual Self entering into full realization, ceases in any sense to be the individual Self, but merges into and becomes again the eternal and absolute Brahman, without parts, unbeginning, undecaying, unchanging.438

The problem for the Rishis, and for us today, is that normal human senses and memory were evolved in order to sense, reflect, and remember external phenomena. Any experience of this Brahman, of God, the "big *Puruṣa*" is not fully registered by normal human biosensory qualia systems (eye, ear, taste, touch) nor can the experience be clearly recorded and stored in human memory because, in part, it is definitely outside of both time and space.

Aurobindo qualifies the term "Nirvana," by pointing out that while Buddhists might interpret this "lack of recording of experience" as a "Void" during this highest experience, another way of describing the beyond-visual experience is to say that it leads to a "luminous ecstasy" of infinite light as Aurobindo says here:

> The culmination of knowledge by the superseding of our divided and fallible intellect with something greater must lead not to utter darkness and blank vacuity but to the luminous ecstasy of an infinite Consciousness. Not the annihilation of Being, but utter fullness of Being is our Nirvana.

Thus we see that human rational knowledge really cannot begin to penetrate into nor to accompany the serious seeker into this experience of a new kind of knowledge, the knowledge of God, the direct knowledge of the Brahman, the Absolute Self, the "*big Puruṣa.*" Here indeed the word *knowledge* itself becomes a problem for us.

According to Aurobindo's discussion of Vedanta, there are at least three different types of knowledge: knowledge by experience, knowledge by hearing (or reading), knowledge by *becoming one with* the object of knowledge. The one-dimensional human intellect, fed by sequential word tokens, when encountering deeper levels of transcendent experience, is superseded. Verbal knowledge becomes obsolete, and shuts down "at a point where the Knower, Knowledge and the Known become one."[439]

Knowledge of Brahman Beyond All Domains

In the ultimate state of union, the "Knowledge of Brahman Beyond All Domains," the Upanishads tell us that the individual *puruṣa* has realized the Supreme Being as himself as Aurobindo here explains:

> The individual Self entering into full realization, ceases in any sense to be the individual Self, but merges into and becomes again the eternal and absolute Brahman, without parts, unbeginning, undecaying, unchanging.[440]

This state of being, he says, is called *Laya,* the highest state of knowledge-being-bliss, extinction from separation, beyond phenomena. He goes on to say that it is obvious that here words and even memories cease to have meaning and are not needed. It is a condition that is perfectly pure and absolutely infinite in all dimensions. He comments that an approach to this state often creates anxiety and fear if approached by the average "undisciplined imagination" of present-day humanity by those who are uncomfortable even in brief moments of silence, let alone in the more rarified psychotropic contemplative states attainable through advanced psychodynamic practices.

The normal human senses never glimpse this state because they have evolved over many millions of years to sense externalities in the world of gross, material, relatively large-scale objects, and to filter out and hide a myriad of finer, higher bandwidth activities of consciousness. Such is the power of Maya working through avidya. But there is a mistaken assumption that this state of *Laya,* of "consciousness without an object," is a state of dark emptiness. On the contrary, says Aurobindo of the experience, the state is not a blank empty vacuum but (with a slight dig at Buddhism): "this experience is the luminous ecstasy of an infinite Consciousness, not the annihilation of Being, but utter fullness of Being is our Nirvana."[441]

And it is here that Aurobindo gives a description which later in *The Life Divine* he will call, the "method of Vedantic knowledge:"

> For the final absolution of the intellect can only be at a point where the Knower, Knowledge and the Known become one, Knowledge being there infinite, direct and without media. And where there is this infinite and flawless knowledge, there must be, one thinks, infinite and flawless existence and bliss.[442]

Metaphor of the Porch

But even here, in this last (the fourth) state of the Self there are *stages* and *degrees* by which experience can vary. To describe these stages, Aurobindo here chooses a visual metaphor. He asks us to visualize different viewpoints as seen from an individual standing on a porch. He describes the various ways a person might see things while standing near on the porch near the entrance (here the entrance between space-time and the eternal, between little self and Big Self).

For practical purposes we may speak of three stages, the *first* when we stand at the entrance of the porch and look within; the *second* when we stand at the inner extremity of the porch and are really face to face with the Eternal; the *third* when we enter into the Holy of Holies, as described here by Sri Aurobindo:

> The first stage, when we stand at the entrance of the porch and look within, is attainable through yoga, and the person who attains this stage returns a *Jivanmukta*, "one who lives and is yet internally released from the bondage of phenomenal existence." The person who reaches the second stage, standing at the inner extremity of the porch and face to face with the Absolute Eternal, we call a *Buddha* or Avatar. But here, entering into the Holy of Holies, says

Aurobindo, "From the third stage none returns, nor is it attainable in the body."[443]

The Five Levels of Brahman

Before beginning detailed discussion of the mysterious Trinity of *Saccidānanda*, Aurobindo, describes what he has perceived to be the full range of Brahman's manifest reality, derived from the psychonautical discoveries of the ancient Indian sages and verified in his own experiences. The early explorers of the transcendental psyche came to the consensus that when these deeper dimensions of reality are experienced by an individual human, there are **five levels** or operational modes that can be navigated as described in Fig. 25.

The Unknowable
Tuneable during Asamprajñata Samādhi:
Enstasis or 'Consciousness Without An Object'

Parabrahman
Tuneable during Samprajñata Samādhi:
Saccidānandam

Brahman Prajñā
Tuneable during advanced concentration:
Dhyāna ("Zen") or Entheogens

Brahman Hiranyagarbha
Tuneable during Dream State

Brahman Virat
Tuneable during Liturgical Activities

Figure 25. *Five Levels of Absolute Brahman.*

The objective of these early contemplative Vedic forefathers in articulating this five level map was solely to help other psychonauts to navigate the wide oceans of consciousness by identifying and articulating distinct regions for future explorers. One can see a similar objective in the work of 14th and 15th century naval explorers, who struggled to produce highly valued "rutters," written charts and guidelines much sought after by Spanish and Portuguese explorers who had the courage to sail into unfamiliar oceans at the far edges of the unknown.

It is worth describing these five levels in some detail.

Level 1 – "The Unknowable" – At the top of the diagram, the most exalted or deepest level of Brahman, is "The Unknowable," congruent with what David Bohm refers to as the "implicate order" (discussed in detail in Chapter III), and Teilhard de Chardin's "Omega point" (discussed in Chapter IV).

Level 1, "The Unknowable," is *outside of* space-time and thus beyond relative consciousness. The non-temporal state of Brahman can only be reached by the human soul during the deepest stages of contemplative, entheogenic, or shamanic trance wherein the seer has been able to *completely detach* from the suspended ego. Here mind fluctuations and memory have come to a halt, and limited self-identification vanishes in an ultimate communion with transcendent nonduality, what Bohm calls "the Whole." To reach this absolute mode of being requires arriving at a state of what has been called elsewhere *enstasis,* or by one mathematician, "consciousness without an object."[444] But for explorers attempting to map the navigation of consciousness, this state is far too deep, as nothing conceptual can be brought back as food for thought. The poet T.S. Eliot expresses the problem clearly:

> I can only say, there we have been: but I cannot say where
> And I cannot say, how long, for that is to place it in time.[445]

Level 2 – "The Parabrahman" – Just before the entrance to "The Unknowable" Brahman, lies the realm or state of "Parabrahman." Here the prefix *param* in Sanskrit may be translated as the word "different," and thus Parabrahman signifies a state of consciousness/being that is slightly "different" than the pure unknowable Brahman.

It is this difference in the Parabrahman level that provides the contemplative the ability to maintain awareness of *both* the transcendent nondual domain *and* the immediate, imminent domain of space-time simultaneously, as if having one foot in each realm. Referring back to the metaphor of the porch, one could say that here the psychonaut is standing in the doorway, neither totally within Brahman, nor totally external to Brahman.

It is useful to note that this level of experiencing Brahman is what is meant by "an experience of God" in many religions, as it is reachable to a limited extent by human beings through various means of communion. Sages and seers have been able to experience Parabrahman through yogic techniques, ritual, ingestion of plant entheogens, or through falling into this extraordinary psycho-physiological state through intense mental or physical activity.

The experience of Parabrahman, though transcending space-time, allows some vestigial co-reflecting focus of awareness to remain in time, during which memory functions sufficiently such that when returning to normal consciousness, something can be said about the experience. It is primarily from encounters within this state that we have received the most significant written and verbal accounts of God handed down to us by mystics and saints throughout the ages.

Aurobindo says, with a bit of Edwardian-phrased humor, that *something* can be understood of Parabrahman because "always if *the liberal use of loose metaphors* is not denied, it can be practically brought within the domain of speech."[446] Due to the almost inexpressible impact of the effulgent Brahman state, normal human language cannot begin to describe the experience, and it is poetry with its "loose metaphors" that comes closest to capturing the phenomenon in words. There is an enormous difficulty in the use of human language to communicate metaphysical experience, and we are reminded of another passage from T.S. Eliot's poem *The Four Quartets*:

> Words strain,
> Crack and sometimes break, under the burden,
> Under the tension, slip, slide, perish,
> Decay with imprecision, will not stay in place,
> Will not stay still.[447]

Level 3 – "Brahman Prajñā" – At this level the experience of Brahman is fully within space-time, though beyond the normal ranges of ego consciousness. The contemplative psychonaut is able to tune into the radiant cosmos, to resonate with the Whole within all of the regions of space-time, and through such resonance to "bring back" knowledge and wisdom through the immediate experience of the Whole, free of normal local mental limitations. This reminds us of the myth of Prometheus who was able to "steal fire" from Mt. Olympus and bring it back to mankind.

This is the region explored by psychonauts through ingestion of psychotropic substances or psychophysical exercises. It is within the *prajñā* level of consciousness that individual humans are able to encounter beings in other levels of space-time, ancestors, alien entities and civilizations so well described in Olaf Stapledon's novel, *The Star Maker*, and by the writer and psychonaut Terence McKenna in books such as *True Hallucinations*. The Brahman Prajñā also the domain discussed by occultist in the 19th and 20th centuries, and one currently being explored by parapsychologists.

Level 4 – "Brahman Hiranyagarbha" – It is this level that is experienced nightly during human "dream state," though it can also be reached through various contemplative practices and is the stage that must be passed through before reaching Brahman Prajñā. According to the rishis it is possible to navigate within this dream state, which is a repository of a myriad of levels of consciousness entered into by all sentient beings in the space-time region of existence. It is often experienced as an intersection between higher levels of Brahman and the individual human consciousness, and though memory and normal ego operation function at a reduced level, it is often possible to recall experiences within this realm after resuming normal operations of awareness.

Level 5 – "Brahman Virat" – Also known as "Master of the Waking Universe," it is here that God is approachable through liturgical activities during which, through repetition and concentrated emotional effort, the normal waking ego can be fairly easily transcended to reach the immediacy of the Brahman Virat stage of consciousness. When this state is entered into by the practitioner through prayer, meditation, or music there is a strong taste or hint of the subtle feelings of the joy, consciousness, and bliss that can be experienced with entrance into the higher levels, and in particular it is an adumbration of the full experience of the Parabrahamn, the mysterious Trinity of *Saccidānanda*.

After describing these five levels of Brahman, Sri Aurobindo now turns to focus more specifically upon Level 2, that of the Parabrahman in which the Holy Trinity fully manifests in its active form to those who seek. He tell us that Vedanta describes this Parabrahman "in two great trilogies, subjective and objective," the first trilogy being of course Sat, Cit, Ananda (Fig. 26). Here it is important to note that this Trinitarian structure of the Parabrahman can be found underlying a multitude of relationships in the world of space-time, and as such has been revered for many centuries by Indian mystics with the term *Saccidānanda*.

Sat
Being

Existence
Causal

Saccidānandam

Subtle

Gross

Bliss

Consciousness

Delight
Ananda

Self Reflection
Cit

Figure 26. Hypostases of *Saccidānanda*.

Sri Aurobindo tells us that "Sat and Cit are really the same," and they are both, at the same time, Ananda or delight. Here we "equate Being (Ananda) with the pleasure of self-reflection or Conscious Existence." *Saccidānanda* is Parabrahman and has three attributes or hypostases, as shown in the diagram: (1.) Absolute Existence, Being, Sat, but also (2.) Pure Awareness, Absolute Consciousness, Cit, and finally (3.) Pure Ecstasy, Absolute Bliss, Ananda. Parabrahman as *Saccidānanda* can be regarded fundamentally as a three component hypostasis (similar to the Christian Trinity). This is the great teaching of Vedanta.

But these three hypostases are *not completely imminent* in our material universe of space and time. They live, reside, exist, or take their being somehow in the intermediate realm or dimension that lies between the inexpressible infinities of

Brahman and the quite expressible limitations of the material, time bound world of galaxies, stars, and zebras. They function as a bridge for human consciousness between the imminent and the transcendent, between the nondual implicate order and the space-time explicate order. And this Trinity of Sat-Cit-Ananda (grammatically elided into the single Sanskrit word *Saccidānanda*), this Parabrahman now understood more clearly in its triadic nature, manifesting most fundamentally as the Trinity of *Saccidānanda*, has both a subjective, inward turning side (Fig. 27), and an objective, outward turning side (Fig. 28).

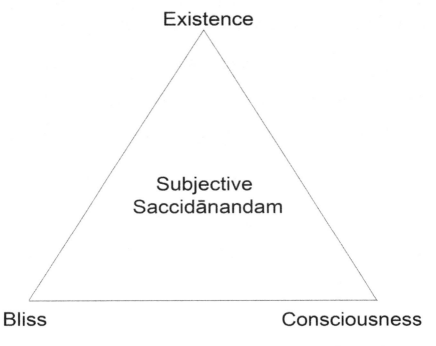

Figure 27. Subjective (inward turning) *Saccidānanda*.

Subjectively, Saccidānanda is a self-contained hypostasis of Existence-Consciousness-Bliss, approachable and able to be resonantly experienced (if not completely "knowable" by the mental rational human mind) by human sages, shamans, and Rishis, and modern psychonauts.

Objectively however, Saccidānanda can also be understood, Aurobindo tells us, by use of the three Sanskrit terms *satyam, jñana, anantam.* Brahman is *satyam,* or Reality, and is a term encountered widely in Indian philosophy and metaphysics; the word satyam itself defines Reality or Truth in these discussions. *Jñana* on the other hand is Brahman's objective Knowledge hypostasis. "Brahman is absolute *jñanam,* direct and self-existent, without beginning, middle or end, in which the Knower is also the Knowledge and the Known."[448] Finally, he tells us, "Brahman is *anantam,* Endlessness, including all kinds of Infinity."

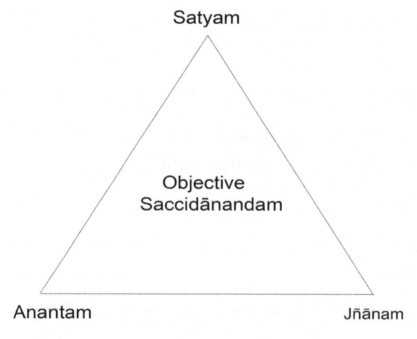

Figure 28. Objective (outward turning) *Saccidānanda.*

The Vedantic Theory of Maya

Brahman projects a luminous shadow of Itself that is called the Parabrahman. Under the play of Maya, the One becomes the Many. "But why? To what purpose?" asks Aurobindo, and he immediately gives one possible philosophical explanation:

> The Absolute One, it is argued, passes through the cycle of manifestation, because He then returns to His original unity enriched with a new store of experiences and impressions, richer in love, richer in knowledge, richer in deed.[449]

The questions then arose of how and why the One became the Many. "Why did the Absolute turn His face toward Evolution?" asks Aurobindo. Why did that which is beyond Causality "need to act on a purpose," and "what was the nature of the process." The answer, it was discovered, lies in a power or force they named Maya.

Maya: The Energy of the Absolute

What is Maya and how and where might it have come into existence? The term Maya is commonly interpreted as indicating illusory appearance that makes the phenomenal world seem "real" to us. But according to Aurobindo, the Upanishads tells us that Maya, a function of the Parabrahman, precedes phenomena and is a force that is outside of space-time.

> The birth of Maya, if it had any birth, took place on the other side of phenomena, before the origin of time, space and causality; and is therefore not cognizable by the intellect which can only think in terms of time, space, and causality.[450]

Maya must then be an objective action, a function of Parabrahman turning outwardly. The action of Maya is analogous to the working of a prism at the very source of creation. Through Maya the Brahman is refracted into the three rays, the emerging primary spectrum called *Saccidānanda*. Brahman finds itself split by Maya into a diffraction pattern of Existence, Consciousness, and Delight, releasing the powers of Sat, Cit, and Ananda to create the universe. Brahman morphs into Saccidānanda, the one becomes many.

And though they remain One in origin, the many now awaken to the transformations of Maya. They discover the endless possibilities in relating with one another in an evolving, spiraling, reciprocal fashion. Accordingly we may say that with Maya's transformation, Brahman finds delight in existence, and discovers delight in consciousness. Likewise it can be said that Brahman is now enjoying awareness of the consciousness of existence, consciousness of delight and the delight of existence. Brahman has discovered joy, the exuberance of creation, the discovery of infinite delight in being, the exuberant thrills of consciousness in an infinite universe.

As this flowing transformation into phenomena deepens, the single *Puruṣa* differentiates into an infinity of separate *puruṣa* beings. Parabrahman is the luminous shadow of the Absolute projected in itself by itself, and Maya is similarly the dark shadow projected by the Absolute in Parabrahman.[451] Seen from the viewpoint of Ananda, it is the Will of Parabrahman that is dividing itself into innumerable forms each of which represents itself "As individual selves solely for the pleasure of existence or Will to live."[452]

The Function of Vidya and Avidya

But still not answered is why the Parabrahman who is absolute knowledge should limit himself. Why should "the pure ultra-Spiritual *un-refine* Itself into the mental and material."[453] Sri Aurobindo's answer is that this is necessary for free creativity to commence in the form of imagination. He tells us that the Vedantic sages had identified the two polar functions that power creative action as it blossoms in the universe; these are expressed in the Sanskrit terms *vidya* and *avidya*, roughly translated, "knowledge" and "ignorance." It is this dynamic duo, *vidya* and *avidya*, knowledge and ignorance, working as a tag team similar in operation to the popular "good cop/bad cop" paradigm, through which Parabrahman is able to discover the delight of consciousness as it transforms through exercises of imagination and pure creativity.

Aurobindo gives several examples of the necessity of *avidya*. Without *avidya* we might see before us a complex conglomeration of whirling energy vortexes of different frequency, atomic nuclear patternings of holographic vibration. But through the power of *avidya* we are able to ignore this and focus instead upon what we see to be a brown stone; thus avidya acts as a filter. Again, without *avidya,* when we go for what otherwise would seem to be a casual walk down a path in the woods, we might instead perceive that we were walking upside down on the spherical body of the planet, our actual motion on an ellipse about the sun at 70,000 miles per hour combined with our circular motion about the planetary axis at 1,000 mile per hour.

Avidya is thus required for filter, focus, imagination, for creation, and must be present in every operation of normal human consciousness. Avidya allows the human to co-create the universe through the arts and the sciences and through sheer consciousness. Aurobindo talks about Shakespeare's imaginations and the origin of his creative images:

> These mighty images live immortally in our minds because Parabrahman in Shakespeare is the same as

Parabrahman in ourselves; thought, in fact, is one, although to be revealed to us, it has to be bodied forth and take separate shapes in sound forms which we are accustomed to perceive and understand.[454]

We see also that Avidya is also inherent in engendering the Delight that arises in approaching Ananda, the Bliss of existence, and we see in nature a "fundamental impulse toward phenomenal existence, consciousness, and the pleasure of conscious existence, though the deepest bliss is after all that which she left and to which she will return."[455]

A summarizing diagram relating the arc of Brahman is presented in Fig. 29, where our everyday space-time of butterflies and zebras (on the right) is symbolized as a projection by Maya refracted into the three beams of Sat-Cit-Ananda feeding a Taoist yin–yang symbol. According to Sri Aurobindo, the nondual, unmanifest (avyakta) and indescribable Level 1 Brahma (the "Unknowable God the Father" on the left) resides in a nondual, non-spatial, non-temporal condition called Avyakta, or "unmanifest." Another way to interpret the diagram would be to see that God the Father on the left is connected to God the Son (space-time) on the right, through the transformational bridge of the Holy Spirit, Parabrahman.

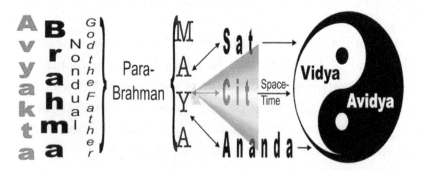

Figure 29. *Vedantic relationships from Avyakta to Avidya.*

We are reminded of the image of Vishnu sleeping on the cosmic ocean of Avyakta, and dreaming the universe. It is Parabrahamn (in the center) that bridges Avyakta and Maya, linking the nondual eternal on the left with spacetime on the right, and within space-time we see the vidya-avidya duo, "me and my shadow," interlocked and spinning in the yin–yang symbol, exhibiting an unending cyclical flow of the energies of creation and destruction, light and darkness.

Avyakta as Concealed *Puruṣa*

Avyakta is a Sanskrit term that indicates a state prior to manifestation in space, time, or causality. Avyakta, as observed by Vedantic seers, is said to be that state of non-temporal, non-spatial manifestation of Brahman, which is not prior to time but outside of time, not outside of space but having no outside nor inside, nondual and nonlocal everywhere and everywhen. According to sages who wrote the 7th century *Avyakta Upanishad,* this Avyakta is of an intelligent and joyful nature, consisting of a superpositioning of all of the three elementals of the Parabrahman: Sat, Cit, and Ananda.

Spirit and matter, Purusha and Prakriti, are indissolubly welded together simply because they are "the one thing viewed from two sides." Spirit takes the shape and appearance of matter through the powers of Avidya (ignorance, obscuration) and Vidya (clarity, knowledge) and the gross material universe is rendered forth from the Parabrahman which, in the course of evolving phenomena, enters into three states or conditions" Sat, Cit, and Ananda, which are called in one passage "His three habitations" and in another, "his three states of dream."[456]

Words fail here, of course, and at this point Sri Aurobindo recalls an image of Avyakta to describe these ethereal relationships in the form of a mythical image of the Golden Egg

(Fig. 30), related in the Purāṇas (literally the "ancient or old" folk tales of India, recorded as early as 200 CE).[457]

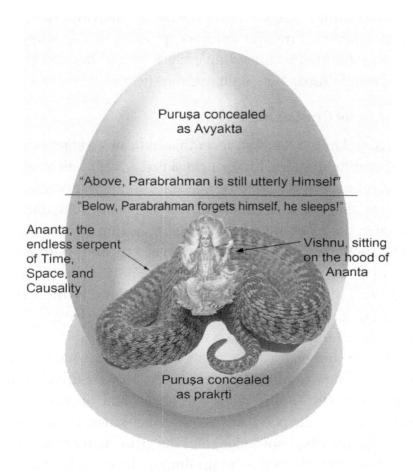

Figure 30. *Avyakta as the Golden Egg of the Purāṇas.*

Let us then imagine Avyakta as an egg, the golden egg of the Purāṇas full of the waters of undifferentiated existence and divided into two halves, the upper or luminous half filled with the upper waters of subjective ideation, the lower or tenebrous half with the lower waters of objective ideation. In the upper half Purusha is concealed as the final cause of things, in the lower half he is concealed as Prakriti, the material cause of things.[458]

If we rotate the Golden Egg ninety degrees counterclockwise, a similar cosmological relationship can be seen in Fig. 31, where "Purusha concealed as Avyakta" is now seen as "Purusha Non-local Causal Implicate Order" and "Purusha concealed as Prakriti" now becomes "Atman Local Explicate Order," on either side of a Fourier transform process bridging the two in an endless feedback loop (discussed fully in the next chapter).[459]

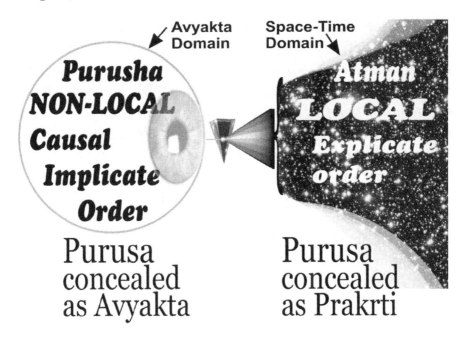

Figure 31. *Two Regions and a Holoflux Bridge.*

Thus the Whole, both seen and unseen, both space-time as well as other dimensions, enfolded within the Implicate Order, can be seen as a process consisting of three parts or movements, described by Christian saints as "the Father, the

Son, the Holy Spirit," and which the ancient Vedic Seers described by combining three terms into one, *Saccidānanda*.[460]

Implicate Father and Explicate Son

The diagram in Fig. 31 implies that one way to see the Holy Trinity may be as two domains bridged by pure energy:

- Region 1 – "God the Father"/"The Implicate Order"

- Region 2 – "God the Son"/"The Explicate Order"

- Flux – "The Holy Spirit"/"Holoflux Energy"

In the diagram we see the transforming flux (Spirit) processing between two orders of being in "an undivided flowing movement without borders."[461] The consciousness Identity at the left in the diagram can be expressed as a *spectrum of holoflux energy* in Bohm's "implicate order" (as discussed in the next Chapter). In the conceptual map of Vedanta, this is termed, the single all-seeing Purusha, while Christian use the phrase "God the Father."

A continuous energy transformation (the Spirit) between left and right regions (i.e., between "God the Father" and "God the Son") is depicted as a prism at the center of the diagram. To the right in the diagram, our space-time local region, might be called "The Son" by Christian theologians. In fact there has been much controversy over the publications of Matthew Fox, a formerly Dominican priest (now Anglican) with a PhD in medieval theology, for his conception of the "Cosmic Christ" in what he called "Creation Spirituality."[462]

If gender is considered and overlaid upon the configuration (see Fig. 32), it can be seen that the Holy Trinity is also reflected in the universal human conditions of Being,

Mind, and Love, known in Vedanta as Sat-Cit-Ānanda, with Ananda => Feminine/Love, and Cit => Masculine/Mind.

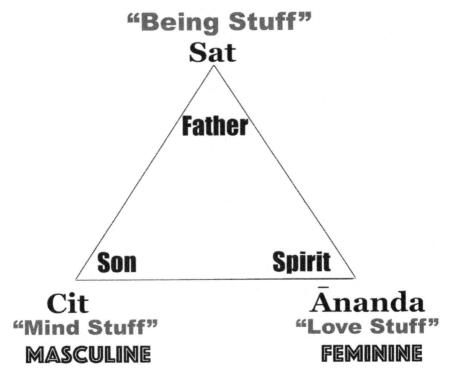

Figure 32. *The Sat-Cit-Ananda Trinity as Being-Mind-Love.*

Aurobindo's Trinity and *The Supermind*

Aurobindo's experiential understanding of the Trinity largely agrees with that of Teilhard de Chardin, as can be seen here from Aurobindo's thousand-page opus, *The Life Divine*:

> The Trinity is the source and basis of all existence and play of existence, and all cosmos must be an expression and action of its essential reality.[463]

Aurobindo's understanding of the Trinity is a modern one, though in full agreement with the concepts of the Vedantic Trinity, expressed in the Sanskrit as *Saccidānanda*. Aurobindo frequently uses the term *Saccidānanda* in his writing, telling us that an experience of *Saccidānanda* is possible through a state of consciousness which he calls "the Supermind," a term which appears to be identical to one of Teilhard de Chardin's, who himself uses the term "Noosphere" to refer to the same intermediary link. It is access to Saccidānanda, through networking with the Supermind (or the Noosphere), that will afford the individual human psyche the full experience and knowledge of the Holy Trinity during contemplative prayer.

During my retreat with Fr. Bede Griffiths in South India, not far from the town of Pondicherry, where Sri Aurobindo had lived his final fifty years, I recall singing local hymns at the end of each mass, using words both from English as well as the Tamil language. I noticed in particular the many refrains offering up praise and thanks to the Holy Trinity, ending with the word "*Saccidānanda,*" a term I had first heard years earlier, studying Aurobindo's *Life Divine.*

Practically speaking, the Supermind designates a configuration of consciousness toward which each individual human psyche has the potential to grow and eventually to access, assuming sufficient effort and will have been applied. Metaphysically, Aurobindo uses the term Supermind to designate the bridge, link, or interface between our normal everyday consciousness (our "thinking meat" mind) and that region of pure nondual infinite Being termed *Saccidānanda*, outside of space-time. We suggest that Aurobindo's Supermind is congruent with Teilhard de Chardin's *Noosphere*, David Bohm's "*Active Information*," and also with the Christian notion of an experience of "*the Spirit.*" Each one of these might be seen as one of the three hypostases of the Holy Trinity, the other two being "the Father" and "the Son."

According to this hypothesis, when the individual human psyche resonates with, links, or communes with the Supermind, it knows itself to be One by immediacy, having reached the rarified condition of nonduality. It has at this stage reached the integral mode of consciousness or awareness. At this moment there arises an omni-dimensional mode of nondual awareness, beyond that of normal space-time observations which rely upon the exterior human sensory systems. Aurobindo tells us that we (or "I" or "we") then see "without any process of construction . . . the totality:"

> The Supermind distinguishes by a direct seeing without any mental process of taking to pieces the peculiarities of the thing, form, energy, action, quality, mind, soul that it has in view, and it sees too with an equal directness and without any process of construction the significant totality of which these peculiarities are the incidents.[464]

According to Aurobindo the knowledge of Supermind can eventually be reached through accumulated experience and evolutionary growth which, according to many schools of Indian philosophy, may take multiple incarnations, but is the goal of each soul. A similar belief can be found in Christianity in the belief that eventually the individual soul will find God and link, through the Holy Spirit, with God the Father (Bohm's Implicate Order), and with God the Son (Bohm's Explicate Order, also called the "Cosmic Christ" by Matthew Fox), or both simultaneously.[465] In bridging the two, the three become one, even within what was formerly believed to be an individually separate soul.

Summary of Sri Aurobindo's Vedantic Trinity

Sat ->   God the Father, Logos
Cit ->   The Cosmic Christ Consciousness
Ananda ->   The Holy Spirit, Love, Touch

IV. Trinitarian Quantum Physics

Understanding Sri Aurobindo's explanation of the states and stages associated with the Vedantic Trinity can be challenging, partially due to the liberal use of Sanskrit terms. In mapping experience, languages, even our own, fall far short of expressing the experience itself. The problem is clearly that a word simply points to something else that is *not* the word itself, and certainly not the experience itself. Words retrieve the unique interpretation we assign to each term as it is used within our own particular cultural moment in history. Each word is then further filtered by our own local biases, and spun even further by our unique personal histories. Again we find this idea in the words of T.S. Eliot, "Words strain, crack and sometimes break, under the burden."[466]

Sri Aurobindo realized this and often commented on the superiority and immediacy of "knowledge by experience" as contrasted with knowledge merely read about or heard through the slippery media of words and languages; it is for this reason that he frequently urged his readers to practice direct contemplative exercises, to learn to communicate with a deeper silence in what he termed "integral yoga," in order to achieve a direct authentic experience of numinous reality.[467]

Quantum Physics and the Triple Brahman

Nevertheless, words and diagrams can be quite useful if one is able to approach the same subject from multiple perspectives; accordingly, this chapter presents an approach to a description of the Trinitarian configuration of the cosmos set forth by the modern theoretical physicist, David Bohm, who in his description of the dynamic operation of the universe offers a map of the "Whole" as an integration of three primary dimensions or domains. He does this in what might be called the language of Trinitarian quantum physics.

David Bohm: Physicist and Mystic

Born on a farm in Pennsylvania in 1917, at the time of his death in 1992, Bohm had risen to the rank of a distinguished Professor Emeritus of Theoretical Physics at Birkbeck College, University of London. His early research career had begun at the University of California in Berkeley, where he completed his dissertation in plasma physics in 1944 under Robert Oppenheimer at the Lawrence Radiation Laboratory in Berkeley.[468]

In the same way as Aurobindo had sought for a comprehensive map of the relationship between the eternal and the immanent (the assumed dual aspects of reality) through consideration of ancient metaphysical texts, Bohm sought for something that was missing in quantum theory, the relationship between matter and consciousness. Bohm derided physicists who seemed to show no interest in the *meaning* of the quantum world, those who used quantum mechanics merely as a mathematical tool for effectively predicting results in nuclear physics experiments. At the same time, Bohm perceives that reality lies beyond appearances, that it is the creative process of a whole, beyond theorizing, even given the repeatable appearances of scientific measurement:

> The quantum jump or quantum leap is a creative process . . . . I called it the implicate order because it's the order of enfoldment that counts not the movement in a line. It manifests in the explicate. What we thought was the essence is now the appearance . . . . Namely, that the particle which was thought to explain the reality is now seen as an appearance. The essence of the true being is unknown. Even the implicate order is merely a

concept, so even that should turn out to be an appearance. But we say be bringing in deeper more penetrating appearances we understand better, but we are never going to grasp the whole. Even a unified theory will only be an appearance.[469]

In his approach, Bohm stresses that the distinction between information and meaning is an important one. Unlike many physicists, whom he criticized for being information intoxicated, Bohm felt it of the utmost importance to search for meaning behind the information, and not to regard quantum mechanics simply as some exotic branch of calculation methodology. Understanding the underlying ontology behind quantum mechanics, Bohm felt, was a key to understanding the relationship between matter and consciousness, and here Bohm criticizes Bohr, the founder of quantum mechanics, who had won the Nobel Prize in 1913 for his quantum theory in modeling the hydrogen atom:

> Bohr's approach is to say nothing can be said about quantum mechanics at all other than to use it is a calculator, but my approach is to give it another appearance, more meaning. In the mechanical order it is hard to get much meaning.[470]

In the middle of his career as a theoretical physicist, Bohm's search for the underlying meanings to quantum theory was enriched through an introduction to a contemplative approach to the mind and consciousness expressed in the ideas of Jidu Krishnamurti. In 1961, while a professor of physics at Bristol University, Bohm attended a conference in London to hear a series of Krishnamurti lectures on perception, a topic that, as a quantum physicist, greatly interested Bohm. During the prior year, Bohm had become interested in theories of consciousness and perception expressed in the writings of philosophers and mystics, and had begun reading books on Yoga, Buddhism, and the work of the mathematician P. D. Ouspensky, a follower of the mystic G. I. Gurdjieff.[471] Public knowledge of his new interest resulted in further loss of credibility among Bohm's critics in the United States, as recounted here by his colleague and biographer, the physicist F. David Peat:

> When his former colleagues in the United States learned of this change of interest, it caused them considerable distress. In the years that followed, some lamented that Bohm had gone "off the rails," that a great mind had been sidetracked, and the work of an exceptional physicist was being lost to science.[472]

Bohm, however, was completely serious in his search for an understanding of quantum theory, even though the quest had led him into these areas of philosophy, psychology, and mysticism. Bohm's driving interest can be seen in the first paragraph of *The Undivided Universe: An Ontological Interpretation of Quantum Theory*, completed in 1992, only weeks before he suffered a fatal heart attack; here he expresses his passion to understand the mysteries that continue to lie behind quantum theory, rather than regarding the theory simply as something "which which we know how to use."

> The formalism of the quantum theory leads to results that agree with experiment with great accuracy and covers an extremely wide range of phenomena. As yet there are no experimental indications of any domain in which it might break down. Nevertheless, there still remain a number of basic questions concerning its fundamental significance which are obscure and confused. Thus for example one of the leading physicists of our time, M. Gell-Mann, has said "Quantum mechanics, that mysterious, confusing discipline, which

none of us really understands but which we know how to use."[473]

To understand Bohm's approach to quantum theory it is useful to examine their development in the context of the complexity of his life. Born in Pennsylvania in 1917, Bohm took an early interest in science, having become an avid reader of science fiction by the age of seven. After graduating in physics and receiving the school's Mathematics Prize from the University of Pennsylvania, he accepted a fellowship to enter graduate studies at Cal Tech. Within a year he found himself dissatisfied with the seemingly exclusive focus on problem solving at Cal Tech, a focus which seemed to discount Bohm's passion for seeking an understanding of what must be underlying ontological realities, favoring instead the development of mathematical models and their manipulation.[474] In 1941 Bohm met with J. Robert Oppenheimer at the University of California, Berkeley, having heard that in addition to being a brilliant theoretical physicist, the thirty-seven year old Oppenheimer encouraged wide ranging intellectual discussion among his grad students and postdoctoral researchers. Bohm soon after accepted a fellowship offer from Oppenheimer to study at Berkeley, and in 1941 Bohm moved from Los Angeles to begin graduate work in plasma research at Berkeley.[475]

After a year of intense collaboration with other physicists at the laboratory, often working more than sixty hours a week, Bohm gave his first presentation of the ideas he had thus far developed to model the complex nature of plasma, but early in the presentation, as he began to try to convey his new ideas to Oppenheimer and the rest of his committee, something unexpected occurred:

A naturally shy person, as he began to speak he nonetheless felt that everything was going extremely well. Soon he had the sensation that he was going beyond physics into something almost mystical, to the point where he felt himself in direct contact with everyone in the room. He was convinced that each individual consciousness had been transcended so that his audience was also sharing this experience. [476]

This intense feeling was overwhelming, leading immediately to a deep depression, and Bohm took a leave of absence, during which he was unable to work or study for almost an entire year.[477]

Even more problematical for Bohm during the first year of work on his dissertation under Oppenheimer was his growing interest in several activist antiwar groups, including the Committee for Peace Mobilization, the Campus Committee to Fight Conscription, and the Young Communist League, and "it was noted that Bohm had been involved in organizing activities for the Communist party and had distributed copies of Earl Browder's *Victory—and After*."[478] These associations and activities were later to haunt him.[479]

The Communist party in the United States had peaked at about 30,000 members in 1941, having grown steadily during the Great Depression due in part to the rapid growth of labor unions, but also because Communism was seen as a clear enemy of Fascism.[480] In November 1942, Bohm joined the Communist party in Berkeley, but membership was not particularly exciting or eventful, as Bohm later described to the historian Martin Sherwin during an interview: "The meetings were interminable, discussing all these boring attempts to stir up things on the campus which didn't amount to much."[481]

Back at Berkeley in 1943, Bohm completed his doctoral research project, an effort to develop a mathematical theory with which to model the dynamics of plasmas, a poorly understood phenomenon that greatly intrigued Bohm:

> As he studied the plasmas he became struck by their extraordinary nature. They began to take on, for him, the qualities of living beings. When physicists studied a plasma by introducing an electrical probe, it would generate a charged sheath around the probe and neutralize its effects. It was as if the plasma were protecting itself and preserving its internal status.[482]

Bohm completed his project, and the results were considered by Oppenheimer to be spectacular; the calculations that Bohm developed in his thesis were able to model accurately the behavior of uranium fluoride plasma in an electric arc, and led directly to an elegant technique for separating U^{235} from U^{238}, a critical step in the Oppenheimer's effort toward building a nuclear bomb.[483]

Unfortunately, shortly before the publication of his dissertation, Bohm's previous political activities caught up with him. It was suddenly apparent that his affiliation with Communism made it impossible for him to obtain a security clearance, while paradoxically the importance of his own dissertation for the war effort led to it being considered highly classified:

> The scattering calculations (of collisions of protons and deuterons) that he had completed proved useful to the Manhattan Project and were immediately classified. But without security clearance, Bohm was denied access to his own work; not only would he be barred from defending his thesis, he was not even allowed to publish his own thesis.[484]

Oppenheimer was accordingly forced to petition the University of California Regents to rule on an exception to academic policy in order to approve Bohm's doctoral dissertation without allowing it to be published. The Regents assented and Bohm was awarded his doctorate and permitted to remain working at the Lawrence Laboratory, where he continued to focus his intense intellect upon the behavior of plasma flow and the mathematics of flux movement.[485] Here in an interview, Bohm describes his early interests and work with Oppenheimer during the period 1943–1946:

> When I worked at the Lawrence Laboratory, after taking my PhD, I became very interested in the electron plasma. This is a dense gas of electrons that exhibits radically different behavior from the other, normal states of matter and it was a key to much of the work the laboratory was doing at the time. My insights sprang from the perception that the plasma is a highly organized system, which behaves as a whole. Indeed, in some respects, it's almost like a living being. I was fascinated with the question of how such organized collective behavior could go along with the almost complete freedom of movement of individual electrons. [486]

Unfortunately, Bohm's early flirtation with Communism made the suppression of his dissertation only the first of what would eventually be a series of challenges to his academic career. Nevertheless, in 1947 the young physicist was hired as an assistant professor by Princeton University. During the relocation to New Jersey, he found a room near campus, and soon met his neighbor, another Princeton professor, the 57-year-old Albert Einstein, who, like Bohm, objected to quantum mechanics for its "lack of an objective description."[487] Bohm's clarity on this topic was no doubt helped by the many discussions he had with Einstein in his days at Princeton.[488]

During his time at Princeton, Bohm also continued his research on the mathematics of plasma dynamics, while giving classes and public lectures on quantum mechanics, but he refused to accept the majority view which was, and remains to this day, a primary focus upon consistent mathematical calculations.

> For the majority of physicists, all that is needed is to work with the self-consistent mathematical formalism, which, in some mysterious way, correctly predicts the numerical results of actual experiments. But after lecturing on the subject for three years, Bohm thought that this was not a satisfactory position to adopt so he decided to try to get a better understanding of the subject by writing a definitive textbook in which the physical aspects of the mathematics would be emphasized.[489]

Bohm worked furiously in his spare time on this major textbook that was to be a full interpretation of quantum theory, grounded both in mathematics and conceptual clarifications, which he hoped would resolve major unanswered problems within the quantum theory.[490] He also began working on a reinterpretation of quantum theory in a paper of his own, which he called the "hidden variable theory." His textbook was published in 1951, and the paper in 1952, but in October 1951 Bohm fled the United States for Brazil, his reputation having been seriously affected by the politics of McCarthyism, and under the fear of being jailed for Contempt of Congress.[491]

In late 1949, while working on the final chapters of his book, Bohm had been served with a summons, a subpoena ordering him to appear before Senator Joseph McCarthy at the House Un-American Activities Committee. At the hearing, Bohm was asked to identify which of his previous numerous colleagues at Berkeley had been interested in Communism. Not wishing to incriminate his friends and colleagues, Bohm repeatedly had his attorney plead his "right to silence" under the Fifth Amendment to the United States Constitution. Notwithstanding, on December 4, 1950, Bohm was arrested at his home for Contempt of Congress, and though he made bail and was released, the administration at Princeton University peremptorily suspended him from "all teaching and other duties" for the duration of the trial.[492]

The publicity associated with the McCarthy hearings soon led to Bohm's dismissal from his position at Princeton, and subsequent inability to find employment in the United States. With letters of reference from Einstein and Oppenheimer, Bohm was offered a position in the physics department of the University of Saõ Paulo, the largest university in Brazil, then in the throes of development and expansion, during which had been seeking to attract a prominent quantum physicist from a mainstream American university.[493] Bohm decided to accept the position and prepared to make a hasty departure for Brazil, a day described here by his biographer:

> On the October day in 1951 when Bohm left the United States, thunderstorms and hurricane-force winds swept across New Jersey and New York. The flooded streets made it difficult for him to reach the airport . . . . On board the aircraft while taxiing to takeoff, he heard an announcement that the plane would return to the terminal because of an irregularity in the passport of one of the passengers. Already highly nervous, Bohm wondered if he was going to be arrested. The problem, however, concerned another passenger, who was removed from the flight.[494]

In December 1951, two months after his arrival in Brazil, the US consulate in São Paulo confiscated Bohm's passport, effectively stripping him of his US citizenship, and making it impossible for him to leave Brazil other than to return to the United States.[495]

Undeterred, with his passion for learning undiminished, Bohm continued to work, and he was soon fluent in self-taught Portuguese, sufficiently fluent to lecture at the University of São Paulo.[496] He was especially encouraged by favorable peer reviews of his recent US publication of *Quantum Theory*, a 646-page textbook interpreting quantum theory, and which begins in the first paragraph to emphasize the importance of familiarity with Fourier analysis:

> It seems impossible, however, to develop quantum concepts extensively without *Fourier analysis*. It is, therefore, presupposed that the reader is moderately familiar with Fourier analysis.[497]

Theory of Hidden Variables

But perhaps the greatest significance of *Quantum Theory* lies in the fact that Bohm presents, once again, but this time in a major text book, his theory of hidden variables: "Perhaps there are hidden variables that really control the exact time and place of a transfer of a quantum, and we simply haven't found them yet."[498] Einstein's major objection to the quantum theory was its almost complete lack of an objective description, and it was this that Bohm addressed in his new interpretation.[499]

At Princeton, Bohm and Einstein had agreed that there must be underlying processes yet to be discovered. Quantum mechanical calculations, while they work in the prediction of experimental evidence, treat particle actions collectively; in a similar way as taking temperature measurements are used to predict the motion of billions of gas molecules. In neither case can actual particle motion be mapped or predicted at the real dimensions being examined. Einstein and Bohm felt there must be principles that affect motion at a lower scale than that addressed by the collective mathematics of quantum mechanics (or temperature measurements).

This assumption has been the object of severe criticisms, notably on the part of Einstein, who has always believed that, even at the quantum level, there must exist precisely definable elements or dynamical variables determining (as in classical physics) the actual behavior of each individual system, and not merely its probable behavior . . . . The suggested interpretation provides a broader conceptual framework than the usual interpretation, because it makes possible a precise and continuous description of all process, even at the quantum level. This broader conceptual framework allows more general mathematical formulations of the theory than those allowed by the usual interpretation. Now, the usual mathematical formulation seems to lead to insoluble difficulties when it is extrapolated into the domain of distances of the order of 10^{-33} cm or less. It is therefore entirely possible that the interpretation suggested here may be needed for the resolution of these difficulties.[500]

In his paper on hidden variables can be seen Bohm's early fascination with the physics of the greatest depths of scale, far below the normal range at which even quantum mechanics is applied, down at distances of the Planck length (approximately 10^{-33} cm), a scale at which "classical notions such as causality or distance between events cannot be expected to be applicable."[501] The Planck constant is discussed in detail in Chapter 5.

Motion of "Particles" in Space-Time

Bohm explains apparent linear motion with an ontology derived from quantum theory when he speculates that, rather than manifesting as a solid, continuous particle in space–time, "the proton takes the form of a wave that collapses inward from all space," like a whirlpool in water.[502]

Similarly, in a conclusion that is contrary to the conventional assumption that electrons and protons are well-defined particles, Bohm describes the apparent motion of protons and electrons as:

> a continuous process of inward collapse and outward expansion. Therefore, every elementary particle collapses inward from the whole of space. In fact, each elementary particle is a manifestation of the whole universe.[503]

While his textbook on *Quantum Theory* was generally well received, and subsequently used in undergraduate courses on quantum mechanics worldwide for its clarity of language, analogy, and supporting calculus, the concept of *hidden variables*, described in the book and in his 1952 paper published exclusively on the "hidden variables" was pounced upon almost universally by quantum physicists, as being incompatible with the largely prevailing "Copenhagen interpretation."[504] In Copenhagen, during 1925 and 1927, Niels Bohr and two of his young students, Heisenberg and Pauli, at a series of meetings and conferences, both formal and informal, had developed what was later to be called the Copenhagen Interpretation of quantum mechanics, a conjectural descriptive explanation of what the working mathematical equations seemed to imply.[505] To most physicists, having worked under general agreement for over 20 years under the Copenhagen interpretation, Bohm's hidden variable theory was seen as being almost heretical, a direct challenge to the Copenhagen interpretation; yet from Bohm's point of view, it was the Copenhagen approach, with its heavy reliance on mathematical probability theory, that was random.[506] In this, Albert Einstein, Bohm's former neighbor, friend, and mentor at Princeton, can be seen in full agreement; Einstein is quoted here in a 1926 letter to Max Born, where he comments on the recently published Copenhagen interpretation, and expresses special concern regarding the deep reliance of probability theory in quantum mechanics:

> Quantum mechanics is certainly imposing. But an inner voice tells me that it is not yet the real thing. The theory says a lot, but does not really bring us any closer to the secret of the "old one." I, at any rate, am convinced that He does not throw dice.[507]

The prevailing consensus, in accord with the Copenhagen interpretation, holds that quantum events are indeterminate and discontinuous, and therefore the physics of process is not linearly predictable at quantum scales of matter, and that only probability mathematics works in predicting outcomes. Bohm opposed this axiom with his conviction that the process of the universe cannot be attributed to purely random statistical activity, but that there is an underlying order and comprehensive connectivity, a unity to the cosmos, a wholeness not predicted by mere probability theory.[508]

In his hidden variable theory, however, Bohm assumes the universe to be coherent and predictable, and considers the apparent randomness to be misleading, proposing instead that there must exist hidden variables operating at sub-quantum levels, hidden forces and processes operating at lower levels, below the currently assumed lower limit of matter, and not yet accessible with current instrumentation. Understandably, Bohm's new theory of hidden variables was immediately rejected by the community of physicists, in part for political reasons (Bohm's earlier communist affiliations), but primarily due to the firm attachment to the consensual acceptance of the Copenhagen interpretation and the predictable results proven by use of quantum mechanical calculations.[509]

At best, Bohm's new theory was ignored, but some went so far as to accuse him of being a Trotskyite and a traitor; one physicist termed Bohm's work "juvenile deviation," and another called Bohm "a public nuisance."[510] This strong reaction against Bohm's *hidden variable* hypothesis even led his own one-time supervisor, mentor, and hero, Robert Oppenheimer, to gather a meeting of physicists at Berkeley in 1953 with the objective of disproving Bohm's theory; the meeting closed with Oppenheimer being heard to say, "If we cannot disprove Bohm, we must continue to ignore him."[511]

In 1955, Bohm left Brazil to accept a position as a physics professor at the Israel Institute of Technology in Haifa, where he meets his future wife, Saral, an artist. In 1957 Bohm and Saral left Israel where Bohm accepted a position at Bristol University in England. In London, that same year, Bohm presented his mature version of the hidden variable concepts, which he had first begun to develop in 1952 in *Quantum Theory*. In his London paper Bohm introduced the idea of processes occurring at sub-quantum levels, operating at considerably smaller dimensions than those at which quantum mechanical calculations modeled the activity of atomic particles. This was the beginning of Bohm's conceptualization of the implicate order, through considering the possible ontological reality of dimensions far below the quantum dimensions being explored by quantum mechanics.

During his second year in England, Bohm presented a series of lectures at London University detailing his hidden variable theory; the lecture was attended by a young doctoral student in physics, John Bell, who had become interested in mathematical approaches to the nonlocality problem in quantum mechanics. Bell, encouraged by Bohm's theories, went on to develop a mathematical proof of nonlocality, a phenomenon that has since been verified several times in rigorous experiment.[512] It is of interest to note that Bell said, of Bohm's theory, "No one can understand this theory until he is willing to see psi as a real objective field rather than just a probability amplitude."[513]

Bohm did not limit his intellectual pursuit exclusively to physics. During his three years at Bristol University he began to read widely in areas of speculative philosophy and soon became acquainted with the process philosophy of Alfred North Whitehead (1861–1947), the Cambridge mathematician turned Harvard philosopher. One evening, according to Bohm, while reading *Process and Reality*, he experienced what seemed to be an epiphany, a visualization of infinity in the image of a large number of silvered spherical mirrors, each one reflecting all of the others, a cosmos composed of an infinity of reflections, and of reflections of reflections: "Every atom was reflecting in this way, and the infinity of these reflections was reflected in each thing; each was an infinite reflection of the whole." [514] The influence of this image can be found 20 years later in Bohm's understanding of what he had by then come to call, "the Implicate Order." The image of mirrors reflecting the whole is echoed in *Wholeness and the Implicate Order* in the following passage, which describes Bohm's concept of the holomovement:

> In certain ways this notion is similar to Leibniz's idea of monads, each of which "mirrors" the whole in its own way, some in great detail and others rather vaguely. The difference is that Leibniz's monads had a permanent existence, whereas our basic elements are only moments and are thus not permanent.[515]

At Bristol in the early 1960s, during his wide-ranging reading in philosophy and Eastern metaphysics, Bohm was introduced to the writings of the Russian mathematician P. D. Ouspensky, who had written several books on the metaphysics of the mystic G. I. Gurdjieff.[516] In 1962 Bohm managed to meet in London with J. G. Bennet, himself a mathematician as well as an authority on Gurdjieff; the two corresponded over the next several years, but "their connection was broken," as Bohm's biographer says, in a footnote:

> Bohm became increasingly critical of Gurdjieff's emphasis upon the essential separation of an observing consciousness. For Bohm there was a "total awareness" that lies beyond consciousness and is the field in which creativity operates.[517]

Krishnamurti and Meditation

It was also while at Bristol University that Bohm first became acquainted with the philosopher Jidu Krishnamurti. In the Bristol public library, Bohm's wife, Saral, discovered a book in the philosophy section discussing the topics of perception and thought, and brought it home as of possible interest. Bohm was immediately fascinated by what Krishnamurti had to say:

> My first acquaintance with Krishnamurti's work was in 1959 when I read his book *First and Last Freedom*. What particularly aroused my interest was deep insight into the question of the observer and the observed . . . I felt that it was urgent for me to talk with Krishnamurti directly and personally as soon as possible. And when I first met him on one of his visits to London, I was struck by the great ease of communication with him, which was made possible by the intense energy with which he listened and by the freedom from self-protective reservations and barriers with which he responded to what I had to say . . . it was in essence of the same quality as that which I had met in contacts with other scientists with whom there had been a very close meeting of minds. And here, I think especially of Einstein who showed a similar intensity and absence of barrier in a number

of discussions that took place between him and me. After this, I began to meet Krishnamurti regularly and to discuss with him whenever he came to London.[518]

In 1961, Bohm left Bristol University to accept the offer of Chair of Theoretical Physics, offered to him by J. D. Bernal, the head of the physics department (and a dedicated Marxist) at Birkbeck College, University of London. In that same year Bohm, for the first time, arranged a private conversation with Krishnamurti in London. The two continued their dialogues, at first privately, and then eventually in public venues, before audiences in London, Switzerland, and later in Ojai, California.[519]

In Switzerland in 1965, the first public recordings were made of a series of dialogues between Krishnamurti and Bohm. Undoubtedly Bohm's previous reading experience of Whitehead, Hegel, Ouspensky, and Indian philosophy had prepared him well for these flowing dialogues with Krishnamurti, and likely influenced his own conceptualizations. In addition to published books containing transcripts of many of these dialogues, numerous video and audio recordings have been released; a recent YouTube search on "Krishnamurti" and "Bohm" pulls up 32,000 results.[520]

It was in 1967, during the "Summer of Love," that Bohm and his wife, at the urging of Krishnamurti, both became vegetarians and took up the daily practice of meditation. Bohm was particularly interested in Krishnamurti's teaching on the process of "dying to thought" in which the physical brain no longer gives energy to the movement of thought process in the brain.[521] According to Krishnamurti, it is this incessant conditioned mental thought process that masks and conceals the silence within which the less conditioned consciousness process might be perceived, and within which new modes of "non-verbal thought" might operate. Bohm here describes his own understanding of Krishnamurti's teaching on the process of meditation:

> Krishnamurti has observed that the very act of meditation will, in itself, bring order to the activity of thought without the intervention of will, choice, decision, or any other action of the "thinker." As such order comes, the noise and chaos which are the usual background of our consciousness die out, and the mind becomes generally silent . . . . In this silence, Krishnamurti says that something new and creative happens, something that cannot be conveyed in words, but that is of extraordinary significance for the whole of life. So he does not attempt to communicate this verbally, but rather, he asks of those who are interested that they explore the question of meditation directly for themselves.[522]

It is easy to imagine how Bohm's exceptional, trained capability (as a theoretical physicist) for focus on abstractions served to reinforce his growing capabilities in the practice of formless meditation. Bohm soon established a daily period in the early morning during which he would walk slowly in the park or countryside while watching the movement of this thoughts, not allowing himself to become distracted or "caught up" in their content; this practice continued throughout his life.[523]

The Implicate Order

It is of interest to note that within two years of beginning his daily meditation walk, Bohm conceptualized a significantly new idea, the "implicate order," which ontologically strengthened his hidden variables theory. By 1969 the subjects of topology, nonlocality, and pre-space had come to the forefront of discussion within the physics department at the

University of London, and as his colleague, the physicist B. J. Hiley recalls, Bohm had a breakthrough in his understanding: "Suddenly, a new idea emerged from Bohm, apparently entirely out of the blue . . . Bohm called it the *implicate order*."[524]

Bohm identified this implicate order as being the source of the hidden, sub-quantum variables which he hypothesized were providing the causality underlying the operation of quantum mechanics, and he began an effort to model the effect of the implicate order mathematically.[525] In 1925, Werner Heisenberg (1901–1976) had taken a similar view:

> Heisenberg, who at age twenty-four, was young even by physics standards, tried to save classical mechanics by abandoning it at Nature's bottom rung. Inside the atom, he declared, not only do particles and electron orbits have no meaning, but neither do even such basic classical properties as position, momentum, velocity, and space and time. And because our imaginations require a space–time container, this atomic world cannot be easily pictured.[526]

But Heisenberg's approach fell by the wayside when the Copenhagen approach proved so successful in predictive calculations of nuclear particle trajectories using probabilities. Decades later, Bohm pursued alone a similar idea, and in 1980 published *Wholeness and the Implicate Order*, in which is revealed both the mathematics and a mature conceptual model for his proposed implicate order, a model based not on "things" considered as objects, nor restricted solely to phenomena in a Cartesian space–time order, but rather modeling a lens-like flowing of simultaneous enfolding and unfolding dimensions between two orders, an implicate order and an explicate order, as Bohm explained:

There is the germ of a new notion of order here. This order is not to be understood solely in terms of a regular arrangement of *objects* . . . . Rather, a *total order* is contained, in some *implicit* sense, in each region of space and time. Now, the word "implicit" is based on the verb "to implicate." This means, "to fold inward." So we may be led to explore the notion that in some sense each region contains a total structure "enfolded" within it.[527]

Bohm went so far as to describe the implicate order as the ground within which the entire universe is enfolded at each and every "point" in space–time, as the Finnish philosopher Paavo Pylkkänen, a former student and friend of Bohm's, explains clearly:

Just think of all the atoms and particles that constitute your body. We are used to thinking about them as tiny little things that just passively sit there. But quantum field theory, as interpreted by Bohm, suggests otherwise. There is a sense in which each particle in your body enfolds information about the whole universe . . . . There is also a sense in which information about each particle in your body is enfolded throughout the universe.[528]

However, Bohm's focus of interest clearly ranged beyond the conventional boundaries of physics, into theories of mind, thought, and consciousness. It is easy to conclude that Bohm's dialog with Krishnamurti influenced the expansion of this focus, bringing to the forefront for Bohm issues of thinking and mind. But with his deep understanding of quantum theory, Bohm was able to see a direct connection between thought, consciousness, and the implicate order, as can be discerned in his description of the thinking process, recorded in a 1990 interview:

234

And that's how the thinking process goes, it's enfolded in your consciousness, it unfolds to a certain thought, folds back, and then the next thought appears, different; a series of thoughts not too different seems to be continuous.[529]

In imagining this process as an "enfoldment," we are led to the obvious next question, "Enfoldment into what?" And Bohm's non-Cartesian answer then, is enfoldment *into something within*, enfoldment into the implicate order. How then might this be conceptualized? Imagine the universe at the lowest possible spatial range. Moving to ever-smaller dimensions, to the very bottom of the dimensional scale, we encounter the end of space, according to accepted quantum theory, at a limiting length, below which length has no meaning.[530] Thus this implicate order, located at the center, everywhere, can be seen as the ground, base, or center out of which dynamically springs the space–time continuum itself, the explicate order.

The Sub-Quantum Order

Bohm applied the term "sub-quantum order" to that order of physics which he viewed as expressing the underlying causal reality *from which* quantum mechanics operates, calling this approach "going beyond the quantum theory."[531] While quantum mechanical theory works well for predicting the path of nuclear particles in dimensional ranges around 10^{-15} meters, the theory places a heavy insistence on pure probability considerations, and this randomness had always bothered Bohm. As early as 1952, in his textbook, *Quantum Theory,* Bohm states:

We have come to the point of view that the wavefunction is an abstraction, providing a mathematical reflection of certain aspects of reality, but not a one-to-one mapping.[532]

He further argues that the ontological cause is to be discovered at lower levels, below quantum mechanical dimensions, and that "quantum theory is inconsistent with the assumption of hidden causal variables" governing processes at the lowest, sub-quantum levels.[533] At the end of the Introduction to his 1993 book, Bohm predicts the failure of the "current laws of physics" at the Planck length:

> The idea is that there will be a stochastic sub-quantum and sub-relativistic level in which the current laws of physics will fail. This will probably first be encountered near the Planck length of 10^{-33} cm . . . . This idea is connected with our ontological interpretation by means of a model of a particle as a sequence of incoming and outgoing waves, with successive waves very close to each other . . . . One of the main new ideas implied by this approach is that the geometry and the dynamics have to be in the same framework, i.e. that of the implicate order.[534]

This leads us to the observation that there exist three sets of framework-dependent mathematical models, applicable in three ranges: (1) Newtonian mechanics, operating at human dimensions, in the 10^0 meter range, (2) quantum mechanics, operating at nuclear particle dimensions, in the 10^{-15} meter range, and (3) Bohm's "hidden variables," operating at the boundary of space–time, in the 10^{-35} meter range. Here Bohm reiterates an observation he had previously made regarding the important significance of the dimension 1.616×10^{-33} cm, the Planck length, and designated with the symbol ℓ_P in quantum theoretical calculations.[535] Over a decade earlier, in a 1980 publication, *Wholeness and the Implicate Order*, Bohm, in discussing the calculation of what is called "the zero-point energy" for point in space, provides another explanation for the significance of this 10^{-33} cm distance:

> We come to a certain length at which the measurement of space and time becomes totally indefinable. Beyond this, the whole notion of space and time as we know it would fade out, into something that is at present unspecifiable . . . . When this length is estimated it turns out to be about 10^{-33} cm. This is much shorter than anything thus far probed in physical experiments (which have gone down to about 10^{-17} cm or so). If one computes the amount of energy that would be in one cubic centimeter of space, with this shortest possible wavelength, it turns out to be very far beyond the total energy of all the matter in the known universe.[536]

It is here then, in the region of the Planck length at 10^{-33} cm, that Bohm predicts that there will be found *a boundary* separating an outer, *explicate order* from an inner, *implicate order*. There will also be seen gaps of, at minimum, 10^{-33} cm between each and every concentric shell that might be surrounding the central area, a spherical locus of Planck length diameter ℓ_p. This is in accord with the founding quantum theory of Max Planck (1858–1947), first published in 1900, in which he proposed that a photon could have only distinct, fixed energy states, separated by integers, which he termed "quanta."[537] Bohm uses such quantum theoretical considerations to point out a fallacy still held by many, the classical Cartesian assumption that space is continuous:

> What of the order between two points in space? The Cartesian order holds that space is continuous. Between any two points, no matter how close they lie, occur an infinite of other points. Between any two neighboring points in this infinity lies another

infinity and so on. This notion of continuity is not compatible with the order of quantum theory. . . . Thus the physicist John Wheeler has suggested that, at very short distances, continuous space begins to break up into a foam-like structure. Thus the "order between" two points moves from the order of continuity to an order of a discontinuous foam.[538]

According to Bohm, at the ultimate bottom level of these subdivided infinities, between two points in space, like an end-of-stop bumper terminating a railroad track, will be found a cosmologically fixed boundary at the Planck length of 10^{-33} cm, beyond which no further subdivision is meaningfully possible. It is here, at this smallest of possible spatial coordinates, that we encounter the origin of the dimension of space that finds its maximum in the diameter of the currently expanding universe (the bandwidth continually increasing, at the speed of light).

Viewed another way, to use the depths of the ocean as a metaphor (Fig. 33), Bohm's region of sub-quantum mechanics can be viewed as being at the bottom of a dimensional ocean with a floor significantly below the depths of the region mapped and explored by the mathematics of quantum mechanics or the measurements of Newton.

The image reveals three ranges along the vertical (depth) axis: (1) classical Newtonian physics, (2) Quantum physics, and (3) Bohmian physics. The laws and relationships governing each of these three approaches to physical reality is only operational within a distinct scalar ranges, with the entire range separated by over 10^{15} orders of magnitude.

In a real sense, Bohm was plumbing this depth of dimensional physics, far below the level at which conventional quantum theory is applied, at depths of scale considerably below those of the dimensions of a Monarch butterfly wingspan, a uranium atom nucleus, a proton, or a calculated electron (photon) diameter.

238

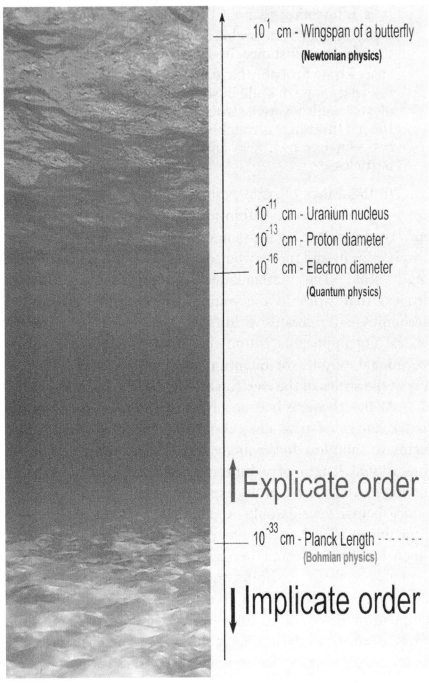

Figure 33. *Sub-quantum ocean floor metaphor.*[539].
Bohm comments on the depths of this range:

It is interesting to note that between the shortest distance now measurable in physics (10^{-16} cm) and the shortest distance in which current notions of space–time probably have meaning (10^{-33} cm), there is a vast range of scale in which an immense amount of yet undiscovered structure could be contained. Indeed this range is roughly equal to that which exists between our own size and that of the elementary particles.[540]

In this range of scales, quantum mechanics is a "thing" that is applicable only within a limited, intermediate range, halfway down the scale, somewhere between the human biosphere scale and the very bottom of space–time at the Planck length scale. The mathematical models (and operational physics) that work in one range (for example, Newtonian mechanics as it operates within the human body parts) are in general not applicable within the other ranges (such as the operational physics of quantum mechanics, which operates only at the scales of the electron and proton.

At the absolute bottom of Fig. 33's ocean floor lies the Planck length of 10^{-33} cm., above which the explicate order begins to manifest increasingly larger scale ranges until the dimensional length of a butterfly (about 1 cm) is reached, floating on the surface of the explicate order's scale. Of course, a more inclusive scale would expand upwards to include the size of the universe, with a diameter of 10^{26} meters, and the human dimensional range would then be seen to lie approximately half way between these two limits, the size of the universe (10^{26} m) and the Planck length (10^{-35} m).[541] Fig. 34 shows such a complete range of scales, from the maximum diameter of the universe (currently expanding at the speed of light) down to the Planck length where space ends and the implicate order begins.

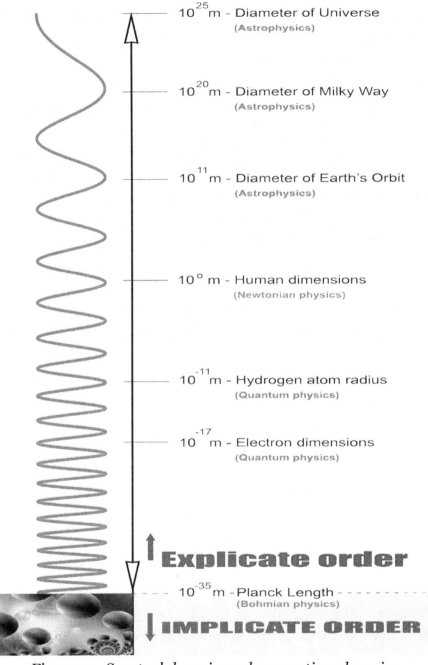

10^{25} m - Diameter of Universe
(Astrophysics)

10^{20} m - Diameter of Milky Way
(Astrophysics)

10^{11} m - Diameter of Earth's Orbit
(Astrophysics)

10^{0} m - Human dimensions
(Newtonian physics)

10^{-11} m - Hydrogen atom radius
(Quantum physics)

10^{-17} m - Electron dimensions
(Quantum physics)

Explicate order

10^{-35} m - Planck Length
(Bohmian physics)

IMPLICATE ORDER

Figure 34. *Spectral domain and space–time domain.*

Another foundation upon which Bohm's model of the universe grew can be seen in his vision of an endless infinity of ordered fields, as he describes here:

> We may suppose that the universe, which includes the whole of existence, contains not only all the fields that are now known, but also an indefinitely large set of further fields that are unknown and indeed may never be known in their totality. Recalling that the essential qualities of fields exist only in their movement we propose to call this ground the *holomovement*. It follows that ultimately everything in the explicate order of common experience arises from the holomovement. Whatever persists with a constant form is sustained as the unfoldment of a recurrent and stable pattern, which is constantly being renewed by enfoldment, and constantly being dissolved by unfoldment. When the renewal ceases the form vanishes.[542]

Fields need not exist only within space–time. Einstein's theory of general relativity posits ten fields to describe the movement of gravity in four dimensions.[543] As early as 1919 a German mathematician, Theodor Kaluza, sent Einstein a paper proposing an extremely small fifth dimension in which additional frequency and phase fields could provide a solution to resolve Einstein's struggle to resolve the connection between gravity and electromagnetism.[544] In 1926 the Swedish physicist Oskar Klein "drawing on quantum mechanics, calculated the size of this compact dimension, arriving at a number that was tiny indeed—around 10^{-30} cm in circumference."[545] The theory became known as the Kaluza-Klein theory, offering the potential of extra fields in an additional dimension as a promising approach to resolving Einstein's search to connect gravity and electromagnetism. Einstein wrote to Kaluza, saying he liked the idea "enormously" and in fact continued working with the theory for the next 20 years; ultimately, however, the Kaluza-Klein theory was discarded because of its prediction of a particle so small that it could not be proven to exist using any foreseeable technology.[546]

But by the same token it has also been impossible to *disprove* a cosmological reality existing at such small dimensions, and it is here, at the limiting space–time scale of 10^{-33} cm, that Bohm hypothesizes the *implicate order*.[547] Diagrammed in Fig. 35 is Bohm's implicate order to the left, in the frequency domain, and Bohm's explicate order to the right, in the space–time domain, dynamically linked in a mathematical pattern called the Fourier Transform.

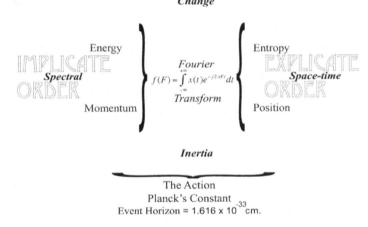

Figure 35. *The implicate/explicate order transform.*

This connecting Fourier transform function describes the reciprocal flow of radiating information between the implicate order and the explicate order. This is a two-way flow which operating at an event horizon, the Planck limit of 10^{-33} cm (or if measured in meters, 10^{-35} m), in a process which Bohm terms the "holomovement," and which, he tells us, is grounded in the implicate order:

The implicate order has its ground in the holomovement which is vast, rich, and in a state of unending flux of enfoldment and unfoldment, with laws most of which are only vaguely known, and which may even be ultimately unknowable in their totality . . . . Nevertheless, the overall law (holonomy) may be assumed to be such that in a certain sub-order, within the whole set of the implicate order, there is a totality of forms that have an approximate kind of recurrence, stability, and separability. Evidently these forms are capable of appearing as the relatively solid, tangible, and stable elements that make up our "manifest world."[548]

Holomovement and Holoflux

In 1978 Bohm discusses these concepts with remarkable clarity during a Harvard conference on "Science and Mysticism: Exploring the New Realities." After his presentation, which he called, "The Implicate Order: The Holodynamic Model of the Universe," Bohm was interviewed by Renée Weber for *ReVision* magazine, and here he expresses the difference between holography and the holomovement, and introduces the term "holoflux":

> **Weber**: Could we begin by clarifying the difference between the holomovement, the holograph and the implicate order?
>
> **Bohm**: Holomovement is a combination of a Greek and Latin word and a similar word would be holokinesis or, still better, *holoflux*, because "movement" implies motion from place to place, whereas flux does not. So the *holoflux* includes the ultimately flowing nature of what is, and of that which forms therein. The holograph, on the other hand, is merely a static recording of movement, like a still photograph: an abstraction from the holomovement. We therefore cannot regard the

holograph as anything very basic, since it is merely a way of displaying the holomovement, which latter is, however, the ground of everything, of all that is. The implicate order is the one in which the holomovement takes place, an order that both enfolds and unfolds. Things are unfolded in the implicate order, and that order cannot be entirely expressed in an explicate fashion. Therefore, in this approach, we are not able to go beyond the holomovement or the *holoflux* (the Greek word might be holorhesis, I suppose) although that does not imply that this is the end of the matter.[549]

Bohm hypothesizes that consciousness must operate dynamically in a holonomic fashion, driven by a quantum potential wave, and that the information guiding motion in space–time must originate from ano*ther order*, the implicate order, which lies outside of the commonly perceived explicate order of the space–time domain.[550] From early in his career, Bohm had tried to visualize the motion of quantum "particles," not moving in linear sequential tracks as viewed in a cloud chamber, but as oscillating in and out of space–time.[551]

Bohm, here in a 1990 interview recorded for a Dutch television, not only proceeds to describe this movement or "holomovement" as *superseding* the so-called "particle" phenomena of quantum mechanics, but in doing so, he emphasizes the reality of the whole, the *continuum of mind and matter*, and discusses the general implications of this for perception:

> **Bohm**: Now, I saw that you could understand the quantum mechanics in terms of that process. That instead of saying an electron, for example, is a particle just moving along, you could think that there is a wave coming in, enfolding, or it's really unfolding at a point, it's enfolded in the whole universe. Then it folds back. Then another wave comes in, at a slightly

different point. You get a series of points that are very close together so we imagine they're a particle, right? But, because of that wave nature, from which it comes, you understand, the wave/particle nature, that is, it's a wave.[552]

Support for this view is found in an interpretation of holodynamics put forth by a consciousness researcher at UC Irvine, Gordon Globus, who describes Bohm's holodynamic process as follows:

> There are two primary phases of this holodynamics according to Bohm: *implication* and *explication* . . . . Implication is the "enfolding" of world to the whole and explication is the cotemporaneous "unfolding" of world from the whole. Each moment of unfolding/enfolding has a brief duration . . . . The world is explicate order continually unfolded from implicate order, rather than explicate order persisting.[553]

And what then might be the temporal rate of such an oscillation or "brief duration" of unfolding of the world in space–time? Here again it is the Planck constant that sets the limiting boundary condition. The Planck second, or "Planck time," calculated to be 5.44×10^{-44} seconds, is the smallest conceivable time interval consistent with quantum theory, and below this interval time has no meaning. If indeed time is granulated at such a limit, then the cosmos may be created, destroyed, and recreated a staggering number of times per "human second." In the limiting case, space–time reality can be seen to emerge from an implicate order into an explicate order, from flux into space–time, at a recurring clock cycle every 5.44×10^{-44} seconds, only to collapse out space-time and back into the implicate order in alternate intervals between each of these sub-quantum clock cycles. Such a cyclic pattern of unfolding potential accords well with Bohm's description of the holomovement here, in a 1990 paper:

> All things found in the unfolded, explicate order emerge from the holomovement in which they are enfolded as *potentialities*, and ultimately they fall back into it. They endure only for some time, and while they last, their existence is sustained in a constant process of unfoldment and re-enfoldment, which gives rise to their relatively stable and independent forms in the explicate order.[554]

Meaning, Form, and Information

In developing an appreciation for the ontological and cosmological implications of quantum theory, Bohm discovered great importance in maintaining a clear distinction regarding three terms: meaning, form, and information.

He describes the essential significance of form as being the conveyor and shipping container of embedded meaning:

> What is essential for a form to constitute information is that it shall have a meaning . . . . The form in the radio wave thus literally "informs" the energy in the received . . . this form is then *transformed* ("form carried across") into related forms of sound and light.[555]

How then is the meaning unpacked from the shipping container? How is information related to meaning? Bohm says that for information to become meaning requires, specifically, what Bohm terms "Active Information."[556]

> The basic idea of active information is that a *form*, having very little energy, enters into and directs a much greater energy. This notion of an original energy form acting to "inform," or put form into, a

much larger energy has significant applications in many areas beyond quantum theory.[557]

For Bohm, active information is the state in which a receiving energy is informed by the *form* of a transmitted energy, the receiving energy is "in-formed." Here he gives as an example a radio wave of electromagnetic energy being "in-formed"

> In the radio wave, the form is initially inactive, but as the form enters into the electrical energy of the receiver, we may say, that the information becomes active. In general, this information is only potentially active in the radio wave, but it becomes actually active only when and where there is a receiver which can respond to it with its "own energy."[558]

Bohm goes on to say that the operation of active information can be detected in nature outside of the human context, and can be seen, for example in the action of RNA as it decodes information locked in the form of DNA:

> It is assumed that the DNA molecule constitutes a code (i.e. a language), and that the RNA molecules "read" this code, and are thus in effect "informed" as to what kind of proteins they are to make.[559]

Finally, Bohm identifies the *activity* of the energy in the receiving entity as the *meaning*, (i.e., the active information flow *is* the meaning):

> I would like to suggest then that the activity, virtual or actual, in the energy and in the soma *is* the meaning of the information, rather than to say that the information affects an entity called the mind, which in turn operates somehow on the matter of the body.[560]

What Bohm is implying here is that perhaps there is, in actuality, no "thing" that can be called mind, that there is no "entity called the mind," but that, rather, it is the *active information* itself, sourced in the implicate domain, that is informing the region of the explicit domain, directly. Bohm concludes:

> The thinking process unfolds certain explicate thoughts, then folds back into the implicate, and then the next thought appears, the entire process forming a series of thoughts, which, seeming not too different, appear to be flowing in a continuous stream.[561]

Active Information and the Quantum Potential

To better understand "active information," imagine that from each Planck length diameter "point" or "holosphere" in the universe (but outside of space–time) radiating waves of information encoded energy emerge from the implicate domain at the center, radiating outward into space–time in expanding shells. Active information, like conceptual thought, does not need to be of great magnitude to be the effective cause of relatively large orders of magnitude of effect in the explicate domain. An example given by Bohm is the action of a tiny electrical signal that guides the flight of a large ship, airplane, or missile in flight. Here he provides a common example of how, even in the explicate world, a source of active information, comprising relatively minute quantities of energy, can effectively influence a receiver operating at considerably higher energy levels:

> As an example, let us take a radio wave, whose form carries information representing either sound or pictures. The radio wave itself has very little energy. The receiver, however, has a much greater energy (e.g. from the power source). The structure of the

radio is such that the form carried by the radio wave is imposed on the much greater energy of the receiver.[562]

Here Bohm claims that it is not the magnitude of energy that is important for active information to be effective, but *only the form itself,* guiding larger sources of energy in the explicate system. Bohm developed his mathematics of active information by deriving a potential function directly from the Schrödinger equation in quantum mechanics, and designating it as Q, the "quantum potential":[563]

> As time went on, Bohm emphasized the role played by the quantum potential. The quantum potential— whose influence depends on its overall form and not on its strength—is totally unlike anything previously postulated in physics.[564]

In order to prove that there is *real* causation acting in quantum mechanics, rather than accepting the commonly held theory that it is all probability and stochastic process, Bohm proposed that a quantum potential (Q) also acts upon quantum particles such as electrons and protons and states that this Q function

> expresses the activity of a new kind of implicate order. This implicate order is immensely more subtle than that of the original field, as well as more inclusive, in the sense that not only is the actual activity of the whole field enfolded in it, but also all its potentialities, along with the principles determining which of these shall become actual.[565]

Bohm derives the quantum potential mathematically by taking derivatives of quantum mechanical Hamiltonian models of particle motion to give the following equation for the quantum potential.[566]

$$Q = \frac{-\hbar^2 \, \nabla^2 \, |\psi|^2}{2m \, |\psi|^2}$$

Equation of the Quantum Potential.[567]

In Bohm's equation of the quantum potential (Q) of active information, the function ψ is the quantum field or "wavefunction" derived from Schrödinger's equation, $\hbar$ is Planck's constant, and m is the mass of the electron or "particle."[568] The symbol ∇ is called a "curl," and this symbol indicates an infinitesimal rotation of multidimensional coordinates (usually three or more) around a common origin, in order to obtain the differential motion of the wave in space–time. Bohm here points out what appears to be of special importance:

> what is mathematically significant in the above equation is that the wavefunction is found in both the numerator and the denominator . . . . The fact that ψ is contained both in the numerator and the denominator for Q means that Q is unchanged when ψ is multiplied by an arbitrary constant. In other words, the quantum potential Q is *independent of the strength, or intensity,* of the quantum field but *depends only on its form.* This is a particularly surprising result.[569]

Of great significance for Bohm is that fact that Q, the quantum potential, is seen to be independent of strength, or signal energy magnitude. This provides support for his insistence on causality, by implying that there is a formal cause, independent of magnitude, below the postulated randomness that is otherwise implied by the probabilistic calculations of quantum mechanics, and here Bohm concludes:

"In the causal interpretation, the electron moves under its own energy, but the information in the *form* of the quantum wave directs the energy of the electron."[570]

This can be visualized in the figure below, (Fig. 36, "Active Information and the Quantum Wave"), in which the function Q, sourced in the implicate order, molds or in-forms the quantum wave ψ in the explicate order. Here the metaphor of waves influencing the course of a ship is applicable.

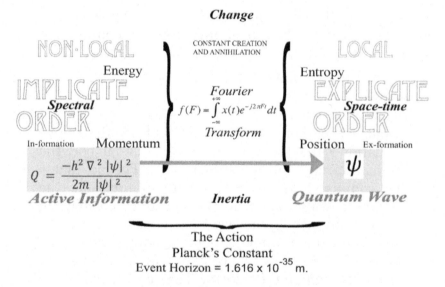

Figure 36. *Active Information and the Quantum Wave.*

In fact, a "pilot wave theory" similar to Bohm's active information model was proposed by de Broglie in 1927, though his idea was immediately criticized by the skeptical Wolfgang Pauli for being untestable.[571] In consequence, de Broglie abandoned his suggestion in favor of probability theory, but some years later Bohm brought up the idea again when he published, in 1952, "A Suggested Interpretation of the Quantum Theory in Terms of 'Hidden Variables.'"[572]

In the figure, the Active Information function can be seen to be guiding the Quantum Wavefunction. Bohm here provides another example of *form* as active information in everyday human experience:

> It is clear, of course, that the notion of active information also applies directly to human experience. For example, when the form of a road sign is apprehended in the brain and nervous system, the form is immediately active as meaning.[573]

But not all information is active, and Bohm refers to information which is not active as *virtual information,* "the activity of meaning may be only virtual, rather than actual. Virtual activity is more than a mere potentiality . . . it is a kind of suspended action."[574] And until it is made explicate as active information, this virtual information exists only in the implicate domain.

Indeed, Bohm's logic leads him to the conclusion that consciousness, at least of the nonactive kind, is of, or resides "within," the implicate order (though, of course, the word "within" has no clear meaning for the spaceless, timeless implicate order.) And while he speaks of the actual "substance" of consciousness as residing primarily in the implicate order, he sees the ranges of "human experience" of consciousness residing in reality as a whole, in a continuum of the implicate/explicate orders:

> In some sense, consciousness (which we take to include thought, feeling, desire, will, etc.) is to be comprehended in terms of the implicate order, along with reality as a whole . . . the actual "substance" of consciousness can be understood in terms of the notion that the implicate order is also its primary and immediate actuality.[575]

Bohm goes on to point out that some forms of information *from within* the implicate order are perceived, or can be perceived, by modes of consciousness in the explicate order: "Evidently this order is *active* in the sense that it continually flows into emotional, physical, and other responses." And here he provides as an example, music: "In listening to music, *one is therefore directly perceiving an implicate order.*"[576] But it is not only in listening to music that consciousness resonates in the implicate order, but also in ordinary, everyday experience, as Bohm says, perhaps even further:

> A great deal of our difficulty comes from the fact that we accept the idea that not only matter, but all of our experience as well, is in the explicate order, and then suddenly we want to connect this up with consciousness, which is of a totally different order . . . we should consider the nature of ordinary, everyday experience. I say that it is totally misunderstood, that it is actually part of the implicate order . . . in that order everything contacts everything else and thus there is no intrinsic reason why the paranormal should be impossible.[577]

In a 1978 interview at the Krishnamurti center in Ojai, by which time Bohm had been practicing meditation for over a decade, Bohm comments on distinctions between different modes of consciousness, and how it may be possible to experience the implicate order as a mode of consciousness which is timeless:

> **Question**: When mystics use the visualization of light they don't use it only as a metaphor, to them it seems to be a reality. Have they tapped into matter and energy at a level where time is absent?

Bohm: It may well be. That's one way of looking at it. As I've suggested the mind has two-dimensional and three-dimensional modes of operation. It may be able to operate directly in the depths of the implicate order where this timeless state is the primary actuality. Then we could see the ordinary actuality as a secondary structure that emerges as an overtone on the primary structure . . . . The ordinary consciousness is one kind of music, and the other kind of consciousness is the other kind of music.[578]

The Sense of "I" and the Implicate Order

Bohm argues that none of this indicates that consciousness and the world of matter are absolutely separate, as assumed by Cartesian dualists. Consciousness and matter form a continuum, a whole, as Bohm says here in the final words of his last book, *The Undivided Universe*, and he uses the metaphor of a mirror:

> At no stage is there a break in this process . . . . There is no need, therefore, to regard the observer as basically separate from what he sees, nor to reduce him to an epiphenomenon of the objective process. Indeed, the notion of separateness is an abstraction and an approximation valid for only certain limited purposes. More broadly one could say that through the human being, *the universe is making a mirror to observe itself* . . . . All proposals are points of departure for exploration. Eventually some of them may be developed so far that we may take them as working hypotheses.[579]

Here it may be useful to examine the conception of dualism versus monism. In Fig. 37, "Dualism vs. Monism," Cartesian dualism, denoted to the left, contrasts with three positions of Monism; Bohm's "neutral monism" can be seen in the lower right on the diagram, where matter and mind are both shown as derivative (both are in Bohm's explicate order of space–time), while the fundamental "3rd substance" would be Bohm's implicate order.

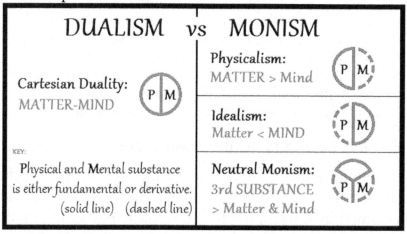

Figure 37. *Dualism vs. monism*. Graphic by Dewynne (2012). Reprinted under the terms of a Creative Commons CC0 1.0 Universal Public Domain Dedication. Image retrieved from Wikimedia Commons.

In an interview videotaped in Amsterdam in September of 1990, by the Dutch Public Television Network, Bohm discusses the phenomenon of the sense of Self, that sense that individuals have of being "I," and in his interview he states clearly that this sense of self is a *product* of thought, and not the real situation. Rather, he points to the implicate order as being the source of deeper reality, as being the true "I," "the Me" which we all assume to be so very unique:

> **Bohm**: Remember, thought is conditioned reflex at a very high subtle level. It just goes by itself, but it has in it the thought that thought is being produced by a center, which it calls "Me." And all the feelings, which should belong to that center, are thrown onto Consciousness as if from "Me," right?
>
> **Interviewer**: And our society reinforces that.

Bohm: Everybody says the same thing, like everybody sees the same rainbow, everybody sees the same "Self," whether it's there or not.

In fact, it becomes all-important, the concept is regarded as central and supremely important. All sorts of powerful feelings will arise if it's questioned. You see, now, it all goes on by itself...and, you see... ...there's a deeper being, I say, which can...which is...that being which may be able to reveal itself anew...rather than being a fixed being...it's deep in the Implicate Order...in the Infinite.

Interviewer: So, thought creates "the Me," rather than "Me" creating the thought?

Bohm: Yes. If you don't see that happening, you will treat that as real and give it apparent reality. The whole being will take actions on that basis which seems to be coming from the center.[580]

The Whole: Cosmology and Consciousness

Bohm's interest in what he frequently termed "the Whole" went beyond what virtually all physicists normally consider to be the "cosmological whole" (i.e., the space-time universe within which experiments can be conducted). Bohm sought to understand the structure and dynamics of a greater whole, which not only includes the four dimensions of space-time phenomena, but *all eleven dimensions* predicted by Edward Witten's "M-theory," including the dimension of consciousness itself.[581]

Bohm was forthright in his inclusion of consciousness as an important aspect of his cosmology. According to Bohm there is a two-phase reciprocal movement or holomovement at the boundary of (between) the implicate order and the explicate order,[582] and in a 1978 interview, he states unequivocally, "Let me propose that consciousness is basically *in* the implicate order."[583]

In the closing words of his final published work, Bohm reifies his proposal that consciousness and quantum mechanics are connected, that "they have the implicate order in common."[584]

> Several physicists have already suggested that quantum mechanics and consciousness are closely related and that the understanding of the quantum formalism requires that ultimately we bring in consciousness in some role or other . . . the intuition that consciousness and quantum theory are in some sense related seems to be a good one . . . . Our proposal in this regard is that the basic relationship of quantum theory and consciousness is that they have the implicate order in common.[585]

Bohm's Waves for All Points

David Bohm saw a similar process underlying what proponents of quantum mechanics theorized to be simply "quantum jump" of energy, and here in an interview, he describes the reality as waves coming in to a point and waves coming out of a point, for all points in the holoplenum:

> **Angelos**: Could we... Again, the term "quantum" itself has its base in?
>
> **Bohm**: Well, the "quantum"... That's one of the features of "quantum"... The quantum has its base in the fact that energy is transferred in discrete jumps or "quanta" rather than continuously...
>
> **Angelos**: I see.
>
> **Bohm**: Now, you can see that some sort of quantum appears here... the wave comes to a point, then there

is a jump to another point. See one thing—according to quantum theory—was that the electron could go from one state to another without passing in between. Now you said: That is an utter mystery, right? But you see, if the wave comes in to this point... then it spreads out... it could come in to another point. So, therefore, it needn't look so mysterious.[586]

To more fully grasp the relationship of consciousness to the implicate order and the explicate order, two visual metaphors are now considered: the metaphor of the micro black hole, and the metaphor of the Yin/Yang symbol.

Metaphor of the Quantum Black Hole

It is appropriate here to use the image of a quantum black hole as a visual metaphor for realizing the topology of the implicate order.

> Micro black holes, which have also been called quantum mechanical black holes, quantum black holes, or mini black holes, are hypothetical tiny black holes .... It is possible that such quantum primordial black holes were created in the high-density environment of the early Universe (or Big Bang). [587]

Visualizing the implicate order as a micro black hole, we can perhaps view its boundary as a spherical event-horizon shell, marking the limits of an "external," explicate order and the outer limits of an "internal," implicate order. Below the surface of such a sphere, of diameter equal to the Planck length, lies a transcendental implicate order, while outside the quantum black hole begins a universe of the explicate order, replete with time and space.

With this image in mind, it is appropriate here to review the topological understanding of a "point." The conventional definition of a point is a mathematical one, that it has no diameter at all, or that it is a sort of sphere with an infinitely small diameter. But in a cosmological understanding of the point, considering that below the Planck length there is no space as we know it, the closest approximation to a point in space–time that can be identified is that of a micro black hole of Planck length diameter 10^{-35} m.

Metaphor of the Yin/Yang Symbol

Bohm's cotemporaneous enfolding/unfolding process can be visually captured in the Yin/Yang symbol (Fig. 38), attributed historically to Chinese Taoist sages of the third century BCE.[588]

Figure 38. *Implicate/explicate as yin/yang.*[589]
Graphic by Alkari (2013).

In the Yin/Yang symbol, one side can be taken to represent a timeless, spaceless implicate order, and the other side can be seen as the expressed space–time explicate order. And yet each one is also at the heart of the other (designated by the central dots in each of the two regions of the Yin/Yang symbol).

Summary of David Bohm's Quantum Trinity

Implicate Order ->   God, Brahman, The Void

Explicate Order ->   Christ-Consciousness

Active Information ->   Holy Spirit

V. Summary: The Integral Trinity

We began this book in search of resonance among various cultural expressions of what is generally known as "The Trinity" and conclude with the table below.

	1st Person	2nd Person	3rd Person
Religions			
Christianity	"The Father"	"The Son"	"The Holy Spirit"
Islam*	"The Meaning"	"The Name"	"The Gate"
Vedanta	"Existence" (*Sat*)	"Consciousness" (*Cit*)	"Love" (*Ananda*)
Buddhism	TheTranscendent (*Dharmakāya*)	The Immanent (*Nirmaṇakāya*)	The Clear Light (*Sambhogakāya*)
Philosopher-Mystics			
Pierre Teilhard de Chardin	"Omega"	"The Christic"	"Energy"
Sri Aurobindo	"Supermind"	"Mind"	" The Gnostic Being"
David Bohm**	"The Implicate Order"	"Space-Time Domain"	"Active Information"
William Tiller	"God Self"	"Personality Self"	"Soul Self"
Henri Bergson	"Élan vital"	"Duration"	"Intuition"
Patañjali	Brahma	Citta	Atman
Sigmund Freud	Super-Ego (das Über-Ich)	Ego (das Ich)	Id (das Es)
Rudolf Steiner	Causal	Etheric	Astral
Carl Jung	"The Self" Source Energy.	"Ego #1" Male: Left-hemisphere	"Ego #2" Female: Right-hemisphere
Shelli Joye	Frequency Domain	Electric Domain	Magnetic Domain

* Shiite Alawites
** Quantum Physics

This summary table offers a comparative view of 14 Trinitarian structures associated with four major religions and the writings of ten philosopher-mystics (all ten writing in the 20th century, with the exception of the Indian philosopher-mystic Patañjali, who is thought to have lived during the 4th century BCE).

In an integrated pictorial summary, the multiple Trinitarian configurations explored in this book can also be seen combined within the schematic diagram below:

The perspectives offered here are certainly not meant to form a definitive map in our exploration and understanding of the Trinity. However, in overlaying these multiple concepts, and in viewing them integrally as various feasible approaches supported by both science and tradition, a deeper and richer understanding of the Trinity may begin to emerge. Here again it is especially useful to be reminded of the words of the integral East/West scholar, the Jesuit Spanish priest, Raimundo Panikkar.

> We are not saying that the idea of the Trinity can be reduced to the discovery of a triple dimension of Being, nor that this aspect is a mere rational discovery. We are only affirming that the Trinity is the acme of a truth that permeates all realms of being and consciousness and that this vision links us together.[16]
>
> Raimundo Panikkar, *The Trinity and the Religious Experience of Man*, 1973, xi.

---

[16] Raimundo Panikkar (1918-2010), son of a Spanish Roman Catholic mother and a Hindu Indian father (a renowned upper caste leader from South India and an active freedom fighter during British colonial rule), completed three separate doctoral programs in the following order: philosophy, chemistry, theology.

About the Author

Shelli Renée Joye was born on the island of Trinidad in the British West Indies, and grew up in London and northern Virginia. Accepting a scholarship in Physics from Rice University, she completed a Bachelor of Science in Electrical Engineering. After working with Dr. John Lilly in research involving interspecies communication between dolphins and humans, she began a lifelong exploration of the interface between consciousness, yoga, electromagnetic theory, and mathematics.

She was awarded an M.A. in Asian Philosophy from the California Institute of Asian Studies under the guidance of the founder, Dr. Haridas Chaudhuri, and in the early '90s she studied with Fr. Bede Griffiths at Shantivanam in Tamil Nadu, South India.

Dr. Joye completed a Ph.D. program in the Philosophy, Cosmology, and Consciousness program at the California Institute of Integral Studies under the guidance of Drs. Allan Leslie Combs, Brian Swimme, and Dean Radin. She has been a Camaldolese Benedictine Oblate since 1992, and currently leads a contemplative life at 4500 feet above sea level near Mt. Lassen in the Cascade mountains of northeastern California.

About the Viola Institute

The Viola Institute is a non-profit corporation established to promote consciousness research and to foster an integral, ecumenical, science-based approach to spiritual traditions, religious practices, and the numinous arts. To this end, the Institute sponsors art exhibitions and publishes works of nonfiction around the themes of contemplative practice, comparative religion, and consciousness studies. A primary goal of the Viola Institute is to consciousness research and retreat centers in northern California and in Gualdo di Sopra, a forested countryside near Assisi, Italy.

For more information, or to make a tax deductible contribution contact:

The Viola Institute
35366 Wild Turkey Lane
Viola, CA 96088

References

Abi-Talib, *Al-Saheefah Al-Alawiyah or The Alawite Book*. London: Forgotten Books.

Archibald, Douglas N. 2010. *The Story of Trinidad. Vol. I: The Age of Conquest, 1498-1623, Vol. II: The Age of Settlement 1624-1797*. Trinidad and Tobago: Aleong and Montgomery.

Sri Aurobindo Ghose. 1949. *The Life Divine*. 3rd ed. New York: India Library Society.

———. 1955. *The Synthesis of Yoga*. Pondicherry: Sri Aurobindo International University Centre.

———. 1972. *Hymns to the Mystic Fire*. Pondicherry: Sri Aurobindo Ashram.

———. 1972. *The Upanishads: Texts, Translations and Commentaries*. Pondicherry: Sri Aurobindo Ashram.

———. 1997. *Tales of Prison Life*. Pondicherry, India: Sri Aurobindo Ashram.

Bailey, Gregory. 2003. *The Study of Hinduism*. Columbia, SC: The University of South Carolina Press.

Barnhart, Bruno. 2001. "Christian Self-Understanding in the Light of the East." In *Purity of Heart and Contemplation: A Monastic Dialogue Between Christian and Asian Traditions*, 291–308. New York: Camaldolese Hermits of America, Inc.

Blofeld, John. 1972. *The Wheel of Life: The Autobiography of a Western Buddhist*. 2nd ed. Berkeley: Shambala.

Bohm, David. 1951. *Quantum Theory*. New York: Prentiss-Hall.

———. 1952. "A Suggested Interpretation of the Quantum Theory in Terms of 'Hidden Variables,' Vol. 1." *Physical Review* 85 (2): 166–93. Retrieved from http://fma.if.usp.br/~amsilva/Artigos/p166_1.pdf.

———. 1965. *The Special Theory of Relativity*. Philadelphia: John Benjamins.

———. 1978. "The Enfolding-Unfolding Universe: A Conversation with David Bohm." In *The Holographic Paradigm and Other Paradoxes: Exploring the Leading Edge of Science*, edited by Ken Wilber, 44–104. Boulder, CO: Shambhala.

———. 1979. *A Question of Physics: Conversations in Physics and Biology*, edited by P. Buckley and F. David Peat. London: Kegan Paul.

———. 1980. *Wholeness and the Implicate Order*. London: Routledge.

———. 1985. *Unfolding Meaning: A Weekend of Dialogue with David Bohm*. London: Routledge.

———. 1986. "The Implicate Order and the Super-Implicate Order." In *Dialogues with Scientists and Sages: The Search for Unity*, edited by Renée Weber, 23–49. New York: Routledge.

———. 1987. "Hidden Variables and the Implicate Order." In *Quantum Implications: Essays in Honour of David Bohm*, edited by B. J. Hiley and F. David Peat, 33–45. London: Routledge.

———. 1989. "Meaning and Information." In *The Search for Meaning: The New Spirit in Science and Philosophy,* edited by Paavo Pylkkänen, 43–85. Northamptonshire: The Aquarian Press.

———. 1990a. "Beyond Limits: A Full Conversation with David Bohm." Interview by Bill Angelos for Dutch public television. Posted March 5, 2011. Retrieved from http://bohmkrishnamurti.com/beyond-limits/

———. 1990b. "A New Theory of the Relationship of Mind and Matter." *Philosophical Psychology* 3 (2): 271–86.

Bohm, David, and Basil J. Hiley. 1993. *The Undivided Universe: An Ontological Interpretation of Quantum Theory.* London: Routledge.

Bohm, David, and J. Krishnamurti. 1985. *The Ending of Time: Where Philosophy and Physics Meet.* New York: Harper Collins.

Bohm, David, and J. Krishnamurti. 1999. *The Limits of Thought: Discussions between J. Krishnamurti and David Bohm.* London: Routledge.

Bohm, David, and F. David Peat. 1987. *Science, Order, and Creativity.* London: Routledge.

Bohm, David, and R. Weber. 1982. "Nature as Creativity." *ReVision* 5 (2): 35–40.

Booth, J. C., S. A. Koren, and Michael A. Persinger. 2005. "Increased Feelings of the Sensed Presence and Increased Geomagnetic Activity at the Time of the Experience During

Exposures to Transcerebral Weak Complex Magnetic Fields." *International Journal of Neuroscience* 115 (7): 1039–65.

Chaudhuri, Haridas. 1954. *The Philosophy of Integralism: The Metaphysical Synthesis in Sri Aurobindo's Teaching.* Pondicherry, India: Sri Aurobindo Ashram Trust.

Chaudhuri, Haridas. 1974. *Being, Evolution & Immortality: An Outline of Integral Philosophy.* Wheaton, Ill: A Quest Book.

Chaudhuri, Haridas, and Frederic Spiegelberg, eds. 1960. *The Integral Philosophy of Sri Aurobindo: A Commemorative Symposium.* London: George Allen & Unwin.

Churton, Tobias. 2011. *Aleister Crowley: The Biography,* London: Watkins Publishing.

Combs, Allan. 2009. *Consciousness Explained Better: Towards an Integral Understanding of the Multifaceted Nature of Consciousness.* St. Paul, MN: Paragon House.

Eliot, Thomas Stearns. 1943. *Four Quartets.* New York: Harcourt Brace.

Fourier, Jean-Baptiste. 1822. *The Analytical Theory of Heat.* English translation published 1878.

Fox, Matthew. 1988. *The Coming of the Cosmic Christ.* New York: Harper One.

Gebser, Jean. 1949. *The Ever-Present Origin: Part One: Foundations of the Aperspectival World.* Translated by J. Keckeis. Stuttgart, Germany: Deutsche Verlags-Anstalt.

Griffiths, Bede. 1973. *Vedanta and Christian Faith.* Clear Lake, CA: The Dawn Horse Press.

———. 1990. *A New Vision of Reality: Eastern Science, Eastern Mysticism and Christian Faith.* Springfield, IL: Templegate.

Heehs, Peter. 2008. *The Lives of Sri Aurobindo.* New York: Columbia University Press.

James, William. 1950. *The Principles of Psychology,* 2 vols. New York: Dover.

———. (1909) 1998. *A Pluralistic Universe: Hibbert Lectures on the Present Situation in Philosophy.* New York: Longmans, Green.

Joye, Shelli R. 2016. *The Pribram–Bohm Holoflux Theory of Consciousness: An Integral Interpretation of the Theories of Karl Pribram, David Bohm, and Pierre Teilhard de Chardin* (Doctoral dissertation). Available from ProQuest Dissertations and Theses database. (UMI No. 1803306323).

———. 2017. *Tuning the Mind: Geometries of Consciousness.* Viola, CA: The Viola Institute.

———. 2017. *The Little Book of Consciousness: Holonomic Brain Theory and the Implicate Order.* Viola, CA: The Viola Institute.

Jung, Carl G. 1968. "Psychology and Alchemy." In Vol. 12 of *The Collected Works of C. G. Jung.* Edited and translated by Gerald Adler and R. F. C. Hull. 2nd ed. Princeton, NJ: Princeton University.

———. (1946) 1969. "A Psychological Approach to the Dogma of the Trinity." In Vol. 11 of *The*

Collected Works of C. G. Jung, translated by R. F. C. Hull, 159–234. 2nd ed. Princeton, NJ: Princeton University.

———. (1946) 1969. "On the Nature of the Psyche." In Vol. 8 of *The Collected Works of C. G. Jung*, translated by R. F. C. Hull, 159–234. 2nd ed. Princeton, NJ: Princeton University.

Keats, John. (1818) 2010. *Endymion: A Poetic Romance*. Whitefish, MT: Kessinger.

Khanna, Madhu. 1979. *Yantra: The Tantric Symbol of Cosmic Unity*. London: Thames & Hudson.

Kropf, Richard W. 2015. *Einstein and the Image of God: A Response to Contemporary Atheism*. Johannesberg, MI: Stellamar Publications.

Leroi-Gourhan, Andre. 1968. *The Art of Prehistoric Man in Western Europe*. London: Thames and Hudson.

Lilly, John. 1972. *Programming and Meta-Programming the Human Biocomputer: Theory and Experiments*. New York: The Julian Press.

———. 1988. *The Scientist: A Metaphysical Autobiography*. Berkeley, CA: Ronin Publishing.

———. 2007. *The Deep Self: Consciousness Exploration in the Isolation Tank*. Nevada City, CA: Gateways Books.

Lossky, Vladimir. (1944) 1949. *The Mystical Theology of the Eastern Church*. Translated by James Clarke, Cambridge, UK: James Clarke & Co.

Merrill-Wolf, Franklin. 1973. *The Philosophy of Consciousness Without an Object*. New York: Julian Press.

McKenna, Terence. 1993. *True Hallucinations: Being an Account of the Author's Extraordinary Adventures in the Devil's Paradise*. New York: HarperCollins.

Merton, Thomas. 1948. *The Seven Story Mountain*. New York: Harcourt.

Mishra, Rammurti. 1973. *The Yoga Sutras: Textbook of Yoga Psychology*. New York: Anchor Press.

Muller, Julius Eduard. 1880. "File:Tropenmuseum_Royal_Tropical_Instit ute_Objectnumber_60008905_Een_groep_ Arowakken_en_Karaiben_in_fe.jpg" (graphic file). September 9, 2009. Wikimedia Commons. Retrieved from https://upload.wikimedia.org/wikipedia/com mons/5/57/Tropenmuseum_Royal_Tropical _Institute_Objectnumber_60008905_Een_g roep_Arowakken_en_Karaiben_in_fe.jpg

Needleman, Jacob. 2005. *The Gospel of Thomas: The Gnostic Wisdom of Jesus*. Rochester, VT: Inner Traditions.

Ouspensky, P.D. 1949. *In Search of the Miraculous: Fragments of an Unknown Teaching*. New York: Harcourt.

Panikkar, Raimundo. 1973. *The Trinity and the Religious Experience of Man: Icon—Person— Mystery*. New York: Orbis Books.

———. 2010. *The Rhythm of Being: The Gifford Lectures*. New York: Orbis Books.

Pribram, Karl H. 1991. *Brain and Perception: Holonomy and Structure in Figural Processing*. Hillsdale, NJ: Lawrence Erlbaum.

Radhakrishnan, Sarvepalli. 1957. *History of Philosophy Eastern and Western: Volume I*. London: George Allen & Unwin, Ltd.

———. 1971. *Indian Philosophy: Volume II*. London: George Allen & Unwin, Ltd.

Roy, Dilip Kumar. 1952. *Sri Aurobindo Came to Me*. Pondicherry: Sri Aurobindo Ashram Trust.

Spiegelberg, Frederic. 1951. *Spiritual Practices of India*. San Francisco: The Greenwood Press.

Stapledon, Olaf. 1968. *Last and First Men and Star Maker*. New York: Dover.

Taimni, I.K. 1961. *The Science of Yoga: The Yoga-Sutras of Patañjali in Sanskrit with Transliteration in English and Commentary*. Madras: The Theosophical Publishing House.

Teilhard de Chardin, Pierre. (1916) 1968. "Cosmic Life." In *Writings in Time of War*, translated by René Hague, 14–71. London: William Collins Sons.

———. (1916) 1978. "Christ in Matter." In *The Heart of Matter*, translated by René Hague, 61–67. New York: Harcourt Brace Jovanovich.

———. (1917) 1978. "Nostalgia for the Front." In *The Heart of Matter*, translated by René Hague, 168–81. New York: Harcourt Brace Jovanovich.

———. (1918a) 1978. "The Great Monad." In *The Heart of Matter*, translated by René Hague, 182–95. New York: Harcourt Brace Jovanovich.

———. (1918b) 1978. "My Universe." In *The Heart of Matter*, translated by René Hague, 196–208. New York: Harcourt Brace Jovanovich. ———. (1923) 1966. "Hominization." In The Vision of the Past, translated by J. M. Cohen, 51–79. New York: Harper & Row.

———. (1931) 1969. "The Spirit of the Earth." In *Human Energy*, translated by J. M. Cohen, 93–112. New York: Harcourt Brace Jovanovitch.

———. (1937) 1969. "The Phenomenon of Spirituality." In *Human Energy*, translated by J. M. Cohen, 93–112. New York: Harcourt Brace Jovanovitch.

———. (1941) 1976. "The Atomism of Spirit." In *Activation of Energy*, translated by René Hague, 21–57. London: William Collins Sons.

———. (1942) 1976. "Man's Place in the Universe." In *The Vision of the Past*, translated by J.M. Cohen, 216–33. New York: Harper & Row.

———. (1943) 1969. "Human Energy." In *Human Energy*, translated by J. M. Cohen, 113–62. New York: Harcourt Brace Jovanovitch.

———. (1944) 1976. "Centrology: An Essay in a Dialectic of Union." In *Activation of Energy*, translated by René Hague, 97–127. London: William Collins Sons.

———. (1945) 1959. "Life and the Planets." In *The Future of Man*, translated by Norman Denny, 97–123. New York: Harper & Row.

———. (1946) 1976. "Outline of a Dialectic of Spirit." In *Activation of Energy*, translated by René Hague, 143–51. London: William Collins Sons.

———. (1948) 1975. "My Fundamental Vision." In *Toward the Future*, translated by René Hague, 163–208. London: William Collins Sons.

———. (1949) 1956. "The Formation of the Noosphere II." In *Man's Place in Nature: The Human Zoological Group*, translated by René Hague, 96–121. New York: Harper & Row.

———. (1950a) 1978. "The Heart of Matter." In *The Heart of Matter*, translated by René Hague, 15–79. New York: Harcourt Brace Jovanovich.

———. (1950b) 1976. "The Zest for Living." In *Activation of Energy*, translated by René Hague, 229–43. London: William Collins Sons.

———. (1951a) 1976. "The Convergence of the Universe." In *Activation of Energy*, translated by René Hague, 281–96. London: William Collins Sons.

———. (1951b) 1976. "A Mental Threshold Across Our Path: From Cosmos to Cosmogenesis." In *Activation of Energy*, translated by René Hague, 251–68. London: William Collins Sons.

———. (1951c) 1975. "Some Notes on the Mystical Sense: An Attempt at Clarification" In *Toward the Future*, translated by René Hague, 209–11. London: William Collins Sons.

———. (1953a) 1976. "The Activation of Human Energy." In *Activation of Energy*, translated by René Hague, 359–93. London: William Collins Sons.

———. (1953b) 1976. "The Energy of Evolution." In *Activation of Energy*, translated by René Hague, 359–72. London: William Collins Sons.

———. (1953c) 1976. "The Stuff of the Universe." In *Activation of Energy*, translated by René Hague, 375–83. London: William Collins Sons.

———. (1953d) 1976. "Universalization and Union." In *Activation of Energy*, translated by René Hague, 77–95. London: William Collins Sons.

———. (1954) 1956. "The Nature of the Point Omega." In *The Appearance of Man*, translated by J.M. Cohen, 271–73. New York: Harper & Row.

———. (1955) 1976. "The Death-Barrier and Co-Reflection, or the Imminent Awakening of Human Consciousness to the Sense of Its Irreversibility." In *Activation of Energy*, translated by René Hague, 395–406. London: William Collins Sons.

———. 1956. *The Appearance of Man*. Translated by J. M. Cohen. New York: Harper & Row.

———. 1959. *The Phenomenon of Man*. Translated by Bernard Wall. New York: Harper & Row.

———. 1960. *The Divine Milieu*. New York: Harper & Row.

———. 1961. *The Making of a Mind: Letters from a Soldier–Priest 1914–1919*. Translated by Rene Hague. New York: Harper & Row.

———. 1962. *Letters from a Traveler*. New York: Harper & Row.

———. 1964. *The Phenomenon of Man*. New York: Harper & Row.

———. 1965. *Building the Earth*. Translated by Noël Lindsay. Wilkes-Barre, PA: Dimension Books.

———. 1968. *Letters to Two Friends 1926–1952*. New York: New American Library.

———. 1969a. *Human Energy*. Translated by J. M. Cohen. New York: Harcourt Brace Jovanovitch.

———. 1969b. *Letters to Leontine Zanta*. Translated by Bernard Wall. New York: Harper & Row.

———. 1971a. *Christianity and Evolution: Reflections on Science and Religion*. Translated by René Hague. London: William Collins Sons.

———. 1971b. *Pierre Teilhard de Chardin: L'Oeuvre Scientifique*. Edited by Nicole and Karl Schmitz-Moormann. 10 vols. Munich: Walter-Verlag.

———. 1972. *Lettres Intimes de Teilhard de Chardin a Auguste Valensin, Bruno de Solages, et Henri de Lubac 1919–1955*. Paris: Aubier Montaigne.

———. 1976. *Activation of Energy*. Translated by Rene Hague. London: William Collins Sons.

———. 1978. *The Heart of Matter*. Translated by René Hague. New York: Harcourt Brace Jovanovich.

———. 2003. *The Human Phenomenon*. Translated and edited by Sarah Appleton-Weber. Portland, OR: Sussex Academic. First published 1955.

Temple, Richard. 1991. *Icons and the Mystical Origins of Christianity*. London: Element Books.

Tiller, William. 2007. *Psychoenergetic Science*. Los Angeles: Pavior.

Whicher, Ian. 1998. *The Integrity of the Yoga Darsana: A Reconsideration of Classical Yoga*. New York: State University of New York Press.

Wilber, Ken. 1977. *The Spectrum of Consciousness*. Wheaton, IL: Theosophical Publishing House.

———. 1996. *A Brief History of Everything*. Boston, MA: Shambhala.

Wood, Ernest E. 1948. *Practical Yoga: Ancient and Modern*. New York: E.P. Dutton.

Yau, Shing-Tung, and Steve Nadis. 2010. *The Shape of Inner Space: String Theory and the Geometry of the Universe's Hidden Dimensions*. New York: Basic Books.

Appendix A: The Fourier Transform

Two domains, the time domain (t_d) and the frequency domain (f_d), are of essential importance in the field of information theory and signal communication. On the first page of an undergraduate electrical engineering textbook on network analysis and synthesis, Kuo states:

> In describing signals, we use the two universal languages of electrical engineering—*time* and *frequency*. Strictly speaking, a signal is a function of time. However, the signal can be described equally well in terms of *spectral* or *frequency* information. As between any two languages, such as French and German, translation is needed to render information given in one language comprehensible in the other. Between time and frequency, the translation is effected by the *Fourier series* and the *Fourier integral*.[590]

In his book *Brain and Perception*, Pribram used almost the same words as Kuo in discussing methods by which a Fourier transform operates in mathematical physics. Here Pribram reaches the same conclusion as Kuo:

> It is reasonable to ask: What advantage does the organism gain by processing in the spectral transform domain? The answer is efficiency: The fact that correlations are *so easily achieved* by first convolving signals in the spectral domain and then, inverse transforming them into the space–time domain. Thus Fast Fourier Transform (FFT) procedures have become the basis of computerized tomography, the CT scans used by hospitals.[591]

This emphasis on the significant role of Fourier transform mathematics in electrical engineering and neurophysiological research can also be found in quantum physics (e.g., on page 1 of Bohm's own 646-page textbook, *Quantum Theory*):

> The development of the special mathematical techniques that are necessary for obtaining quantitative results in complex problems should take place, for the most part, either in a mathematics course or in a special course concerned with the mathematics of quantum theory. It seems impossible, however, to develop quantum concepts extensively without Fourier analysis. It is, therefore, presupposed that the reader is moderately familiar with Fourier analysis.[592]

Accordingly it is worthwhile to examine in detail the nature of the Fourier series and Fourier integrals, and in particular to explore their relation to imaginary numbers and the Maxwell equations that map the flow of electromagnetic energy in space–time.

Leonhard Euler and Imaginary Numbers

The two domains related by the Fourier transform, the time domain and frequency domain, had been "discovered," explored and developed as early as 1735 by Leonhard Euler (1707–1783), a Swiss mathematical genius who not only defined the concept of a "function," (Euler was the first to write $f(x)$ to denote a function driven by a variable), but also named and defined numerous mathematical symbols widely used today including the constant "pi," in Greek, the letter π; he had determined through calculation that if the diameter of a circle is 1, its circumference on the other hand is an irrational number, 3.14159265 . . . which "for the sake of brevity" he said he will call π.[593] Euler's most important work published work is a two-volume textbook written in 1748, *Introductio ad Analysin Infinitorum* (*Introduction to Infinite Analysis*).[594]

In the *Introductio*, Euler announced the dramatic discovery of a deep connection between exponential functions, trigonometric functions, and imaginary numbers . . . Euler unveiled numerous discoveries about functions involving infinite theories . . . and proposed definitions and symbols that have since become standard, including π and e.[595]

An example can be seen here in his choice of a base for an exponential function, which he called e, created by adding up a simple infinite series:

$$e = 1 + \frac{1}{1!} + \frac{1}{2!} + \frac{1}{3!} + \frac{1}{4!} + \frac{1}{5!} + \frac{1}{6!} + \frac{1}{7!} + \frac{1}{8!} + \frac{1}{9!} + \frac{1}{10!} + \frac{1}{11!} + \frac{1}{12!} + \cdots$$

This number e became Euler's base for what he called "natural logarithms," and one of the most important mathematical constants in modern physics.[596] However Euler's greatest contribution to mathematical physics was his proof of a direct mathematical connection between the *time domain* and the *frequency domain*. The Nobel Prize winning physicist, Richard Feynman, has called Euler's discovery, "the gold standard for mathematical beauty," and "the most remarkable formula in mathematics."[597]

Mathematicians in the early eighteenth century, following Newton, sought for expressions and patterns in pure mathematics that could be shown to mirror physical phenomena observed in nature. With his photographic memory and "rare ability for concentration," Euler was able to perceive patterns in mathematical series and relationships that resulted in a prodigious number of proofs (at his death Euler had published more than 40 folio volumes on mathematics). Euler's biographer put forth his own theory on the spectacular success of this prodigy:

The phenomenon of Euler is essentially tied to three factors: first to the gift of a possibly unique memory . . . at an advanced age, he demonstrated that he could repeat the Aeneid of Virgil from beginning to end without hesitation, and for every page in the edition he could indicate which line was the first and which the last. Secondly, his enormous mnemonic power was paired with a rare ability of concentration. Noise and hustle in his immediate vicinity barely disturbed him in his mental work: "A child on his knees, a cat on his back, this is the way he wrote his immortal works" reports his colleague, Thiebault. The third factor of the "mystery Euler" is simply his steady, quiet work.[598]

Prior to Euler's discovery, there had never been a way to mathematically connect the timespace (t_d) dimension with the nontemporal frequency (f_d) dimension. His discovery resulted from his investigation into an obscure field of mathematics (discovered by Greek mathematicians, but first called "imaginary numbers" by Descartes by way of ridicule) in which Euler defined the square root of minus one as the letter "i" (for "imaginary").[599] Thus the letter i designates the square root of minus one:

$$i = \sqrt{-1} ,$$

(or conversely, $i^2 = -1$)

Euler found this imaginary number to be a great mathematical tool because multiplying "i" times "i" (i.e., squaring "i"), simply reverses the sign of an expression. This feature can be used to reverse the signs of various elements in a series expansion, and thus allowed Euler to develop and explore a wide range of equalities in mathematical expansion series. Use of this imaginary number as an operator, combined with his copious memory led directly to his discovery, in 1735, of

284

what is now called Euler's Law: a direct relationship between real numbers and imaginary numbers. Depicted in Cartesian coordinates, the horizontal axis of real numbers, commonly labeled the "time" axis, is widely used in physics and mathematical charting, while the vertical, "imaginary" axis, is widely used in electrical engineering because it governs so well the mathematics of complex-plane calculations which are ubiquitous in contemporary electronic devices, during the translation of digital to analog signals and vice versa.[600]

In his *Introductio ad analysin infinitorum*, Euler announced the discovery of a connection between exponential functions, trigonometric functions, and imaginary numbers.[601] Perhaps the best way to appreciate the beauty in the discovery of Euler's Law is to go through its derivation.[602]

Derivation of Euler's Law

Euler was fascinated by what are called "infinite series," expressions by which trigonometric values can be expressed, and more importantly, calculated. By summing a series of arithmetical terms, the value of a sin or cos of an angle can be calculated to any degree of precision by approximating them as the sum of a series of arithmetic values. Obviously an entire infinite series could not be calculated, but approximations were acceptable because it allowed the creation of large tables of values that were in widespread demand for use by engineers in the sixteenth century throughout Europe.[603]

Euler spent countless hours developing various infinite series, in the attempt to discover connections and relationships among the patterns. Two of these series especially intrigued him, the Scottish mathematician Colin Maclaurin's infinite series expansion of the sine and the cosine functions, both shown partially expanded as follows:

$$\sin x = x - \frac{x^3}{3!} + \frac{x^5}{5!} - \frac{x^7}{7!} + \frac{x^9}{9!} - \frac{x^{11}}{11!} \cdots$$

$$\cos x = 1 - \frac{x^2}{2!} + \frac{x^4}{4!} - \frac{x^6}{6!} + \frac{x^8}{8!} - \frac{x^{10}}{10!} \cdots$$

Note that the "factorial sign" (!) represents the product of all numbers starting from the indicated number down to 1, (i.e., 3! = 3 x 2 x 1 = 6), and also that the ellipsis (...) in each of the expressions above indicate an infinite series of additional factors, which follow the same pattern of progression. When Euler discovered an infinite series expansion for his own natural logarithm (the base used widely in nuclear physics, was later named "e" for Euler), he noticed how the Maclaurin's series seemed similar to the pattern of expansion of his own discovery of the e^x expansion:

$$e^x = 1 + x + \frac{x^2}{2!} + \frac{x^3}{3!} + \frac{x^4}{4!} + \frac{x^5}{5!} + \frac{x^6}{6!} \cdots$$

Euler noticed that this was strangely similar to the Maclaurin expansions for cos x and sin x added together; the result of such an addition (shown below, the sum of the two series at the top of this page) is identical to the expansion of e^x, except where minus signs appear.

$$\sin x + \cos x = 1 + x - \frac{x^2}{2!} - \frac{x^3}{3!} + \frac{x^4}{4!} + \frac{x^5}{5!} - \frac{x^6}{6!} - \frac{x^7}{7!} + \frac{x^8}{8!} + \cdots$$

For many months Euler struggled to unlock the secret of what seemed to be a remarkably close connection. Finally, it dawned on him that the relationship might find closure if he could find a way to use his imaginary number "i," the square root of minus 1 to change signs.

Substituting "*ix*" for "*x*" everywhere in his equation (an allowable substitution, since by the rules of algebra any valid expression can be substituted for "*x*"), he found that wherever "*i²*" could be identified and factored out, the sign for that expression would reverse, and he quickly saw that his expansion would then more closely match that of the expansion of *cos x + sin x*.

To recapitulate, here again is Euler's original infinite expansion of the natural logarithm that he had previously discovered:

$$e^x = 1 + x + \frac{x^2}{2!} + \frac{x^3}{3!} + \frac{x^4}{4!} + \frac{x^5}{5!} + \frac{x^6}{6!} \,...$$

Wherever there is an "*x*" in the above equation, Euler substituted "*ix*,"

$$e^{ix} = 1 + ix + \frac{(ix)^2}{2!} + \frac{(ix)^3}{3!} + \frac{(ix)^4}{4!} + \frac{(ix)^5}{5!} + \frac{(ix)^6}{6!} \,...$$

Wherever he found an "*i²*" Euler converted this to its value, "-1":

$$e^{ix} = 1 + ix - \frac{x^2}{2!} - \frac{ix^3}{3!} + \frac{x^4}{4!} + \frac{ix^5}{5!} + \cdots$$

Rearranging the results slightly, we can see the original patterns of *cos x* and *sin x* expansion on the left, now seen as equal to Euler's e^{ix} (on the right): this equation is known as "Euler's Law":

$$e^{ix} = \left(1 - \frac{x^2}{2!} + \frac{x^4}{4!} + \cdots\right) + \left(ix - \frac{ix^3}{3!} + \frac{ix^5}{5!} + \cdots\right)$$

Now we factor out the *i* from the right side of the equation to get the following result:

$$e^{ix} = \left(1 - \frac{x^2}{2!} + \frac{x^4}{4!} + \cdots\right) + i * \left(x - \frac{x^3}{3!} + \frac{x^5}{5!} + \cdots\right).$$

The expressions now within the brackets are simply the Maclaurin expansion series for $\cos x$ and $\sin x$, and the entire expression can now be written as:

$$e^{ix} = \cos x + i * \sin x$$

The amazement generated by this discovery was that for the first time a solid, derivable mathematical link had been established between e, the natural exponential function, the imaginary number i, and trigonometric geometry; the discovery was published in 1735 by Euler:

$$\boldsymbol{e^{ix} = cos\, x + i * sin\, x}$$

Euler's Law.[604]

Notice how both sides of Euler's Law contain both real numbers ($\boldsymbol{x}$) and imaginary numbers ($\boldsymbol{i}$). Euler's Law maps the intersection of the axis of real numbers with the angular frequency axis of imaginary numbers on a single intersecting plane, allowing us to model mathematically the real world of timespace/frequency phenomena of quantum electrodynamics. Euler's Law has since become the basis of electronic communication technology within which our society is currently enmeshed.[605]

During the eighteenth century this field, "complex mathematics," remained an obscurity, until "rediscovered" by physicists such as Maxwell, Tesla, and Marconi in the late nineteenth century; the mathematics of imaginary numbers became an essential tool for modeling an invisible electromagnetic reality, and more importantly, provided a direct way of calculating, predicting, and modulating the electromagnetic energy oscillations and waves associated with the newly emerging technologies of alternating current. [606] Nevertheless, it was Euler who first established the mathematical beachhead into the Real–Imaginary domain, and this relationship was eventually found, perhaps mysteriously, to mirror electromagnetic realities in space–time.[607]

Integral Operator and Fourier Transform

Seventy-four years after Euler published his famous theorem, Jean Baptist Joseph Fourier (1768–1830), expanding upon Euler's mathematical discovery, published what came to be known as the Fourier series and the Fourier Transform, in a paper entitled *The Analytic Theory of Heat*.[608] Before describing the Fourier Transform, it is useful to begin by examining the word "integral" through the perspective of history. The word integral itself stems from a mathematical sign, a convention that was first introduced by Gottfried Wilhelm von Leibniz (1646–1716) as a stylized, elongated letter *S* which he used as shorthand for the Latin word *Summa* (translates "sum" or "total") to denote something that originates from a summation.[609]

Both Leibniz and Isaac Newton (1643–1727) seem to have developed the fundamental concepts of integral calculus simultaneously, but Newton's notation of using a vertical mark to indicate summation became the cause of considerable notational confusion (a vertical slash is "easily confused with the numeral, '1,' or with a bracket, or with the letter 'I'"), and over the next 15 years, Leibniz's elongated letter *S* found preference among mathematicians to denote "summation."[610] The word "integral" itself was coined by Jacob Bernoulli (1654–1705), so that the *S* notation could more easily be discussed in mathematical conversation and in lectures.[611]

However it was not until 1822, when Jean Baptiste Joseph Fourier introduced the notation of upper and lower limits to the integral operator symbol, that the full power of integral calculus was unleashed, making possible the development of his "Fourier series."[612]

A full century after Euler, it was Fourier, working at the time as Napoleon's governor of Egypt, who managed to link the real and imaginary axes by building upon Euler's Theorem. While Euler had provided the initial link between the frequency and timespace domains, it was Fourier, during his experimental investigation of heat flow, who developed the mathematics to model the thermodynamic properties of energy, and was able to derive a mathematical operation of integral calculus that expressed accurately the energy transformations between a time domain (t_d) and a frequency domain (f_d).[613]

It is our thesis here that the mathematics expressed in the Fourier transform can also be understood as a link between a physics of space–time (t_d) and an actual frequency domain (f_d).

The Fourier and inverse Fourier transforms are shown in the following equations:

$$f(t) = \int_{-\infty}^{+\infty} X(F)e^{j2\pi Ft}\,dF \qquad f(F) = \int_{-\infty}^{+\infty} x(t)e^{-j2\pi Ft}\,dt$$

Fourier integral transform of a continuous time function into the frequency domain (f_d).   Fourier integral transform of a continuous frequency function into the time domain (t_d).

Fourier Transform/Inverse Transform.[614]

These Fourier transform expressions indicate that any arbitrary function in the timespace domain, $f(t)$, can be transformed into and expressed by an infinite series of frequency spectra functions $X(F)$ in the frequency domain, and conversely, that any arbitrary function in the frequency domain, $f(F)$ can be transformed into and expressed by an infinite series of time functions, $x(t)$.

These Fourier transforms are themselves derived from an underlying series of alternate pure sine and pure cosine waves, as depicted in Equation 6.

$$f(t) = a_0 + \sum_{n=1}^{\infty} \left(a_n \cos\frac{n\pi t}{L} + b_n \sin\frac{n\pi t}{L} \right)$$

The Fourier Series.[615]

A century after Fourier's death, Norbert Wiener made use of Fourier's transform to model and analyze brain waves, and he was able to detect frequencies, centered within different spatial locations on the cortex, that exhibited auto-correlation. Specific frequencies were found to be attracting one another toward an intermediate frequency, thus exhibiting resonance or "self tuning" within a narrow range of the frequency domain (f_d).[616] This discovery led Wiener to conjecture that the infrared band of electromagnetic flux may be the loci of "self-organizing systems."[617]

> We thus see that a nonlinear interaction causing the attraction of frequency can generate a *self-organizing system*, as it does in the case of the brain waves we have discussed . . . . This possibility of self-organization is by no means limited to the very low frequency of these two phenomena. Consider self-organizing systems at the frequency level, say, of infrared light.[618]

Wiener goes on to discuss such possibilities in biology, where he focuses upon the problems of communication at molecular and primitive cellular levels, specifically on the problem of how substances produce cancer by reproducing themselves to mimic pre-existing normal local cells. Molecules do not simply pass notes to one another, and they do not have eyes, so how do they perceive and how do they communicate? Wiener conjectures:

> The usual explanation given is that one molecule of these substances acts as a template according to which the constituent's smaller molecules lay themselves down and unite into a similar macromolecule. However, an entirely possible way of describing such forces is that the active bearer of the specificity of a molecule may lie *in the frequency pattern of its molecular radiation,* an important part of which may lie *in infrared electromagnetic frequencies* or even lower. It is quite possible that this phenomenon may be regarded as a sort of attractive interaction of frequency.[619]

At the end of his classic book on cybernetics, in the chapter, "Brain Waves and Self-Organizing Systems," Wiener suggests further possible studies to "throw light on the validity of my hypothesis concerning brain waves."[620] Wiener goes on to describe the widespread observations of seemingly simultaneous behavior of groups of living organisms such as crickets, tree frogs, or fish, activity that might be attributable to simultaneous synchronization of neuronal networks through resonant tuning within the frequency domain (f_d):

> It has often been supposed that the fireflies in a tree flash in unison . . . I have heard it stated that in the case of some of the fireflies of Southeastern Asia this phenomenon is so marked that it can scarcely be put down to illusion . . . . Could not the same supposed

phenomenon of the pulling together of frequencies take place? However this process occurs, it is a dynamic process and involves forces or their equivalent.[621]

Real–Imaginary and Mandelbrot's Set

In early explorations of the real–imaginary domain model in the nineteenth century, the Danish mathematician Caspar Wessel (1745-1818), and the mathematical physicist and astronomer Johann Carl Friedrich Gauss (1777-1855) independently discovered that two-dimensional Cartesian plots or graphs could be made of the real–imaginary axes, with one axis of real numbers (traditionally illustrated by a straight horizontal line with values increasing from left to right) and a vertical axis of imaginary numbers drawn at a 90-degree angle to the real number axis.[622] In the twentieth century this two-dimensional model has been adopted by electrical engineers to model, analyze, and solve complex problems dealing with transformations between the time (t_d) and frequency (f_d), domains in electrical power and communication engineering.[623] The concept remains at the essential core of engineering calculations for transforming electromagnetic energy into information encoded in light, sound, and multidimensional images.[624]

Perhaps the most fascinating tool for exploring the nature of the interface between the Real–Imaginary domains was developed in 1980 when the Polish–American engineer, Benoit Mandelbrot (1924-2010), created the software to plot an actual image of the two-dimensional interface between space–time and frequency domains close to the origin (defined as the intersecting point where the Real axis equals zero and the Imaginary axis equals zero). His initial impression, upon seeing the first image, was that the computer program had malfunctioned.[625] Subsequent computer plots assured him that these visual patterns were truly there. Images of this region about the time frequency origin have gained interest worldwide and the region itself has come to be known as the Mandelbrot set shown in the figure below. The English mathematical physicist Sir Roger Penrose was so taken by the resulting images that he described them with a sense of almost reverential awe:

> The Mandelbrot set is not an invention of the human mind: it was a discovery. Just like Mount Everest, the Mandelbrot set is just *there*![626]

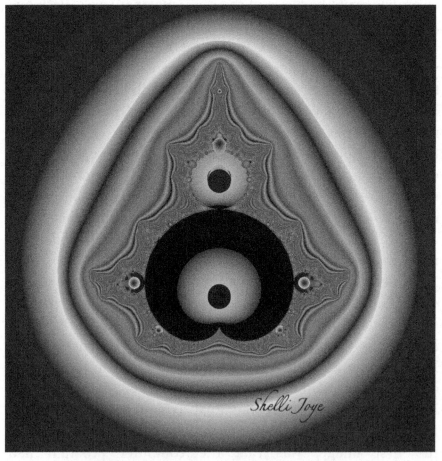

Mandelbrot: Origin of real–imaginary axis.

The Mandelbrot set exhibits remarkable properties. As calculations are done on ever smaller regions on the time–frequency plane, the images appear similar but never completely repeatable, and the viewer begins to sense some sort of biological shapes emerging from this strange world of pure mathematical being. Penrose goes on to say, "The very system of complex numbers has a profound and timeless reality which goes quite beyond the mental constructions of any particular mathematician."[627] The image also is reminiscent, perhaps, of a sitting Buddha!

Exploitation of the basic properties of this mysterious real–imaginary domain have led directly to twenty-first century digital device systems, and accordingly, it is entirely conceivable that they might also be involved in some space-time-frequency spectrum of the psyche, as theorized by Jung: "Psychic processes therefore behave like a scale along which consciousness 'slides.'"[628]

> Using the analogy of the spectrum, we could compare the lowering of unconscious contents to a displacement towards the red end of the colour band, a comparison which is especially edifying in that red, the blood colour, has always signified emotion and instinct . . . The dynamism of instinct is lodged as it were in the nearer ranges of the infra-red part of the spectrum . . . Psychologically, however, the archetype as a spiritual goal toward which the whole nature of man strives . . . as such is a psychoid factor that belongs, as it were, to the invisible, ultraviolet end of the psychic spectrum.[629]

Using Fourier analysis and the Fourier transform, signals can be described either in the time domain or the frequency domain, and they can be quickly transformed back and forth between the two domains. It can be said that they are two different aspects of one and the same thing, energy signals encoded with information content, but potentially existing in either one, or both, of two categorically distinct dimensions. Jung observes the relationship of psyche to matter with the same pattern, noting that they are two different modes of one and the same thing:

> Since psyche and matter are contained in one and the same world, and moreover are in continuous contact with one another and ultimately rest on irrepresentable, transcendental factors, it is not only possible, but also fairly probable, even, that psyche and matter are two different aspects of one and the same thing.[630]

If we assume that the energy of the psyche expresses itself in some category of spectral frequency range within the human biosystem, as Jung has speculated, then a mathematical model of psychic energy activity might be found in the Fourier transform. Humans in contemporary society experience the fruits of the mathematics of the Fourier transform reliably every time a digital communication device is operated.[631]

For example, signal processing chips in cell phones are encoded with what are called fast Fourier transform algorithms, which filter audio voice speech frequency patterns in the space–time domain into a relatively small set of pure frequencies, the individual amplitudes of which are then digitized and transmitted. On the receiving end, a reverse fast Fourier transform unpacks the frequency domain data, transforming them into space–time frequency waves of low voltage circuits, which then drive the vibrating speaker devices by which humans "hear" the re-created audio space–time spectral energy.[632]

Pribram describes this same process as it occurs in the brain, while emphasizing the difference between waves and spectra:

Waves occur in space–time. Spectra do not. Spectra result from the interference among waves—and, by Fourier's insightful technique, the locus of interference can be specified as a number that indicates the "height" of the wave at that point. The number is represented by a Gabor function (or other wavelet.) Frequency in space–time has been converted to spectral density in the transform domain.[633]

Appendix B: Icons and the Holy Trinity

The term *icon* stems from the Greek word *eikon*, which can be translated as *image*. In contemporary usage, the word is most readily found associated with a multitude of tiny graphical images on computer displays, and used as short-hand to select computer files or functions of various types. Traditionally however, icons are recognized within Orthodox Christian churches as images of a religious nature, painted with great care and reverence using egg tempera prepared from natural minerals and clays on flat wooden panels. In this context, the icon is revered as a holy object that not only acts as a visual reminder of various figures and scenes from the Bible, but also can function as numinous doorways, gates, or portals into the transcendental mysteries of the images they portray.

While at first glance icons appear similar to paintings arising from the creative expressions of the artist, the icon should not be associated with the secular world of art and aesthetics, but, as the iconographer Solrunn Nes has written:

> It refers to a spiritual dimension and forms part of a concrete, religious practice. . . Among Orthodox Christians the icon also has a natural function as a private devotional image.[6]

Thus the icons should not be confused with a painting. It does not act as a window through which we might view the visible world through the eyes of an artist. Rather, an icon is above all a metaphysical tool of great power, offering the potential to link the contemplative to an omnipresent yet invisible world, providing a portal to eternity, a bridge to a mystical but very real locus *beyond* space and time. Here the

---

[6]Solrunn Nes, *The Mystical Language of Icons*, 12.

American philosopher Jacob Needleman describes a common experience encountered during the viewing of an icon:

> If one makes the effort to 'just look' at icons, one may undergo a fleeting, but extraordinary experience. From trying to see the icon, one may suddenly sense that one is seen by it. For a moment, we are under the regard of a greater presence.[7]

It is for this reason that icons are regarded as holy mystical instruments or tools, each having a life of its own, bridging our everyday space-time world with light-filled, numinously transcendent dimensions. Our modern scientific culture has been unsympathetic to such mystical tools, tending to relegate them to the margins of our culture or attacking them as heretical. Nevertheless, the origins of the icon are essentially mystical, and harken back millenia, perhaps even to the famous Paleolithic images painted more than 17,000 years ago in caves discovered at Lascaux and Altamira.[8] Iconic images have been found in ancient tombs in Egypt in amazing states of preservation, though originally painted on wood using egg tempera.[9]

The images depicted in icons often reveal heavenly beings such as angels and archangels, and saints found in Bible, but also frequently focus upon the images of historic saints within the Christian churches. The famous 4th century Archbishop of Constantinople, St. Gregory of Nazianzus for example, also known as the "Trinitarian Theologian", has been the source of

---

[7] Needleman, *The Gospel of Thomas: The Gnostic Wisdom of Jesus.*

[8] Leroi-Gourhan, *The Art of Prehistoric Man in Western Europe,* 315.

[9] Temple, *Icons and the Mystical Origins of Christianity*, 7.

numerous icons both in Greece and in Russia. St. Gregory was a powerful orator, and both a clerical and mystical leader of the early church. Here he describes his own experience of the power released through contemplation upon light of the Holy Trinity.

> From the day whereon I renounced the things of the world to consecrate my soul to luminous and heavenly contemplation, when the supreme intelligence carried me hence to set me down far from all that pertains to the flesh, to hide me in the secret places of the heavenly tabernacle; from that day my eyes have been blinded by the light of the Trinity, whose brightness surpasses all that the mind can conceive; for from a throne high exalted the Trinity pours upon all, the ineffable radiance common to the Three. This is the source of all that is here below, separated by time from the things on high.[10]

A characteristic feature of iconography is that the form is depicted consistently with specific rules, equivalent to a language.

Orthodox Christian Icon of the Holy Trinity

Icons are used extensively in all Orthodox Christian churches, both as teaching aids for the congregations (which in earlier centuries were often largely illiterate), as well as for contemplative and liturgical purposes. Traditional Orthodox icons are hand painted using natural pigments and egg yolk, applied to wooden boards, and usually gilded with gold or silver. Their size ranges widely, from several meters tall, suitable for the iconostasis (literally a wall of icons) within the

---

[10] Gregory of Nazianzen, in 'Poemata de seipso I,' P.G., XXXVII, 984-5, as quoted in Lossky, *The Mystical Theology of the Eastern Church*, 44.

church, to smaller icons suitable for accompanying travelers. The icons act as metaphysical doorways or windows into the non-temporal dimensions of the archetypes of which they are the visual image. The most famous is an icon of the Holy Trinity.

The Holy Trinity by Andrei Rublev (Russian, 15ᵗʰ CE).

The Holy Trinity depicted by Rublev in the image is the so-called *Old Testament Trinity*, painted ("written" is the term used by iconographers) in the 15th CE. This image is based on the Old Testament story which describes Abraham receiving three heavenly messengers under the tre of Mamre (Genesis 18, 1-16).

In Rublev's icon we see the angel to the left symbolizing God the Father. The central angel represents Jesus Christ, who blesses the cup as well and accepting it. The angel to the right represents the Holy Spirit, and in the outline beneath his right hand can be seen the image of a descending dove. The tree in the center above Jesus represents the tree of the cross upon which he is sacrificed.[11]

Hindu Tantric Icon of the Holy Trinity

In India, the yantra is a mystical icon that has been widely used for millenia as a metaphysical tool for contemplative practice. The word *yantra* is derived from the Sanskrit root *yam* meaning "to sustain, hold or support" the energy inherent in a particular object, concept, or element. A yantra is basically an abstract geometrical form intended as a 'tool' for meditation practices, for self-development, and for increased awareness.[12]

One of the most famous yantras developed in the context of Kashmir Shaivism, the Sri Yantra. This yantra is a symbol and contemplative tool for understanding the Holy Trinity. The Sri Yantra as an icon us usually painted on wood, consisting of nine interlocking triangles: four upward-pointing triangles represent the masculine forces of nature, or Shiva, and five downward-pointing triangles indicate the feminine nature of

---

[11] Nes, *The Mystical Language of Icons*, 27.
[12] Khanna, *Yantra: The Tantric Symbol of Cosmic Unity*, 11.

reality, or Shakti. Each of the triangles by itself represents different aspects of the Trinitarian nature of of the divine reality of the Holy Trinity abstracted from the Whole.

The image of the Sri Yantra in Fig. 1 was created by the author following traditional iconographical methods, using wood, gold, and hand-ground mineral pigments in egg yolk.

Figure 1 - *A Contemplative Tool (Yantra by author.)*

Associated with each yantra is a specific sound mantra, recited in repetition audibly or inaudibly, which resonates with the yantra and all who have ever linked with it during contemplation, previously or in the future, invoking the cosmic energies of consciousness associated with the yantra.

The Devanagari script of the mantra associated with the Sri Yantra (Fig. 1 below) can be found in a circle just within the inner surrounding row of petals in the yantra. The central point is known as the *bindu,* and can be thought of as representing, and synonymous with, Teilhard de Chardin's "Omega point," the point of entry into Bohm's "implicate order," as discussed earlier in this book.

The Sanskrit scholar Madhu Khanna characterizes the use of yantras in India as follows:

> They are aids to and the chief instruments of concentrated meditative discipline. A yantra used in this context and for this purpose is an abstract geometrical design intended as a 'tool' for meditation and increased awareness.[13]

Among Yantras the Sri Yantra is highly revered as an effective contemplative instrument. It is used as a mnemonic map to provide guidance to the practitioner, a reminder of attributes and issues which should be mastered and overcome in order to facilitate reaching the transformative dimensions experienced at the center of the Yantra.

In the Sri Yantra of Fig. 2 can be seen the "Eight Gates, or eight of essential qualities or obstacles that should be mastered by any serious contemplative, in order to go beyond the "gates" toward the inner dimensions of the yantra.

Cultivating these qualities are important to assisit the practitioner in reaching the state in which they no longer act as afflictions (*klesha*) to hinder the tuning of consciousness into

---

[13] Madhu Khanna, *Yantra: The Tantric Symbol of Cosmic Unity.* (London: Thames & Hudson, 1979), 11.

the more interior dimensions of absolute nonduality, full communion with the Holy Trinity in all its triadic manifestations. The Sri Yantra represents a particular configuration whose power increases in proportion to the abstraction and precision of the diagram, and the ability of the contemplative to maintain a steady focus upon the icon as a whole, leading to resonant union (comm-union) with the Whole of creation, both imminant and transcendent.

Figure 2 - *The Eight Gates of the Sri Yantra*

Index

Endnotes

[1] Photograph by Julius Eduard Muller (1880). Reprinted under the terms of a Creative Commons Attribution ShareAlike 3.0 Unported license. Image retrieved from Wikimedia Commons.

[2] Archibald, *The Story of Trinidad*, 127.

[3] Later named "The Trinity Hills."

[4] Archibald, 119.

[5] Barnhart, "Christian Self-Understanding in the Light of the East," 293.

[6] Ibid.

[7] The Second Vatican Council, known as "Vatican II," (in Latin: *Concilium Oecumenicum Vaticanum Secundum*), was a major conference held in Rome at St. Peter's Basilica in the Vatican between 1963 and 1965 to address the relationship between the modern world and the Catholic Church.

[8] Keats, *Endymion: A Poetic Romance*

[9] *Psychonaut and psychonautics*: (from the Greek ψυχή psyche ["soul", "spirit" or "mind"] and ναύτης naútēs ["sailor" or "navigator"] – "sailor of the soul") refers to a methodology for exploring and mapping subjectively those regions of consciousness communed with during altered states of consciousness (holotropic states), including states induced by meditation, contemplative techniques, entheogenic substances, prayer, or physical exercise; direct exploration involves a *psychonaut* developing the capacity to voluntarily attenuate mental ego activity while maintaining focus upon detected resonances from the "whole," "I," or "Self," both imminant and transcendent.

[10] Lilly, *The Scientist: A Metaphysical Autobiography*, 128.

[11] Blofeld, *The Wheel of Life: The Autobiography of a Western Buddhist*.

[12] Churton. *Aleister Crowley: The Biography*, 108.

[13] Ibid., 149-150.

[14] Ibid., 151.

[15] Ouspensky, *In Search of the Miraculous: Fragments of an Unknown Teaching*.

[16] Ibid., 3.

[17] Samuel Weiser Bookstore, opened in 1926, was known as the oldest most famous metaphysical bookstore in the United States.

[18] Wood. *Practical Yoga: Ancient and Modern*.

[19] Taimni, *The Science of Yoga*.

[20] Whicher, *The Integrity of the Yoga Darsana: A Reconsideration of Classical Yoga*, 42.

[21] Mishra, *Yoga Sutras: The Textbook of Yoga Psychology*.

[22] Chaudhuri and Spiegelberg, *The Integral Philosophy of Sri Aurobindo: A Commemorative Symposium*, 19.

[23] Morin, *Seven Complex Lessons in Education for the Future*, 21.

[24] Gidley, "Evolution of Consciousness as a Planetary Imperative," 224.

[25] McIntosh, *Integral Consciousness*, 180.

[26] Spiegelberg, *Spiritual Practices of India*.

[27] Chaudhuri, *The Integral Philosophy of Sri Aurobindo*.

[28] Chaudhuri, *The Philosophy of Integralism*.

[29] Bergson, *Creative Evolution*.

30 Ibid., 152.

31 Gebser, *The Ever-Present Origin*, xxix.

32 Ibid.

33 Gebser, "Cultural Philosophy as Method and Venture," 78.

34 Feuerstein, *Structures of Consciousness*, 195.

35 Ibid., 194–95.

36 Ibid., 195.

37 Ibid.

38 Ibid.

39 Gebser, *The Ever-Present Origin*, 6.

40 Wilber, *A Brief History of Everything*, 17–18.

41 Wilber, *Integral Spirituality*, 72.

42 Ibid., 87.

43 Wilber, *A Brief History of Everything*.

44 Wilber, *Quantum Questions*.

45 Wilber, *Integral Spirituality*.

46 A hypostasis (Greek: ὑπόστασις) is defined as one of three underlying states or underlying substances that are the source and support of everything manifest in the cosmos and beyond.

47 Jan Assmann, *Of God and Gods: Egypt, Israel, and the Rise of Monotheism*, (Wisconsin: University of Wisconsin Press, 2008), 64.

48 Panikkar, 256.

49 Jung, "A Psychological Approach to the Dogma of the Trinity," 108.

50 Combs, *Consciousness Explained Better*, 1.

51 Robert Fludd, *Utriusque cosmi maioris scilicet et minoris [...] historia, tomus II (1619), tractatus I, sectio*

I, liber X, De triplici animae in corpore visione. Public Domain. Retrieved from https://upload.wikimedia.org/wikipedia/commons/0/0 c/RobertFuddBewusstsein17Jh.png.

[52] James, *A Pluralistic Universe*, 182.

[53] Jung. *The Collected Works of C.G. Jung, vol. 12:44*, 41.

[54] Barnhart, *Purity of Heart and Contemplation*, 291.

[55] Ibid.

[56] Ibid., 304-305.

[57] Both the "Laplace transform" and the "Lagrange multiplier" have found widespread use in engineering calculus, particularly in electrical engineering applications and communication theory.

[58] Connolley, William. 2009. Translation of Fourier's 1827 Memoir." Retreived from "History of Climate Change Science," *https://en.wikipedia.org/wiki/History_of_climate_ch ange_science*.

[59] Fourier, *The Analytic Theory of Heat*, 1.

[60] Bohm, *Quantum Theory*, iii.

[61] Wiener, *Cybernetics: Control and Communication in Animal and Machine*, 72.

[62] Bohm, *Wholeness and the Implicate Order*, 196-7.

[63] Yau and Nadis, *The Shape of Inner Space: String Theory and the Geometry of the Universe's Hidden Dimensions*, 10

[64] Pribram, *Brain and Perception*, 70.

[65] Teilhard, "From Cosmos to Cosmogenesis" in *Activation of Energy*, 257.

[66] Teilhard, "Centrology" in *Activation of Energy*, 103.

[67] Ibid., 106.

[68] Ibid., 104.

[69] Ibid.

[70] "On August 30 2011, Professor Kei Hirose, professor of high-pressure mineral physics and petrology at the Tokyo Institute of Technology, became the first person to recreate conditions found at the earth's core under laboratory conditions, subjecting a sample of iron nickel alloy to the same type of pressure by gripping it in a vice between 2 diamond tips, and then heating the sample to approximately 4000 Kelvins with a laser. The sample was observed with x-rays, and strongly supported the theory that the earth's inner core was made of giant crystals running north to south." from webpage "Structure of the Earth," http://en.wikipedia.org/wiki/Structure_of_the_Earth, accessed 10/27/2011.

[71] Teilhard, *The Phenomenon of Man*, 180-81.

[72] Teilhard, "The Heart of Matter," 39. Essay written in 1954.

[73] Ibid. Italic emphasis added.

[74] Teilhard, "Life and the Planets," 122. Essay written in 1944.

[75] "Contemplation." New Oxford American Dictionary. 3rd ed. 2010. New York: Oxford University Press.

[76] Barnhart, "Christian Self-Understanding in the Light of the East: New Birth and Unitive Consciousness," 304.

[77] Lilly, *Programming and Meta-Programming the Human Biocomputer: Theory and Experiments*.

[78] Lilly, *The Deep Self: Consciousness Exploration in the Isolation Tank*, 49.

[79] Griffiths, *Vedanta and Christian Faith*.

[80] Griffiths, *A New Vision of Reality*, 252.

[81] Griffiths, "Transcending Dualism" in *Vedanta and Christian Faith*, 92.

82 Ibid., 85-89.

83 Ibid., *Programming and Meta-Programming the Human Biocomputer,* 292.

84 Ibid., 296.

85 Ibid., 305.

86 Ibid., 306.

87 Barnhart, "Christian Self-Understanding in the Light of the East," in *Purity of Heart and Contemplation,* 303-305.

88 Teilhard, "Centrology: An Essay in a Dialectic of Union," 99. Essay written in 1944.

89 In this dissertation, I refer to him as Teilhard de Chardin, or simply Teilhard.

90 Teilhard, *The Human Phenomenon,* 2.

91 de Lubac, *The Religion of Teilhard de Chardin*; Henri de Lubac, eventually Cardinal de Lubac, was a Jesuit friend and correspondent of Teilhard's for more than 30 years.

92 Teilhard, *Lettres Intimes,* 269.

93 Teilhard, *The Phenomenon of Man,* xix.

94 Teilhard, *L'oeuvre Scientifique.*

95 B. Cheney, "Has Teilhard de Chardin 'Really' Joined the Within and the Without of Things?," 217.

96 Ibid.

97 Teilhard, "The Stuff of the Universe," 383. Essay written in 1953.

98 Reprinted under the terms of a Creative Commons Attribution ShareAlike 3.0 Unported license. Image retrieved from Wikimedia Commons.

99 King, *Spirit of Fire: The Life and Vision of Teilhard de Chardin,* 1.

100 Ibid., 4.

101 Ibid.

102 Aczel, *The Jesuit and the Skull*, 72.

103 Ibid., 24.

104 Teilhard, *The Heart of Matter*, 25.

105 Ibid., 74.

106 Raven, *Teilhard de Chardin: Scientist and Seer*, 164–65.

107 Bergson, *Creative Evolution*.

108 Teilhard, *The Human Phenomenon*, 149.

109 Teilhard, *The Heart of Matter*, 25.

110 Teilhard, *Letters to Leontine Zanta*, 102.

111 King, *Spirit of Fire*, 38.

112 King, *Spirit of Fire*, 47.

113 Ibid., 49.

114 King, *Pierre Teilhard de Chardin*, 52; *Sidi Marabout*: An Arabic title of great esteem and honor; *Sidi* refers to a North African settled in France; *Marabout* designates a saint and ascetic blessed with divine favor.

115 Aczel, *The Jesuit and the Skull*, 82.

116 Ibid.

117 Ibid., 77.

118 Corte, *Pierre Teilhard de Chardin*, 15.

119 Teilhard, "The Making of a Mind: Letters from a Soldier–Priest 1914–1919," 205.

120 Teilhard, "Nostalgia for the Front," 172.

121 Ibid.

122 Horne, *The Price of Glory: Verdun 1916*, 328.

123 Teilhard, "Christ in Matter," 61. Essay written in 1916.

[124] Tudzynski, Correia, and Keller. 2001. "Biotechnology and Genetics of Ergot Alkaloids."

[125] Teilhard, "Christ in Matter," 61–65. Essay written 1916.

[126] Teilhard, "The Christic," 83. Essay written in 1955.

[127] Ibid.

[128] Ibid., 82–83. Italic emphasis added.

[129] King, *Spirit of Fire*, 59.

[130] Ibid., 116.

[131] Teilhard, "Human Energy," 118. Essay written in 1937.

[132] Teilhard, "My Universe" 197. Essay written 14 April, 1918.

[133] Teilhard, *The Divine Milieu*, 76–77.

[134] Aczel, *The Jesuit and the Skull*, 123–24.

[135] Ibid., 124.

[136] Ibid., 132.

[137] Ibid.

[138] Association for Asian Studies, Southeast Conference, *Annals, Volumes 1–5*, 51.

[139] King, *Spirit of Fire*, 233–34.

[140] Teilhard, "Some Notes on the Mystical Sense: An Attempt at Clarification," 209. Essay written in 1951.

[141] Teilhard, *The Human Phenomenon*, 2.

[142] Teilhard, "Life and the Planets," 123. Lecture delivered in 1945

[143] Ibid., 122.

[144] Teilhard, "My Fundamental Vision," 164. Essay written in 1948.

[145] Ibid., 83. Note that the Eocene Epoch lasted from 56 to 33.9 million years ago.

146 Ibid., 84.

147 Morgan, *Emergent Evolution: Gifford Lectures, 1921–22.*

148 Haisch, *The Purpose-Guided Universe: Believing in Einstein, Darwin, and God.*

149 King, *Spirit of Fire,* 233–34.

150 Ibid.

151 Leroy, "Teilhard de Chardin: The Man," 32.

152 Teilhard, *Letters from a Traveller,* 291

153 Teilhard, "The Zest for Living," 231.

154 King, *Pierre Teilhard de Chardin,* 17.

155 Teilhard, "Centrology: An Essay in the Dialectic of Union," written in 1944.

156 King, *Spirit of Fire,* 213.

157 Teilhard, "The Energy of Evolution," 361–62. Essay written in 1953.

158 Teilhard, "The Activation of Human Energy," 393. Essay written in 1953.

159 Teilhard, *Activation of Energy.*

160 Teilhard, "The Atomism of Spirit," 29. Essay written in 1941.

161 Teilhard, *The Human Phenomenon,* 109.

162 Teilhard, "The Zest for Living," 242. Essay written in 1950.

163 Ibid.

164 Teilhard, "The Activation of Human Energy," 393. Essay written in 1953.

165 Teilhard, footnote 10, "Centrology: An Essay in a Dialectic of Union," 121. Essay written in 1944.

166 Ibid., 120.

167 Teilhard, *Christianity and Evolution*, 56; and *The Appearance of Man*, 33.

168 "Over and above the biosphere there is a *noosphere*."; Teilhard, *The Human Phenomenon*, 124.

169 Samson and Pitt, *The Biosphere and Noosphere Reader*, 3.

170 Teilhard, "The Great Monad," 182. Essay written in 1918.

171 Teilhard, *The Heart of Matter*.

172 Noosphere: from the Greek voῦ ς (*nous*: "sense, mind, wit") and σφαῖ ρα (*sphaira*: "sphere, orb, globe"); Samson and Pitt, *The Biosphere and Noosphere Reader*.

173 King, *Spirit of Fire*, 84.

174 Speaight, *The Life of Teilhard de Chardin*, 117.

175 Teilhard, as quoted in Cuénot, *Teilhard de Chardin: A Biographical Study*, 59.

176 King, *Spirit of Fire*, 84.

177 Bailes, *Science and Russian Culture in an Age of Revolutions*; the term "biosphere" had been in use since as early as 1900, popularized by the Austrian geologist Eduard Suess.

178 Samson and Pitt, *The Biosphere and Noosphere Reader*, 94–95.

179 Vernadsky, *The Biosphere*, 16.

180 Aczel, *The Jesuit and the Skull*, 86.

181 Teilhard, "Hominization," 61. Essay written in 1923.

182 Ibid., 62.

183 Ibid., 73–78.

184 Teilhard, "The Death-Barrier and Co-Reflection," 402. Essay written in 1955.

185 Ibid., 78.

186 Teilhard., 25.

187 Ibid, 24.

188 Teilhard, *The Divine Milieu*, (New York: Harper & Row, 1960).

189 Ibid., 128-129.

190 Teilhard, *The Divine Milieu*, (New York: Harper & Row, 1960), 120.

191 Teilhard, *Christianity and Evolution*, (London: William Collins Sons & Col Ltd., 1969), 160.

192 Teilhard, *The Divine Milieu*, 128.

193 Ibid., 180.

194 Teilhard, "The Christic," in The Heart of Matter, translated by Rene Hague (Florida: Harcourt Brace Jovanovitch, 1976).

195 Ibid., 82.

196 Ibid., 90.

197 King, *Spirit of Fire*, 104.

198 Speaight, *The Life of Teilhard de Chardin*, 135.

199 Radhakrishnan, *History of Philosophy Eastern and Western*, 57.

200 Skrbina, *Panpsychism in the West*, 30.

201 MacKenna, *Plotinus: The Enneads*.

202 Radhakrishnan, *History of Philosophy Eastern and Western*, 115.

203 MacKenna, *Plotinus: The Enneads*, 712.

204 Jung, *Psychology and Alchemy*.

205 Bohm, *Wholeness and the Implicate Order*, 19.

206 Teilhard, "Centrology: An Essay in a Dialectic of Union," 127. Essay written in 1944.

[207] Teilhard, as quoted in Cuénot, *Teilhard de Chardin: A Biographical Study*, 59.

[208] Teilhard, "The Convergence of the Universe," 285. Essay written in 1951.

[209] Samson and Pitt, *The Biosphere and Noosphere Reader*, xi.

[210] Ibid., 2–3.

[211] Allaby and Allaby, *A Dictionary of Earth Science*, 72.

[212] A brane is a geometrical boundary of higher dimensional dimensions spaces. This concept is used in contemporary superstring theory and M-theory; see Susskind, *The Black Hole War*.

[213] Malinski, *Chemistry of the Heart*, 61.

[214] Radio Ukraine; Berg, *Broadcasting on the Short Waves, 1945 to Today*, 43.

[215] Walker, *Three Mile Island: A Nuclear Crisis in Historical Perspective*, 12.

[216] Assuming 7 billion human beings with average heartbeat output of 1.3 watts.

[217] Reprinted under the terms of a Creative Commons Attribution ShareAlike 3.0 Unported license. Image retrieved from Wikimedia Commons.

[218] The data in this chart was recorded from the Geostationary Operational Environmental Satellites 8 and 10, weather satellites in geosynchronous orbit over the east and west coasts of the United States in the days before, during, and after the September 11, 2001, terrorist attacks.

[219] McCraty, Deyhle, and Childre, "The Global Coherence Initiative: Creating a Coherent Planetary Standing Wave," 75.

220 McCraty, Deyhle, and Childre, "The Global Coherence Initiative: Creating a Coherent Planetary Standing Wave," 76.

221 Teilhard, *Christianity and Evolution: Reflections on Science and Religion*, 231.

222 King, *Spirit of Fire*, 97.

223 Ibid., 98.

224 Ibid., 106.

225 Ibid., 106–8.

226 Teilhard, "Letters to Two Friends 1926–1952," 5.

227 Aczel, *The Jesuit and the Skull*, 78.

228 Ibid.

229 Ibid., 79.

230 King, *Spirit of Fire*, 93.

231 Cuénot, *Teilhard de Chardin: A Biographical Study*, 257.

232 Ibid., 258.

233 Leckie, *Delivered from Evil: The Saga of World War II*.

234 Aczel, *The Jesuit and the Skull*, 213.

235 King, *Spirit of Fire*, 230.

236 Aczel, *The Jesuit and the Skull*, 221.

237 King, *Spirit of Fire*, 230.

238 Aczel, *The Jesuit and the Skull*,

239 Ibid., 231.

240 Dunwell, *The Hudson: America's River*, 140.

241 Teilhard, "The Spirit of the Earth," 42. Essay written in 1931.

242 Teilhard, "The Phenomenon of Spirituality," 96–97. Essay written in 1937.

243 Teilhard, "The Nature of the Point Omega," 160.

244 Teilhard, "From Cosmos to Cosmogenesis," 257. Essay written in 1951.

245 Teilhard, "Centrology: An Essay in a Dialectic of Union," 103. Essay written in 1944.

246 Ibid., 106.

247 Ibid., 104.

248 King, *Spirit of Fire*, 164.

249 Teilhard, "The Phenomenon of Spirituality." Essay written in 1937.

250 Skrbina, *Panpsychism in the West.*

251 Teilhard, *Activation of Energy.*

252 Teilhard, "The Phenomenon of Spirituality," 112.

253 Teilhard, *Building the Earth*, 67.

254 Bohm, *Wholeness and the Implicate Order.*

255 An image from a late medieval Byzantine Greek alchemical manuscript Reprinted under the terms of a Creative Commons Attribution ShareAlike 3.0 Unported license. Image retrieved from Wikimedia Commons.

256 Teilhard, "The Phenomenon of Spirituality," 93. Essay written in 1937.

257 Ibid.

258 Ibid.

259 Ibid., 93–94.

260 Ibid.

261 Teilhard, "Human Energy," 130–31.

262 Teilhard, "The Phenomenon of Spirituality," 99.

263 Ibid., 98.

264 Ibid.

265 Ibid., 101.

266 Teilhard's final essay, written shortly before his death in 1955, is entitled, "The Death-Barrier and Co-Reflection, or the Imminent Awakening of Human Consciousness to the Sense of Its Irreversibility."

267 Teilhard, "The Phenomenon of Spirituality," 103.

268 Note that the British spelling "centre" is used here and throughout textual discussion in this chapter, not only because it is in accordance with the spelling found in all published translations of Teilhard's work into English, but more specifically because in the context of Teilhard's metaphysics, the word *centre* is used to designate a "center of consciousness," rather than used simply as an adjective, or a location designator.

269 Teilhard, "The Phenomenon of Spirituality," 104.

270 Ibid., 106.

271 Ibid., 105.

272 Ibid., 106.

273 Ibid.

274 Ibid., 105.

275 Ibid., 107.

276 Ibid.

277 Ibid., 107–8.

278 Data adapted from Teilhard, "The Phenomenon of Spirituality," 105–10. Author's table.

279 Ibid., 108.

280 Ibid., 109–11.

281 Ibid.

282 Ibid.

283 Ibid., 99.

284 Ibid., 101.

285 Ibid., 103.

286 Ibid., 93–94.

287 Gao, *Dark Energy: From Einstein's Biggest Blunder to the Holographic Universe.*

288 Teilhard, "Human Energy." Essay written in 1937.

289 Ibid., 117.

290 Ibid., 118. Emphasis added by author.

291 Ibid., 128.

292 Ibid., 129–30.

293 Jung, "On the Nature of the Psyche," 207.

294 Teilhard, "The Spirit of the Earth," 35. Essay written 1931.

295 Ibid., 33.

296 Teilhard, "Human Energy," 130–31.

297 Ibid., 131.

298 Ibid.

299 Ibid., 138.

300 Ibid., 141.

301 Teilhard, "Cosmic Life," 15; Note that it is here, in Teilhard's earliest known essay, written at Dunkirk in April 1916, that Teilhard first speaks at length about the centres and the sphere: "We are the countless centres of one and the same sphere."

302 Teilhard, *Human Energy*, 143.

303 Ibid., 143–44.

304 Ibid., 144.

305 Ibid., 145.

306 de Lubac, *The Religion of Teilhard de Chardin*, 123.

307 Teilhard, "Life and the Planets." Speech of 1945 published as an essay in 1946.

308 Ibid., 122.

309 Teilhard, *The Human Phenomenon*, 191–93.

310 Teilhard, "Human Energy," 138.

311 Teilhard, "The Activation of Human Energy," 393.

312 Teilhard, "The Nature of the Point Omega," 272–73.

313 Teilhard, "Human Energy," 162.

314 Teilhard, "Centrology," 99.

315 Ibid., 100.

316 Ibid., 101.

317 Ibid., 102.

318 Ibid., 102, n1.

319 Ibid. 102.

320 Ibid., 103.

321 Teilhard, "Man's Place in the Universe," 226. Essay written in 1942.

322 Ibid., 226.

323 Calculated by Drew Weisenberger, a detector scientist at the Department of Energy's Thomas Jefferson National Accelerator Facility. See Weisenberger, "Jefferson Lab Questions and Answers," para. 2.

324 Teilhard, "The Atomism of Spirit," 40.

325 Teilhard, *The Human Phenomenon*, 110.

326 Teilhard, "Centrology," 103.

327 Teilhard, "Universalization and Union," 91. Essay written in 1953.

328 Teilhard, "Centrology," 120.

329 Ibid., 110.

330 Ibid.

331 Teilhard, "Outline of a Dialectic of Spirit," 144.

332 Teilhard, "Centrology," 103.

333 Rescher, *G. W. Leibniz's Monadology.*

334 Teilhard, "Centrology," 104.

335 Ibid., 100.

336 Ibid., 105.

337 Ibid., 106.

338 Ibid., 107.

339 Ibid., 108.

340 Ibid., 109.

341 Sheldrake, *A New Science of Life: The Hypothesis of Morphic Resonance.*

342 Teilhard, "Centrology," 109.

343 Ibid.

344 Ibid.

345 Ibid., 110.

346 Ibid.

347 Ibid., 110–11.

348 Ibid., 111.

349 Ibid.

350 Teilhard, "The Phenomenon of Spirituality," 100.

351 Ibid., 99.

352 Teilhard, *The Phenomenon of Man,* 73–74.

353 Teilhard, "Centrology," 112.

354 Ibid.

355 Ibid.

356 Ibid., 113.

357 Ibid.

358 Ibid.

359 Assistance with these Latin translations was provided by Fr. Thomas Matus, PhD, a Camaldolese Benedictine monk, in an e-mail message to author, August 27, 2015.

360 Teilhard, "Centrology," 114.

361 Ibid.

362 Ibid.

363 Ibid.

364 Teilhard, "The Formation of the Noosphere II," 111. Essay written in 1949.

365 Booth, Koren, and Persinger, "Increased Feelings of the Sensed Presence During Exposures to Weak Magnetic Fields."

366 Teilhard, "Centrology," 114–15.

367 Ibid., 116.

368 Ibid., 115.

369 Ibid., 119.

370 Ibid., 116.

371 Teilhard, "Hominization," in *The Vision of the Past*, 78.

372 Teilhard, "Centrology," 122.

373 Ibid., 116–17.

374 Ibid., 100.

375 Teilhard, "Centrology," 102.

376 Ibid.

377 Goswami, *The Visionary Window*.

378 Gebser, *The Ever-Present Origin*, 37.

379 Ibid., 39.

380 Teilhard, "Centrology," 117.

381 Ibid.

382 Teilhard, *Human Phenomenon*, 2.

383 Einstein, *Autobiographical Notes*, 17.

384 Teilhard, "The Death-Barrier and Co-Reflection," 403.

385 de Terra, *Memories of Teilhard de Chardin*, 42.

386 Teilhard, "The Death-Barrier and Co-Reflection," 402.

387 Ibid., 403.

388 *Atharvaveda–Samhita*, Saunaka recension, I,12.1c: "*Ekam ojas tredhā vicakrame.*"

389 Radhakrishnan. 1971. *Indian Philosophy: Volume II.* London: George Allen & Unwin, 445.

390 Raimon Panikkar, *The Rhythm of Being: The Gifford Lectures*, (New York: Orbis Books, 2010), xviii.

391 Chauduri, *Philosophy of Integralism*.

392 Bohm, *Wholeness and the Implicate Order*.

393 Radhakrishnan, *Indian Philosophy, Vol. II*, 458.

394 Aurobindo, *The Synthesis of Yoga*, 27.

395 Roy, *Sri Aurobindo Came to Me*, 49.

396 Heehs, *The Lives of Sri Aurobindo*, 42.

397 Heehs, 15.

398 Heehs, 32.

399 Heehs, 18.

400 Ibid.

401 Heehs, 24.

402 Ibid.

403 Aurobindo, *Tales of Prison Life*, 37.

404 Heehs, *The Lives of Sri Aurobindo*, 441.

405 The *Arya* was a monthly 64-page journal published by Sri Aurobindo between 1914 and 1921 after his exile by the British to the French colony of Pondicherry.

406 Sri Aurobindo Ghose, *The Upanishads: Texts, Translations and Commentaries*. Pondicherry: Sri Aurobindo Ashram, 1972.

407 "According to post-Vedic tradition, the rishi is a 'seer' to whom the Vedas were 'originally revealed' through states of higher consciousness. The rishis were prominent when Vedic Hinduism took shape, as far back as three thousand years ago." Retrieved from internet URL en.wikipedia.org/wiki/Rishi at 6:57 pm PST 5-14-2012.

408 Aurobindo., 1.

409 Ibid.

410 Aurobindo., 2.

411 Aurobindo., 2.

412 Aurobindo., 4.

413 Aurobindo., 3.

414 Ibid.

415 Aurobindo., 5.

416 Ibid.

417 Ibid.

418 Aurobindo, 44.

419 Aurobindo., 5.

420 Aurobindo., 6.

421 Ibid.

422 Aurobindo., 7.

423 Ibid.

424 Aurobindo., 7.

425 Aurobindo., 9.

426 Ibid.

427 Aurobindo., 10.

428 Aurobindo, 10.

429 Ibid.

430 Aurobindo, 11.

431 Ibid.

432 Ibid. (Italics added)

433 Aurobindo, 12.

434 Ibid.

435 Aurobindo, 12-13.

436 Aurobindo, 13.

437 Monism hold that the universe is ultimately one, rather than ultimately dualistic or pluralistic.

438 Ibid.

439 Aurobindo, 14.

440 Ibid.

441 Aurobindo, 14.

442 Ibid.

443 Aurobindo, 15.

444 Merrill-Wolf, *Consciousness Without an Object.*

445 Eliot, *The Four Quartets.*

446 Aurobindo, 16.

447 Eliot, *The Four Quartets,* 79.

448 Aurobindo, 22.

449 Aurobindo, 24.

450 Aurobindo, 26.

451 Aurobindo, 28.

452 Aurobindo, 31.

453 Aurobindo, 45.

454 Aurobindo, 39.

455 Aurobindo, 42.

456 Aurobindo, 47.

457 Bailey, *The Study of Hinduism*, 139.

458 Aurobindo, 48.

459 Joye, *The Pribram–Bohm Holoflux Theory of Consciousness*, 196.

460 Joye, 271.

461 Bohm, *Wholeness and the Implicate Order*, 172.

462 Fox, *The Coming of the Cosmic Christ*.

463 Aurobindo, *The Life Divine*, 244.

464 Aurobindo, *The Synthesis of Yoga*, 827.

465 Fox, *The Coming of the Cosmic Christ*.

466 Eliot, *The Four Quartets*, 79.

467 Aurobindo, *Synthesis of Yoga*.

468 Peat, *Infinite Potential*.

469 Bohm, *Beyond Limits*, 8:00.

470 Bohm, *Beyond Limits*, 12:55.

471 Peat, *Infinite Potential*, 193–94.

472 Peat, *Infinite Potential*, 194–95

473 Bohm and Hiley, *The Undivided Universe*, 1.

474 Ibid., 31.

475 Peat, *Infinite Potential*, 46.

476 Ibid.

477 Ibid., 47.

478 Ibid., 62.

479 Hiley and Peat, *Quantum Implications*.

480 Peat, *Infinite Potential*, 57–58.

481 Ibid., 58.

482 Ibid., 66.

483 Ibid., 65.

484 Ibid., 64.

485 Plasmas constitute over ninety-nine percent of the matter of the universe—most stars and interstellar gases exist in this fourth state of matter (Peat, *Infinite Potential*, 65).

486 Bohm and Peat, *Science, Order, and Creativity*, xiii.

487 Peat, *Infinite Potential*, 88.

488 Bohm, *The Special Theory of Relativity*, vi.

489 Hiley and Peat, "The Development of David Bohm's Ideas," 4.

490 Bohm, *Quantum Theory*.

491 Peat, *Infinite Potential*, 120.

492 Peat, *Infinite Potential*, 98–99.

493 Baggott, *The Quantum Story*, 305.

494 Peat, *Infinite Potential*, 120.

495 Ibid., 124.

496 Ibid., 126.

497 Bohm, *Quantum Theory*, 1. Italics added.

498 Ibid., 29.

499 Peat, *Infinite Potential*, 86.

500 Bohm, "Interpretation of the Quantum Theory in Terms of 'Hidden Variables,'" 166.

501 Garay, "Quantum Gravity and Minimum Length," 145.

502 Peat, *Infinite Potential*, 48.

503 Peat, *Infinite Potential*, 48–49.

504 Bohm, "Interpretation of the Quantum Theory in Terms of 'Hidden Variables.'"

505 Peat, *Infinite Potential*, 51.

506 Ibid., 52.

507 Born, *The Born–Einstein Letters*, 91.

508 Peat, *Infinite Potential*, 108.

509 Ibid., 148.

510 Ibid., 133.

511 Ibid.

512 Ibid., 168.

513 J. T. Bell, *The Speakable and Unspeakable in Quantum Mechanics*, 128.

514 Peat, *Infinite Potential*, 186.

515 Bohm, *Wholeness and the Implicate Order*, 207.

516 Ouspensky, *In Search of the Miraculous*.

517 Peat, *Infinite Potential*, 213.

518 Bohm and Krishnamurti, *The Limits of Thought*, vii.

519 Peat, *Infinite Potential*, 213.

520 Bohm and Krishnamurti, *The Ending of Time*; and Bohm and Krishnamurti, *The Limits of Thought*.

521 Peat, *Infinite Potential*, 227–28.

522 Bohm and Krishnamurti, *The Limits of Thought*, vii.

523 Peat, *Infinite Potential*, 229.

524 Peat, *Infinite Potential*, 256.

525 Ibid.

526 Crease, *The Great Equations*, 220.

527 Bohm, *Wholeness and the Implicate Order*, 149.

[528] Pylkkänen, *Mind, Matter, and the Implicate Order*, 21.

[529] Bohm, *Beyond Limits*, 8:00.

[530] As discussed shortly, this is the Planck length of 10^{-33} cm.

[531] Bohm and Hiley, *The Undivided Universe*, 9.

[532] Bohm, *Quantum Theory*, 622

[533] Ibid.

[534] Bohm and Hiley, *The Undivided Universe*, 9–10.

[535] See also Chapter 5, "The Planck Constant"; the Planck length of 10^{-33} cm. was first discussed by the German physicist Max Planck, the 1918 Nobel Prize winning originator of quantum mechanics, and is derived from three values: (1) the speed of light in a vacuum, (2) the gravitational constant, and (3) the Planck constant, h, which is required to calculate quantum changes of wavelength as a function of temperature (Bruskiewich, *Max Planck and Black-Body Radiation*).

[536] Bohm, *Wholeness and the Implicate Order*, 190–91.

[537] Bohm, *Quantum Theory*, 18.

[538] Bohm and Peat, *Science, Order, and Creativity*, 311–12.

[539] Data from Benenson, Harris, Stocker, and Holger, *Handbook of Physics*.

[540] Ibid., 86.

[541] Gott et al., "A Map of the Universe."

[542] Bohm and Hiley, *The Undivided Universe*, 357.

[543] Yau and Nadis, *The Shape of Inner Space*, 10.

[544] Ibid., 10–11.

[545] Ibid., 12.

[546] Ibid., 13.

[547] Bohm, *Wholeness and the Implicate Order*, 190.

548 Ibid., 186.

549 Weber, "The Physicist and the Mystic," 187. Italics added.

550 Hiley and Peat, eds. *Quantum Implications: Essays in Honour of David Bohm.*

551 Ibid.

552 Bohm, *Beyond Limits.* The source is an interview with Bill Angelos; the quoted dialogue begins 32:23 into the interview. The interview runs 1:08:13 total.

553Globus, *The Transparent Becoming of World*, 50.

554 Bohm, "A New Theory of the Relationship of Mind and Matter," 51.

555 Bohm, "Meaning and Information," 45.

556 Bohm and Peat, *Science, Order, and Creativity*, 84.

557 Ibid.

558 Bohm, "Meaning and Information," 45.

559 Ibid., 2.

560 Ibid.

561 Bohm, *Beyond Limits*, 5:30.

562 Ibid., 1.

563 Globus, *The Transparent Becoming of the World*, 55.

564 Peat, *Infinite Potential*, 220.

565 Bohm, "Hidden Variables and the Implicate Order," 43.

566 Bohm and Peat, *Science, Order, and Creativity*, 81.

567 Ibid.

568 Ibid.

569 Ibid., 82. Italics added.

570 Ibid.

571 Bohm and Hiley, *The Undivided Universe*, 38–39.

572 Ibid., 399.

573 Bohm, "Meaning and Information," 45.

574 Ibid., 46.

575 Bohm, *Wholeness and the Implicate Order*, 196–97.

576 Ibid., 200.

577 Bohm, "The Physicist and the Mystic," 196.

578 Bohm, "The Implicate Order and the Super-Implicate Order," 45–46.

579 Bohm, *The Undivided Universe*, 389–90. Italics added.

580 Bohm, *Beyond Limits*, 5:30.

581 This eleven-dimensional "M-theory" was first proposed by the mathematical physicist Edward Witten of the Institute of Advanced Study at Princeton in 1995. His hypothesis initiated what has been called "the second superstring revolution" in particle research. Witten suggested the "M" in his "M-theory" should stand for "magic," or "mystery" until the additional dimensions were better understood.

582 Peat, *Infinite Potential: The Life and Times of David Bohm*.

583 Bohm, "The Enfolding-Unfolding Universe," 62.

584 Bohm and Hiley, *The Undivided Universe*, 381.

585 Ibid., 381–82.

586 Bohm, *Beyond Limits*, 7:20.

587 Carr and Giddings, "Quantum Black Holes."

588 Wong, *The Shambhala Guide to Taoism*, 124–31.

589 This is the Taoist yin-yang symbol, with black representing yin and white representing yang. It is a symbol that reflects the inescapably intertwined duality of all things in nature, a common theme in Taoism.

590 Kuo, *Network Analysis and Synthesis*, 1.

591 Pribram, *Brain and Perception*, 73.

592 Bohm, *Quantum Theory*, 1.

593 Crease, *The Great Equations*, 100.

594 Ibid., 98.

595 Ibid., 98–99.

596 Ibid., 100.

597 Feynman, Leighton, and Sands, *The Feynman Lectures*, 211.

598 Fellmann, *Leonhard Euler*, xv.

599 While the "*i*" symbol continues to be used by mathematicians and physicists, electrical engineers use the letter "*j*" to designate imaginary numbers, primarily because they use the letter "*i*" to designate electrical current flow; Kuo, *Network Analysis and Synthesis*, 16.

600 Kuo, *Network Analysis and Synthesis*, 77.

601 Crease, *The Great Equations*, 99.

602 Material in the following section is taken from Crease, "Euler's Equation," in *The Great Equations*, 91–110; mathematical expressions in this section are by author.

603 Crease, *The Great Equation*, 100.

604 Crease, *The Great Equations*, 102.

605 Blakeslee, *The Radio Amateur's Handbook*, 23.

606 Kuo, *Network Analysis and Synthesis*, 14.

607 Crease, *The Great Equation*, 108.

608 Fourier, *The Analytic Theory of Heat*.

609 Crease, *The Great Equations*, 96.

610 Browder, *Mathematical Analysis: An Introduction*, 121.

611 Livio, *The Golden Ratio: The Story of Phi*.

[612] Feynman, Leighton, and Sands, *The Feynman Lectures on Physics*, 271.

[613] Ibid., 286.

[614] Stein and Shakarchi, *Fourier Analysis*, 134–36.

[615] Kuo, *Network Analysis and Synthesis*, 40.

[616] Wiener, *Cybernetics: Control and Communication in Animal and Machine*, 198.

[617] Ibid.

[618] Ibid., 202.

[619] Ibid. Italics added.

[620] Ibid., 200.

[621] Ibid.

[622] E. T. Bell, *Men of Mathematics*.

[623] Kuo, *Network Analysis and Synthesis*.

[624] Ibid., 389.

[625] Mandelbrot, "Fractals and the Rebirth of Iteration Theory," 151.

[626] Penrose, *Concerning Computers, Minds and the Laws of Physics*, 124.

[627] Ibid., 127.

[628] Jung, "On the Nature of the Psyche," 207.

[629] Ibid., 187–213.

[630] Jung, "On the Nature of the Psyche," 215.

[631] Brigham, "The Fast Fourier Transform."

[632] Ibid.

[633] Pribram, *The Form Within*, 109.